JOAN, LADY OF WALES
POWER AND POLITICS OF
KING JOHN'S DAUGHTER

Patri meo
(1945–2018)
Si itaque in aliquo mihi credere velitis,
in hoc mihi fidem adhibere velitis. Valete.

Therefore if you wish to have confidence in me for anything else,
put your faith in me for this. Farewell.
— Joan, Lady of Wales

I Siwan
It will be seen that there are still problems which call for solutions
in the history of this shadowy figure, but I trust that I have done
something to clear the foundations for future building.
— John Edward Lloyd

JOAN, LADY OF WALES
POWER AND POLITICS OF
KING JOHN'S DAUGHTER

Danna R Messer

PEN & SWORD
HISTORY

AN IMPRINT OF PEN & SWORD BOOKS LTD.
YORKSHIRE - PHILADELPHIA

First published in Great Britain in 2020
Reprinted in paperback format in 2021 by
PEN AND SWORD HISTORY
An imprint of
Pen & Sword Books Ltd
Yorkshire – Philadelphia

ISBN 978 1 52679 970 8

Typeset in Times New Roman 11.5/14 by
SJmagic DESIGN SERVICES, India.

Printed and bound in the UK
by CPI Group (UK) Ltd, Croydon, CR0 4YY.

Pen & Sword Books Limited incorporates the imprints of Archaeology, Atlas,
Aviation, Battleground, Digital, Discovery, Family History, Fiction, History,
Local, Local History, Maritime, Military, Military Classics, Politics, Select,
Transport, True Crime, Air World, Claymore Press, Frontline Publishing,
Leo Cooper, Remember When, Seaforth Publishing, The Praetorian Press,
Wharncliffe Books, Wharncliffe Local History, Wharncliffe Transport,
Wharncliffe True Crime and White Owl.

For a complete list of Pen & Sword titles please contact
PEN & SWORD BOOKS LTD
47 Church Street, Barnsley, South Yorkshire, S70 2AS, England
E-mail: enquiries@pen-and-sword.co.uk
Website: www.pen-and-sword.co.uk

or

PEN & SWORD BOOKS
1950 Lawrence Rd, Havertown, PA 19083, USA
E-mail: uspen-and-sword@casematepublishers.com

Contents

Acknowledgments

This has been a journey that has lasted more than twenty years – with many more years surely to come. Though Joan's life seems to be poorly recorded, there are numerous avenues that have been taken to get to this point; and numerous avenues still yet to take. As such, perhaps it's most suitable to acknowledge in the 'Acknowledgments' the fact that much contexualisation appears within the following pages. The old adage that the invisibility in sources doesn't naturally preclude invisibility in life couldn't be more apropos for this woman, or the events that took place in the early thirteenth century between Wales and England. Although various suppositions appear as to Joan's involvement in various instances and her appearances at various events, they are based on evidence that often points to probability or possibility. Ultimately, the goal is to offer additional layers of discussion concerning the history of native Wales and women's involvement as members of society, particularly in the realms of politics. It is a discussion that is long overdue. Of course, any errors are solely of my own doing.

The support I have received from family, friends and colleagues over the years has been unwavering and it's difficult to know where to even begin the humble process of saying thank you. As such, this is kept short and sweet. I want to thank Huw Pryce and Louise Wilkinson for all the guidance and encouragement they've given me, as a long-ago PhD student and as a colleague. Their swift responses to last minute cries for help should especially be recognised. I would also like to thank John Northall for his kind permission to let me use his photographs of Garth Celyn. To my editors Claire Hopkins, for providing me with life-changing opportunities, enthusiasm for all things medieval and a wonderful friendship, and Karyn Burnham whose careful edit and patience deserve more than a few gold stars, an enormous thank you. I also want to give a very warm thank you to Laura Hirst,

Production Coordinator, for her incredible efficiency and for being so wonderful to work with, both as an author and editor.

Most importantly, my heartfelt thanks goes to my stalwart posse of amazing women, some of whom have been in my life for over forty years (you know who you are). You deserve the biggest and most important thanks of all: Athea Merredyth, Linda R. Messer, Jane Anderson, Lucy Chandler, Hannah Clifford, Leslie Hebb, Jen Kochenash, Kelly Langford, Barbara Reyman and Laura Salisbury. You are all Wonder Women. That is all that needs to be said.

Last, but most certainly not least, to Imp for keeping me entertained and for bringing me all the gifts and tokens of love every time the going seemed to get rough. Though, I would prefer flowers rather than baby rodents and avian dinosaurs.

Introduction

It was with great lament that on Monday, 2 February 1237 (Candlemass), the body of the long-reigning consort of the titular prince of Wales was transported from the royal residence of Aber on the north Walian mainland, across the Menai Straits to the ancient holy isle of Anglesey. There on the eastern shores, in the royal demesne of Llanfaes, Joan, Lady of Wales, was buried to views across the dark Irish Sea and formidable Eryri mountains, rearing their lofty summits up to the clouds. In grief over his tremendous loss, her husband, the renowned Llywelyn ap Iorwerth (r. 1195–1240) established the Franciscan house of Barefooted Friars to be built in honour of the soul of his beloved wife. Thereafter, the monastery erected around Joan's final resting place became the royal mausoleum for the successive royal consorts of the princes of Gwynedd.

The death of Joan of England, Siwan to the Welsh, was not just of enormous personal loss for her husband of over thirty years, and their grown children. The king of England was also dealt a great personal blow. The Lady of Wales was his sister and one he was seemingly close to. The impact of her death was also felt politically. Arguably, that sorrowful February Monday is the moment that Anglo-Welsh relations began to tilt slowly on its axis towards an inevitable and permanent decline. Unarguably, her death marked a shift in relations. Without Joan's experience as a diplomat to fall back on, and her position in both the Welsh and English courts as a beloved wife, daugther and sister, the first tremors of change rumbled. Many more powerful tremors followed over the next forty-five years eventually leading to the catastrophic political earthquake of 1282 and the permanent conquest of Wales by England's Edward I (r. 1272–1307).

This is the story of Joan of England, illegitimate daughter of King John (r. 1199–1216) and wife of Llywelyn the Great of Wales. Over the course of a life that spanned close to fifty years, Joan's own power and repute rose to great heights from very humble beginnings. Much lauded for her role in the history of medieval Wales, she was a woman who successfully influenced a generation of Anglo-Welsh politics. Joan fulfilled the traditional expectations of a woman of her royal status, acting as a 'peace-weaver' and merciful conduit between two powerful families. As with many royal woman of the Middle Ages, the situation she found herself in melded the personal and the political. Hers, therefore, is a story that is invariably intertwined with very real personal and political relationships – from relationships that aided in the elevation of her status and that of her own family's on a wider political scale, to one in particular that threatened to destabilise her husband's authority and disrupt the precarious peace between a fragmented Wales and her mighty English neighbour.

As the mother of at least five children, the wife of a husband who was the most powerful Welsh ruler of the Middle Ages, the daughter of a notoriously ruthless king, the sister of a much younger child-king, and in her position as a royal Welsh consort, the breadth of her responsibilities, duties and concerns were tremendous, indeed. Women of the upper echelons of medieval society, and especially royalty, often found themselves in untenable positions as marriage was a political manoeuvre, a means of acquiring allies and attempts to establish peace. Love found in such alliances was believed to be a lucky bonus. As traditional 'weavers of peace', women were literally the gateways between two families who had to privately, and sometimes publicly, negotiate fidelities. Although once married their expected loyalty was to that of their husbands and own family, it was the women of sheer strength who successfully endured, survived and operated within and around the expectations and demands placed upon them by both families. It is not far off the mark to claim that the majority of women were not just survivors of their circumstance, they were women of stamina.

Joan had a penchant for diplomacy given her impressive track record as a successful political envoy from 1211 onwards. Despite of her fame, and infamy, like the majority of women from her time, the fullness or breadth of her story languishes in the shadows of the feats, tragedies and majesties of the powerful men in her life; from her father and husband, to brother, son and lover. But were Joan's own successes and failures simply dictated by those around her, as is often intimated in the pages of the history books in which she appears? Having survived the tumultuous early thirteenth-century and the fraught grandstanding between a Wales ruled by a number of warring native princes and an England ruled by the 'devil's brood', Joan's accomplishments and disappointments were also related to her undertakings defined by her own character and personality. Although her intimate relationships afforded her opportunities to intervene in a highly contentious political realm, over the course of her life she forged an effective political career that seems to have been founded also in strength of character and intelligence.

Without meaning to stumble deep into the caverns of outdated stereotypes, Joan also likely possessed an element of charm, even if it was learnt behaviour. After all, the royal consort in the Welsh court was expected to be the 'hostess with the mostess', hospitality being one of the more renowned and revered customs among the Welsh. These important traditions she would have been quickly educated in upon her arrival as a foreigner and newly-wed in 1205. It was expected that she fulfil them forever more, and to the best of her ability as the female face of Welsh leadership and authority. The reigning Lady of Wales would have been required to carry on conversation with visiting political emissaries, provide entertainment to guests and be involved in public acts of gift-giving – bestowing gifts to guests, in particular, was a time-honoured Welsh custom that was, in reality, an act of recognition of fealty.

Charm, for lack of a better word, was something that her paternal family were often noted for, in amid their infamous and notorious fits of rage. Although it is still unknown who her mother was – a mystery that may never be resolved – as a member of the Angevin dynasty, Joan surely possessed some, if not all of the resolute determination, intelligence and political acumen that defined the legacy of her female forebears from her paternal side – from her grandmother, the renowned and formidable Eleanor of Aquitaine (r. 1154–1189), to her aunts Joanna, queen of Sicily (r. 1177–1189), Eleanor of England, queen of Castile (r. 1170–1214), Matilda of England, duchess of Saxony and Bavaria (r. 1168–1180), and great-aunt, Emma of Anjou (r. 1175–1195) Joan's own predecessor as princess of North Wales and wife of one of Llywelyn's uncles. Her half-sisters were Eleanor, countess of Pembroke and later Leicester (b. *c.* 1215–1275), the wife of the famous Simon de Montfort (d. 1265), Joan Makepeace, Scotland's queen (r. 1221–1238) and wife Alexander II (r. 1214–1249) and Isabella of England, herself Holy Roman Empress (r. 1235–1241). Though, nothing of the sort is recorded in contemporary sources, it is pretty safe to assume that the Lady of Wales, too, possessed at least a modicum of the genetic disposition to fits of rage and haughtiness, never mind stubbornness and a large independent streak, but also the sharp intelligence, resoluteness and strength that so defined the women and the men in her natal family.

Drawing a map of her life, no matter how circuitous the journey, is important for many reasons. Not only does it shed light on a woman whose impact on the history of native Wales was great indeed, but perhaps more importantly, it also sheds light on the very murky and unexplored area of Welsh queenship. Of course, Joan's own story is knitted within the fabric of the stories and relationships with the men in her life. Yet in many ways, evidence points to the fact that she, herself, effected real change in terms of Anglo-Welsh relations and policies stemming from the Venedotian court under Llywelyn's reign. Moreover, the role that she played as a political envoy indicates she carried out duties and expectations associated with royal women within in native Welsh courts.

Before delving further, it is important here to note the deliberate employment of the term 'queen' to refer to Joan throughout this book. It is used for many reasons. In the first instance, although definitions of 'queen' and 'queenship' in a Welsh context seem vague on the outset, as we will see, they are more defined when examined against the background in which their usage appears in both native and normative Welsh sources; sources largely stemming from the twelfth and thirteenth centuries, many contemporary to Joan's lifetime. More importantly, and more apropos to Joan's case in particular, they are also defined by the duties, roles and expectations that the wife of a Welsh ruler were expected to carry out.

Joan's responsibilities, her status, her position and the authority she wielded were not just down to her person or the circumstances that she found herself in. They were also part and parcel of how the office of the queen, at least in North Wales but likely throughout much of Wales, operated. In fact, later in life the eventual change in her title from 'princess of North Wales' to 'Lady of Wales' may have highlighted the elevation of not just Joan's personal position in life, but may also relate real historical change in the status and perception of the office of the Welsh queen. This change in title was a mirror to Llywelyn's own from 'prince of North Wales' to 'prince of Aberffraw and lord of Snowdon'. The choice to embrace these new designations was imbued by the desire to formally declare their royal authority over all others – an authority unmatched in Wales at any time in the Middle Ages.

Joan's status as Llywelyn's consort was set well-above those of her Welsh peers and in the most fundamental of ways, Joan and Llywelyn were queen and king, regardless that titles of 'princess' and 'prince', 'lady' and 'lord' were used. Thus, use of the term 'queen' is a reminder that her status was unparalleled. In many undeniable ways, Joan was a very visible model of a 'Welsh' queen. Remembering this helps us better understand the context of her story and acceptance of her employment of agency and power as a woman. It was not just as a wife, or a mother, or a daughter or a sister that she acted, but also as queen.

As such, although this study follows a chronological approach, beginning with Joan's origins in Normandy in the late 1180s, early 1190s, and follows her career to her death in 1237, it is also defined by an essential thematic strand that is vitally important to understanding who she was: the ideals and practices concerning native Welsh queenship. Interspersed throughout her narrative are examples and stories of other royal consorts in Wales who came before, during and after her as a means of providing a wider backdrop and context. In turn, Joan's own story provides opportunity to illustrate and give voice to other women of Welsh history whose own stories languish in the margins of the master narrative; stories and voices that are much less well known and little understood.

Joan's roles, activities and successes were, in large part, a reflection of her status as the reigning consort of the most prominent of Welsh leaders. Yet, there are numerous native cultural practices and attitudes to contend with when trying to come to terms with what a queen was, her precise position and status in society. Perhaps the largest issue concerns the marital practices in medieval Wales, which differed from much of Western Europe. Concubinage and the recognition of illegitimate children as heirs and successors was a large part of the culture. In fact, Wales had nine different types of legally recognised marital unions and as such, a man could (and often did) have more than one wife. Children of such unions were accepted into society and openly acknowledged as heirs. The first-born son of Llywelyn himself, like Joan, was illegitimate by birth. This Gruffudd ap Llywelyn (d. 1244) spent his entire lifetime fighting for recognition of his privileged status and rights to patrimony, including the successorship to the kingdom of Gwynedd as he found himself in competition with his legitimate half-brother, Dafydd. Llywelyn's decision to choose as his legal heir and successor his son by Joan, largely due to his own legitimate status and blood connection to the English Crown, had a great impact on the cultural and political practices in Wales. For Joan, Llywelyn's decision reflected her own importance and worth, both politically and personally. That Dafydd was chosen as Llywelyn's successor exposes the height of Joan's own perceived status as queen – a worth that was recognised by the English Crown and the papacy when she, herself, was legitimised in 1226.

Themes of identity are also intimately associated with Siwan's story. Did Joan identify herself as a daughter, and sister, of the kings of England? Did she identify herself as a Plantagenet? As Anglo-Norman? Eventually, as 'Welsh'? How were her intimate connections perceived by others? How did these connections affect her identity? Her status? How we remember her? Asking such questions helps us place some of the pieces of the puzzle together by connecting the myriad of shadowy aspects of Joan's life that may be missed otherwise. They also help to position a number of pieces of the puzzle concerning Welsh queenship as her story highlights aspects of Welsh queenship in practice and custom. Joan and queenship go hand-in-hand. Both stories are one. As such, the position of the queen, in particular, is discussed in relation to Joan's own narrative throughout this book. This is a helpful approach to better understanding both subjects when many of the pieces remain lost due to the silence nature of sources.

In medieval Welsh sources, women are identified solely through their lifecycles; they are labelled as the daughters, wives, mothers, widows, sisters, aunts, and nieces of men. In other words, a woman's worth was categorised and identified through relationships, pinpointing the importance of her own position within her natal and marital families. These important classifications helped distinguish a woman's overall social status. For men, property and landholdings defined their status.

The emergence of gender specific research as an all-inclusive discipline, as opposed to the exclusivity and weightiness of women's history as a standalone subject, has been prompted by the urge to know and understand the experiences of women in history through an understanding of the context of their relationships to men. Women's relationships to men are often the only route to undertake in the first instance to studying women's history as it is within these relationships they appear in sources and to which they are intrinsically tied. That the lives of medieval women are often placed within the trajectories of the masculine narrative has created a problematic dichotomy traditionally used to define women and their history: women have been seen as either victims or agents of change, as muted objects or as viragos in control of their own stories. Ultimately, it is a mixture of the two.

As a general rule, medieval sources do little to expose the true intimacy of interactions between individuals making personalities, relationships, aspirations and actions difficult if not nigh on impossible to define in the majority of cases. The ways in which both sexes are often portrayed and represented in medieval sources reveal the complex nature of the intent and purpose behind written records themselves, never mind the complexities associated with actually trying to unravel what the 'truth' or the 'facts' may be. It is because sense of identity, who we are and where we have come from, are so important to us as human beings that the overreaching theme of this book is itself about identity. Such considerations easily coalesce with enduring ontological discussions about the sheer nature of being and human emotions, both of which are certainly crucial to the study of women's and gender history overall.

Lack of information about women in the Middle Ages, even of Joan's standing, is nothing new. Certainly through much of history, little attempt has been made to incorporate women into the stories of humankind and few records exist that discuss women, individual or as a collective, and what their lives were really like. Over the past forty years this exasperating trend has finally gone into reverse for medieval studies. Scholarship continues to reveal the complex nature and interplay between socially constructed gender expectations and stereotypes that we have traditionally accepted as the de facto realities of life. Thankfully, the notion that the 'public' realm of the medieval world was dominated by men while women were forced behind the scenes into the 'private' or domestic realm has been proven to be sorely outdated and just plain erroneous on many an occasion. As we will see, the facts concerning Joan's life as we understand them are the perfect antidote to alleviating such a malaise. That she was successful and respected as a political envoy, there is no doubt. Throughout her life she was sent on many occasions to parlay for peace with the kings of England and, crucially, during times of great upheaval.

The undeniable adage that history is written by the victors holds very true for gender history and certainly skews our perception of individuals and the greater collective. As a woman's historian, one has to learn to read between the blank lines. Joan's life is full of them. Nevertheless, while the appearance of women overall, and Joan specifically, in medieval sources is limited, this does not negate their actual contribution to society in all facets of life: commerce and trade, politics, law, the management of lands, medicine and the arts, family life and the education of children are just a few of the most obvious examples. Any student of history knows that contextualisation of surrounding events and experiences is crucial to a more nuanced understanding of 'facts'.

In an attempt to try to understand as much of the ins and outs of Joan's life as we can, this is an important issue. First, the number of sources stemming from native Wales are extremely small in comparison to elsewhere in Western Europe. It may be argued, however, that the Welsh literary genre was perhaps different. Certainly, the Welsh Triads, *Trioedd Ynys Prydein*[1] (the first written origins of the Arthurian tradition), the tales of the *Mabinogion* and the poetry of the great courtly bards of the twelfth and thirteenth centuries, known as the *gogynfierdd*, exude a distinguished richness in flavour and texture. Variations of such profundity are found in the numerous manuscripts produced in Wales during this time and in such ways that their contribution to the overall lexicon of medieval literature remains unparalleled in many instances.

These sources, which were largely codified during the twelfth and thirteenth centuries, tell us much about Welsh custom and culture and from these we are able to glean information about how royal Welsh courts, queens and kings, vassals and subjects may have operated in many ways. The Lives of Welsh Saints (*Vitae Sanctorum Britanniae et Genealogiae*), the native laws of Hywel Dda (*Cyfriath Hywel Dda*), and the twelfth-century biography of Llywelyn's great-grandfather, Gruffudd ap Cynan of Gwynedd (*Vita Griffini Filii Conani; Historia Gruffudd vab Kynan*) can also be used to capture portraits of court life and courtly expectations. In all of these sources (save, perhaps, for poetry, which is down to mere survival), images of queens and queenship are pervasive: women are associated with legends and power and many enjoy very definite elements of authority in their own rights. Such strong and empowered royal women also feature in the works of Gerald of Wales, based on his travels in the late-twelfth and early-thirteenth century, namely his *Journey Through Wales* and *The Description of Wales* (*Itinerarium Cambriae* and *Descriptio Cambriae*). Although he seemed to enjoy dedicating time to castigating royal wives, we are still able to catch glimpses of how they operated in their courts and throughout their realms. As such, Gerald in particular provides a rich, contemporary illustration of real life in native Wales.

Other types of sources are much less verbose in description by their very nature. Chronicles are a highly used and valuable source of information into past events and are the only Welsh sources in which Joan emphatically appears, albeit a total of three whole times across the different genres. For native Welsh history the primary chronicle, which itself has a few, slightly differing variations, is *The Chronicle of the Princes*, or *Brut y Tywysogion*. In all versions, as well as in the other set of Welsh chronicles, *Cronica de Wallia*, and in the Welsh annals (*Annales Cambriae*), Joan is more closely associated with Llywelyn and his reign than that of her father, King John. She is never associated with her half-brother Henry III (r. 1216–1272). Above all, she is portrayed as the feminine symbol of Llywelyn's power and identity. Llywelyn's distinctiveness is, in turn, symbiotic with a Welsh identity. In fact, all entries in the Welsh chronicles concerning women stress female lifecycles in direct correlation with the more powerful and famous Welsh ruler they are connected to.[2] So, here, depictions of Joan are no exception. We are able to obtain more information, though not much, about her from English chroniclers like Roger of Wendover and Matthew Paris who offer small, but additional anecdotes into Joan's dealings with her father, King John.

Often medieval chronicles and annals are erroneously considered to be statements of 'fact' and an impartial list of events that took place. Yet, this could not be further from the truth. Chronicles and annals stemmed from monasteries, events largely recorded by monks whose mother houses were the beneficiaries of great endowments by the rich and powerful. As such, patronage played a large role in how, which and when events were recorded. The cartulary of Wigmore Abbey in Herefordshire, for instance, received benefaction from the mighty Mortimer dynasty, Marcher lords whose rule on the Welsh March features greatly in the cartulary. Scribes often provided stereotypes of individuals made up of a selection of important attributes shaped by family ideals. Such renderings make it difficult to evaluate a noblewoman's relationships (and man's for that matter), especially within her family due to concerns surrounding land and money. Further, chronicles passed from house to house where events were copied out, elaborated on and added to by individual scribes and patrons. As such, similar to our day and age where discerning the 'facts' through the murky bias of strong political leanings can be fraught with difficulties and frustration, questions about the authenticity of the religious male view concerning women and veracity of the accounts given in chronicles loom large. Perception is everything.

In terms of records of practice concerning the Welsh princes, such as charters, letters and treaties, the number that has survived is so small that Welsh historian Huw Pryce, with the help of Charles Insley, was able to compile and analyse the known acta of all the Welsh princes before 1283 into one amazing volume. It has become the essential bible for anyone interested in the history of native Wales, whether amateur or professional. Documents pertaining to Joan are accessed primarily from English chancery enrolments. Nevertheless, coupled with Llywelyn's acta, they provide great insight into both her possible whereabouts and her involvement in the socio-political and economic dealings of her day as they highlight a connection of business matters. She managed, for example, her own lands and was involved in the arrangement of marriages for her children, never mind her involvement in political diplomacy.

In terms of family interactions, however, the small number of sources provide evidence of the different stages of her family's existence. Surprisingly, much can be taken from the actions and events recorded to help us understand the real variety in relationships and the hows, whens and whys members interacted with one another in the ways they did. This is hugely important as, often, natural human emotions and responses to life's challenges are relegated to the sidelines when it comes to the writing of history; an odd diversion given that humanity and emotions are at the crux of all human interactions. For Joan, specifically, it is through records of practice that we are able to really trace her movements, understand her relationships and her career, and catch a glimpse of who she was as a person.

For the overall condition of women in the Middle Ages, recent studies have shown that although meagre information can be lifted from medieval sources, what does exist can be examined in ways that help paint a clearer picture of their lives, their relationships, the struggles they faced and even the joys they experienced. A woman's relationship with her immediate families, both natal and marital, becomes the utmost important determinant in understanding and evaluating female power and influence. The institution of marriage in Wales, in particular, provided women with considerable power and authority, by means of constructing 'careers' for themselves within the structure of the family and Joan is the superlative example of a woman who enjoyed the great heights of uxorial agency. Marriage often allowed aristocratic and royal women a means of participating in politics and a chance to create their own destinies.[3] For women like Joan, their influences within both their families were influences that had the potential to wield enormous political significance. By far, the most important source related to Joan is dated to the early 1230s and is an amalgamation of all the above.

Notable sources that sometimes offer discernment into a medieval royal or noble woman's own attitudes are personal letters and wills. Though both are rare for the thirteenth century, they offer valuable insight concerning personal beliefs, religion, relationships and even personal possessions by ways of bequests. We have no direct surviving evidence of Joan's religious patronage, though there can be no doubt that, in the least, she gave donations to various monasteries that were important to Llywelyn and probably to those associated with her own manors, in both in England and in Wales. It was an expectation and a way of life, plain and simple. Nor do we have will. What we do have is by far much more insightful and enlightening and much, much more exciting. We have Joan's own voice that speaks to us through the vestiges of time.

In the early 1230s she wrote a letter to her brother Henry, as king of England. In this paragon of a royal correspondence is a true mix of the personal and political. From sending her enduring love to her young brother, to castigating him for his behaviour towards her husband, to an emotive plea for reconciliation, this letter was written in her role as the Lady of Wales. Siwan seems to have been a woman who spoke her own truth and who understood the protocols, remit and authority of her role as wife, as sister, and above all, as queen.

There is only one contemporary source that alludes to this and provides a more descriptive rendering of Joan as an actual person. The English legend known as the *Romance of Fouke le Fitz Waryn* features as part of the corpus of the Matter of Britain dealing with the lives, themes and characters of medieval England. The *Romance of Fouke* is a posthumous biography of Fulk FitzWarin the powerful and daring Marcher lord who famously rebelled against King John in the early 1200s and who the king subsequently outlawed. The romance details Fulk's life as an outlaw and the Marcher lord is arguably seen as the proto-type of Robin Hood. FitzWarin had a difficult relationship with Llywelyn, but the romance tells us that Joan and Fulk's wife, Matilda de Vavasour, were friends. Importantly, Joan makes her grand appearance on centre-stage as the peace-maker between the Marcher lord and the prince of North Wales. There also appears an earlier anecdote to which she secretly informs FitzWarin of her father's interest in resuming relations with Llywelyn. Although this is a highly embellished and legendary biography befitting of the literary genre of the time, that Joan is portrayed with such high regard may speak volumes as to how she was perceived by her peers.

For Welsh and English antiquarians of the Early Modern Era, Joan seems to have been a particularly fascinating character. The dramatisation of the events surrounding her life, most specifically the year 1230 when she was imprisoned after a supposed affair with the powerful Marcher lord William de Braose, whom Llywelyn, in turn, hanged, is greatly enhanced by a number of writers and lovers of Welsh history – many of whom wrote some 500 years after her lifetime and, by extension, imposed their own anachronistic gender biases and expectations on narratives. Nevertheless, these antiquarians should be thanked for their efforts to record local tradition and lore. Without these, Joan's figure would remain in the darkness of the shadows in which she is already shrouded. Characterisations of her stem from being stoic and true to form in acting how a royal (and pious) woman should act, to her being a naïve, lovelorn creature and a conniving traitor. The writings of antiquarians like the sixteenth-century John Leland and eighteenth-century Thomas Pennant have a much more genteel approach to Joan, proffering a quaintness to the quirky customs and legends of the Welsh, than nineteenth-century writers like Louisa Stuart Costello and Thomas Pritchard, especially, who are clear and vociferous in their Welsh nationalist tendencies where the foreign woman Joan and events surrounding her actions are portrayed as being especially vile, vicious and traitorous.

The variations in how Siwan has been portrayed throughout the ages continues in our modern era, where she appears in popular historical novels by writers like Sharon Penman (*Here Be Dragons*), Edith Pargeter (Ellis Peters, *The Green Branch*) and Barbara Erskine (*Child of the*

Phoenix), as a heroine, as a woman suffering the pangs of middle age, or as removed and relatively cold-hearted. In 1956 the Welsh poet and playwright Saunders Lewis wrote the play *Siwan*. Written in the Welsh language, the play follows Joan's liaison with William de Braose to its miserable end and has most recently enjoyed a revival in theatres across Britain, in both Welsh and English.

The use of different sources throughout this investigation stemming from native Wales and England in the Middle Ages, to antiquarian works up to the nineteenth century, tie what minimal information we have on Joan in as neat a bow as possible. Collectively, they provide context to the culture and society in which she lived and help explain her status, her activities and the roles and expectations she faced. They also help us to understand the impact she herself may have had on preserving queenly tradition as the Lady of Wales, if at all. Jointly, they even help us understand what certain silences may mean – whether or not they are weighted with political and social import, or are just in fact, conventional silences concerning the movements and lives of women.

As are all life stories, that of Joan of England's is complicated; the complexities of which are further irritated by a dearth of contemporaneous material related to her. The identity of her mother remains a mystery and is much debated by today's genealogists, as is who her children were, how many she really had and where some even ended up in their own lives. How many times she travelled as an envoy, how many charters she issued and just how fully she participated in effecting Welsh polity can never be fully known. No matter the daunting aspect of approaching such an ill-documented existence, which is a painstaking project indeed, it is one that yields both exciting and long-overdue results.

This study of Joan of England seeks to revise the master narrative of native medieval Wales in the early-thirteenth century – to generate a better and more inclusively nuanced understanding of the history of this fascinating and wild region of Britain and its relationship with England by placing this particularly interesting and fascinating women at the forefront in the sequence of events. The ins and outs of the events concerning Welsh history in the late-twelfth, early-thirteenth centuries are not covered here as they are recounted in great detail, with insightful and scholarly discussions produced by great modern day historians of Welsh history, including R.R. Davies, A.D. Carr and Roger Turvey to name but a small few. Nevertheless, as this book will show, Joan is a viable subject of historical enquiry and an agent of change in her own right. In a number of ways, recorded evidence of her involvement in Anglo-Welsh affairs, as a formal and official envoy, remain not just the first, but sadly the only 'full and complete' accounts that illustrate the role of the Welsh consort in practice. If nothing else, it is for this reason that a study such as this is important.

Although Siwan's role in Anglo-Welsh history has received recognition by historians, she has been still largely relegated to the sidelines; an indication that her role was not entirely critical to the stability and growth of Welsh polity, or peace with England overall. On the flip side, it is sometimes difficult not to naturally overplay our hand and emphatically conclude that Joan was, indeed, a heroine and that if it were not for her, the very fabric native Wales would have been fundamentally altered by the time Llywelyn died in 1240. On balance, however, it is vitally important to understand that the aggregate of Joan's interventions in the early-thirteenth century ensured that she really was a crucial player in the political wranglings between the ruler of Gwynedd and the rulers of England. The famous early-twentieth-century Welsh historian J.E. Lloyd concluded that Llywelyn ap Iorwerth 'had one emissary whose diplomatic services far outran those of the seneschal and who helped him in this capacity for the greater part of his reign. To the assistance of his wife Joan, both as advocate and counsellor, there can be no doubt he was much indebted.'[4] To the assistance of Joan, Lady of Wales, there can be no doubt that the history of native medieval Wales is also much indebted.

Chapter One

Roots and All

'daughter of King John and Queen Clemencia'

By the late twelfth century, the most powerful dynasty in Western Europe was that of the Angevin. The shocking marriage of Eleanor, duchess of Aquitaine, former wife of Louis VII, King of France (r. 1131–1180), and mother of his two daughters, to the son of England's Empress Matilda (r. 1114–1125), Henry II (r. 1154–1189), in 1152 rocked much of Europe. The royal couple's combined comradery, passion and antagonism quickly became legendary, even during their own lifetimes. Eleanor was strong, intelligent, politically perspicacious and fiercely independent, but so was Henry. The product of this combustible combination and ultimate clash of wills was that the leading European dynasty in the mid- to late-twelfth century was fraught with public and private discord. Discord which resulted in, first, the creation, and second, virtual destruction of the vast Angevin Empire. Over the course of a mere sixty-four years, the Angevins suffered greatly, with both loss of lands and, arguably more importantly, family love and loyalty.

The future of Eleanor and Henry's youngest son John, indeed the youngest of eight children, was initially defined by a religious career. Having three older brothers, Henry the Young King (r. 1170–1183), Geoffrey and Richard I (r. 1189–1199), meant any real potential for this particular whelp to wield landed power was minimal, earning him the sobriquet 'Lackland' (Jean sans Terre). By all accounts, it was accepted that he was destined for the church, the fated home for many a young son of the medieval elite. Nevertheless, it seems that John was Henry's favourite and was given much authority in his young life, including the titles of the Count of Mortain and Lord of Ireland. It was during these formative years that John cultivated his understanding of the Welsh and the Marcher lords having been placed in charge of the region as a mere teenager.

1

Joan was likely born out of wedlock when her father was in his late-teens, early-twenties (*c.* 1185–89). Evidence for this is indicated in the April 1226 decree made by Pope Honorious III (r. 1216–1227) formally legitimising Joan, which refers to her birth occurring at a time when King John of England was unmarried, fathering her by an unmarried woman.[1] As John married his first wife Isabella of Gloucester (r. 1189–1199) on 29 August 1189, it is believed that Joan cannot have been born after that date. Although, she certainly could have been as it is by no means beyond the realm of possibilities that the political weight behind Joan's legitimisation overrode any moral contingencies, and that a looseness with the truth was necessary to make sure private agreements and/or expectations at the time of her request were met.[2]

John was said to have been much like his father, donning dark red hair, not overly tall – being about 5 ft 6½ in – and disposed to great, childish fits of rage.[3] As an adult, he was also known for his charm, hospitality, generosity and wit, when it suited him. Nevertheless, King John of England was, and still is, far more notorious than admired for a number of reasons. Contemporary chroniclers were particularly unkind to him, with the Waverly annalist summing up his reign: 'He disinherited some without judgment of their peers, and he condemned others to a dire death; he violated their wives and daughters – his own law was his despotic will'.[4] The way he ruled was seen as arbitrary and not by the law. His infamous paranoia made him spiteful towards those he imagined slighted him. Even his own adherents were not spared his bouts of pettiness and rage. The view of him as a tyrant has been based on his perceived eagerness to exact revenge when insulted, his extravagance and constant need for money, his unsuccessful attempts to mollify nations which only induced fear and unease because of his flawed and largely unsuccessful tactics, his purported cowardice and, conversely, his ambition to hold the Crown in the first place. As one of his own famous biographer's noted, 'He had the mental abilities of a great king, but the inclinations of a petty tyrant'.[5] Some accusations are certainly justified, but recent scholarship has taken a kinder approach to discussing both the man and his reign. He was, indeed, a capable administrator, a remarkable arbiter, and an astute strategist.[6] He was also a doting father.

Nevertheless, King John is a man well known for his penchant for upsetting and insulting his barons. The crimes and misdemeanours documented in the Magna Carta notwithstanding, John was also renowned for more personal, or 'private' insults. One of his especially notorious

2

proclivities was sleeping with the wives and daughters of many an English baron. This, in itself, was a contentious enough issue that likely helped fan much of the disaffection he faced during his reign by leading men in his kingdom. Medieval chroniclers like Roger of Wendover, Gerald of Wales and William of Newburgh attest to John's immoral behaviour, adulterous ways and constant straying into unacceptable amorous realms. In fact, Gerald of Wales actually compared John to 'a robber permanently on the prowl, always probing, always searching for the weak spot where there is something for him to steal'.[7] The anonymous author of *The Legend of Fulk FitzWarin* refers to John as 'a man without conscience' who was 'wicked and perverse and wanton'; hated by 'all good folk' he was a womaniser who, upon hearing of,

> any fair lady or damsel, wife or daughter or earl or of baron, or of any other, he desired her for his pleasure, deceiving her by promises or by gifts, or else carrying her off by force. And for that he was most hated, and by reason of this many of the great lords of England had renounced their homage to the King, and because of this the King was the less feared.[8]

A leading example of this behaviour stems from John's relationship with Eustace de Vesci, lord of Alnwick. When he was younger, John was purportedly taken with Eustace's wife, Margaret of Scotland, half-sister to Alexander II, King of Scotland. Eustace was a 'Northerner' and a powerful landowner, often found in service of John, and Richard before him. Before falling out of favour, as so many of John's familiars seem to have done, Walter of Guisborough tells us that John was set on seducing Margaret only to be thwarted by trickery when a commoner surreptitiously took her place the one night the king eagerly awaited spending time alone with her. A great amount of animosity simmered between the two men, which was perhaps compounded by John's lust of Margaret, and in the end, Eustace de Vesci was one of the leading barons who rebelled against John in 1212 and, finally, in 1215/16.

The judgement by the medieval literati was hardly surprising, or unwarranted in context. Most were monastic writers, who by virtue of vocation, saw the public and private roles of the king essentially as one – the king (like his queen) was supposed to be the pinnacle of integrity, a model of piety and morality. John's known behaviour was, of course, derided, but not unexpected as father and both grandfathers were also renowned for their adulterous affairs. Being seduced by the excitement of immoral and clandestine affairs was in the king's blood.

It is known that John had numerous mistresses throughout his lifetime, with many contemporary references providing curious, suggestive entries about probable relations, rather than overtly naming the women John desired and slept with. One example relates to Joan de Cornhill, the wife of Hugh Neville. Hugh, sheriff of a number areas in England such as Lincolnshire, Hampshire, Hertfordshire, Oxfordshire and Essex was another of John's favourites. He was, in fact, castigated as one of the king's foremost 'evil counsellors', being named in Magna Carta as one of the king's leading advisors. In 1204, Joan de Cornhill promised the king 'two hundred chickens that she might lie one night with her husband'.[9] We also know that Hawise, the countess of Aumale, was one of John's mistresses when she was in her widowhood. She was powerful woman, described by Richard I's chronicler, Richard of Devizes as 'a woman who was almost a man, lacking nothing virile except the virile organs'.[10] Many other references in records are even more vague. We know he had mistresses named Suzanne and Clemencia, yet most remain unidentified, such as the woman in 1212 to whom the king sent roses straight from his justiciar's garden.

What we know of Joan's mother comes from her own obituary found in the Tewkesbury annals which refers to the Lady of Wales as the daughter of King John and 'Queen Clemencia'. There has been much debate concerning the elusive nature of this entry. The title 'queen' in context itself could relate to very different meanings, which adds to the mystery. The Old English '*cwen*', or Old Saxon '*quan*', is related to the Proto-Germanic '*kwenon*', the root of which means 'woman' or possibly even 'wife'. In fact, the Old English use of *cwen* also refers to a 'female serf, hussy or prostitute'. On the swing side of the pendulum, the use of the term *cwen* unquestionably relates to 'queen, female ruler of a state'. Ultimately, the original essence of the label referred not just to a 'wife', but expressly to the 'wife of a king'.

In early medieval Europe, the betrothal of concubines and the status of the defined relationships thereof, were regarded as proper marriages. It was a relatively common practice and even early canon laws that addressed concubinage were ambiguous. In the simplest of terms, such unions were generally accepted if marital affection was evident. Marital affection, as opposed to lust, was viewed as a potential future contract of

4

marriage because it was assumed the union was based on love. As such, couples who cohabitated enjoyed privileges similar to those who were bound by the more formal union of marriage. For concubines themselves, early medieval laws protected their status and, theoretically speaking, these women enjoyed the same legal status as that of the formal wife. A concubine was able to retain gifts and legacies from her partner, hold property and titles in her own name. She was also allowed to receive testamentary bequests from her partner's estate.[11]

The social and, importantly, political acceptance of concubinage among royals ensured that the limited rights these women enjoyed were upheld. Perhaps key to concubines maintaining their rights was the fact that their children were publicly recognised by their fathers who were also rulers. Such recognition of children from concubinous unions meant that the status of the concubine herself was an elevated one; she was de facto a member of the royal household. How could she not be if her first-born son from such a union was allowed to succeed the throne? Such a stance can be summed up by the Merovingian dynasty in early-medieval France who believed that the sheer strength and purity of royal blood itself meant that the practice of concubinage could hardly taint it. Consequently, the status of royal concubines in the imperial household was of an elevated rank.

Throughout Europe during the twelfth-century Renaissance, ecclesiastical ideals towards marriage changed, and the sexual union between a woman and man was seen as a means of constructing, in a sense, both religious and a social order. These orders were based on ideological terms that enhanced religious objectives, ensuring marriage became a spiritual journey – from betrothal to a formal union. Thus, the accepted relationship between a woman and man became one defined through a public ceremonial process; in the least, with a couple being married at the church door. In the wider context, changes redefined and established marriage as a spiritual union based on consent. This was an argument popularised by Peter Lombard who believed that betrothal was different from marriage, being a promise of the future, whereas marriage was a consent regarding the 'here and now'. The papacy backed the consensual theory and, eventually, this became the leading canonical doctrine concerning marriage. It was widely adopted throughout Europe in the High Middle Ages. With the additional rise in the importance and acceptance of the practice of primogeniture during this time, women's status as queens became much more secure because the era of 'serial marriages' came to an end. This allowed the succession of their eldest children to remain unchallenged. Thus, ecclesiastical attitudes towards concubinage (and the sexual roles of women in particular) changed and the church increased its dominance over marital proceedings and rulings concerning the legitimacy of marital unions. By the twelfth century, the practice of concubinage was all but snuffed out across Western Europe. That is not to say, however, that traditional attitudes towards such unions were as easily quelled.

Wales, Ireland and Norse countries, particularly Denmark and Iceland, remained pockets of resistance to the social and ecclesiastical changes in marital practices and attitudes to concubinage that occurred over the course of the twelfth and early-thirteenth centuries. In these societies, there seems to have been little to no stigma attached to concubinage or to the status of the concubine well into the thirteenth century. The marriage to more than one woman was deemed an acceptable means of allying oneself with more than one kindred or dynasty.[12] This was particularly important for rulers who wanted to expand the remit of their authority. Analogous to earlier medieval times, it is questionable as to whether a woman's status was debased by these customs during the High Middle Ages, because all wives maintained a legal status that separated them from concubines.

The culture that Joan herself married into when she wed Llywelyn ap Iorwerth in 1205 was fluid when it came to defining wives and concubines. Welsh practices and attitudes towards marriage had a bearing on her own status as a wife and queen. As a principal matter of policy during Joan and Llywelyn's reign, the practices of concubinage and marriage found themselves at the forefront of great change. They were spectacularly modified by the royal couple for their own personal and political purposes – to preserve their family dynasty and hegemony in Wales – and the way of doing so was to: one) bring the practice of marriage in Wales more in line European standards established in the twelfth century; and two) formally adopt the practice of primogeniture, recognising the first-born legitimate son as a successor. Before the changes introduced by Joan and Llywelyn, essentially all wives were considered equal as is evidenced by the inheritance of *all* sons by such wives.

Although fundamentally based on the concept of consent, Welsh marital customs and laws were unique to much of medieval Europe at this time and, in fact, were distinctly different in a number of ways. Native Welsh law, in fact, defines nine different types of marriage, or 'nine rightful couplings' ('*nau kynywedi teithiauc*') that were considered to be legally binding.[13] Explanations of these 'nine rightful couplings', save for the bottom tier which is essentially forced marriage and rape, stress the woman's choice in defining a union – whether or not she chose to live with the man or continue to live with her family. The fluid nature of definitions and types of marriage suggest that the innate sexual nature of woman and man was recognised and even respected. This is important to keep in mind once delving into the events in Joan's life and how her own experiences were perceived and recorded.

At the top of the tier of marriage types, which promised social and economic advancement, were 'unions by gift of kin' (*priodas* and *agwedi/ agweddi*). At the second level were 'unions not by gift of kin, but with the consent of kin and the woman herself'. *Caradas*, where the women did not have to leave her home at marriage, but who was openly visited by her husband, was probably the most common. Of the other two types related to this category, *deu lysaub*, is believed to have been related to marital unions between step-children or families, while *llathlut goleu* likely pertained to an elopement (where the couple cohabitated together anywhere but in the woman's family home). The publicity of both acts indicates that the woman's family gave consent to these unions.

The third level dealt with 'unions to which the woman's kin do not consent, but to which the woman herself does'. Both of these were enveloped in secrecy. *Llathlut twyll* was probably an elopement and while *beichogi twyll gwreic lwyn a pherth* was a secret marriage where the woman remained at home with her family and did not live with her husband. At the bottom of the pyramid lies the fourth category of 'marriage', which generally deals with lack of consent to a union by the woman or her family. In other words, abductions, forced marriages (*kynnywedi ar liw acar oleu*) or unions based on deceit, particularly of a virgin woman who was tricked into intercourse or raped (*twyll morwyn*).

All of these categories have additional levels of recognised marriage. In the top tier, 'unions by gift of kin', there were two distinct levels, one of which was considered the most formal type of union known as *priodas*. *Priodas* was deemed the most honourable type of union and was the most legally binding.[14] Certainly, by the end of the thirteenth century, it was regarded as the only real type of marriage that was recognised by both Welsh ecclesiastics and jurists and is essentially what we recognise to be marriage today.

Above all, different variations of the Welsh laws imply that the wedded wife, by definition *gwraig briod*, had a much more significant status over that of the concubine, *cywyres* (or perhaps sometimes referred to simply as *gwraig*). Sources like the Life of Gruffudd ap Cynan, the Welsh Triads, chronicles and the genealogical tract related to the princely dynasties, *Achau Brenhinoedd a Thywysogon Cymru*, make clear differentiations between the status in a ruler's 'wife' and that of his 'concubine'.[15] The tractate on the Welsh laws of women, *Cyfraith y Gwragedd*, actually goes as far as to pardon any wife who beats her husband's concubine, even if the beating kills her. This diktat is also found in the legal triads. Interestingly, the rendition of this particular tractate is found in the legal redaction of the Welsh laws from thirteenth-century Gwynedd, known as Iorwerth, which also makes it clear that by this time, a man is *not* to have two wives in the first place. It is no coincidence that this change is found in the Iorwerth redaction, which was written during Joan and Llywelyn's rule.

Much of the ambiguity concerning the status of wives, and queens, is epitomised in the vocabulary used to define 'married woman'; comparable to the ambiguity used to describe the different types of marriages on offer. Similar to eleventh-century Anglo-Saxon culture where the words 'wife' and 'woman' were used interchangeably to refer to a woman of adult status (and/or queen as discussed above), Welsh language used a common term to refer to a woman who was married and/or of adult age: *gwraig*. *Gwraig* had a number of wide ranging meanings varying from 'female of any age' to our modern appreciation of the definition of 'wife'. Ultimately, *gwraig* alluded to a 'sexually experienced female', though the lawyers were quick to acknowledge the difficulty in assessing a woman's legal status based merely on her sexuality, even quipping: 'no one knows what she is, whether maiden or woman, because the signs of childbearing have appeared on her'.[16]

The term *gwraig briod* refers to our perception of what a 'married woman' is and during Llywelyn and Joan's reign this became a very important distinction, specific to their situation; it was one that had a direct effect on the long-term successes of their kingdom. In order for Llywelyn to further strengthen his authority as the leading Welsh leader, it was important for him to be seen to modify Welsh marital practices so they fell more in line with European traditions, namely, openly embracing the practice of primogeniture. Interestingly, the importance and need for this change, which both Joan and Llywelyn adopted as a means of ensuring that their son Dafydd became Llywelyn's rightful successor, was also mirrored in native records that illuminate the evolution of the practice of *priodas* so that it evolved to eventually become the only truly accepted type of marriage and the superior legal union. Nevertheless, evidence of how marriage and concubinage was actually practised in conformity with the laws is meagre. Yet, one fascinating thirteenth-century charter from South Wales, an area largely under Anglo-Norman control by this time, shows that the practice of concubinage was still accepted, and arguably even profitable for the woman in question. A grant of land was made to Margam Abbey by a woman named Margeria a former concubine of a clerk of Kenfig (*Margaria filia Rogeri q[u]ondam c[on]cubina ... Ricardi cl[er]ici de Kenefeg*).[17] The charter itself makes it clear that her label of 'concubine' was one that helped promote her status as a patron.

Thus, there was a commonality in the ambiguity of a woman's status across the board, not only in societies such as Wales that embraced antediluvian practices as a means of underscoring a proud cultural identity, but in many locations in Europe. This is important as marriage was an essential avenue for women to secure a more reputable status in society. For queens, it was about establishing a venerated status above all others. Terms used to identify women in medieval sources, whether as 'wife' or 'queen' were hugely weighted and not always as they seemed. It is against this backdrop that the Tewkesbury entry must be associated in order to highlight the sheer complex nature of figuring out not only who Queen Clemencia was, but how and why Joan's mother was referred to in such a way. John was not married to Joan's mother, if we accept the 1226 papal dispensation for Joan's legitimisation for face value. As such, it is also very likely that the title of 'queen' was bestowed upon Clemencia as a reflection of Joan's own legitimacy, whether Clemencia was actually low-born or not; 'queen' was a title used to further eulogise Joan's own royal standing in both England and Wales at the time of her death in 1237. It is also important to consider that the Tewkesbury entry may be reminiscent of the older, customary attitudes towards royal concubines in Wales in particular. In places like Tewkesbury located on the Welsh March, the acculturation of Welsh attitudes towards marriage was inevitable to an extent, even if practices themselves were not adopted. With this in mind, the monk who wrote the entry may have been under such influences.

Whether or not Clemencia was a queen or a concubine is perhaps a moot point. What is important, however, is trying to establish who she was a person. Clemencia was probably French and this can be deduced using two particular reasonings. One, John was in his late-teens, early twenties when Joan was born, and with only a small handful of possible sojourns to England, he spent much of his time in France between 1187 and 29 August 1189, when he married Isabella of Gloucester in England. And two, Joan seems to have spent her early years in France, probably Normandy, from where she sailed to England in 1203. Never mind that Clemence was a name that was more widely used for women in France than in England. Although she was probably French, that is not to say she did not live in England. There are a number of contenders for which Clemencia gave birth to the future Lady of Wales, but there is enough evidence against most of the candidates to rule them out, save for two.

For instance, the fact that in 1210 a baron from Cumberland by the name Robert de Vaux had to bribe John into silence by giving him five palfreys of the highest standard and an astounding sum of 750 marks in additional amity for purely salacious reasons has erroneously led to Clemence Pinel being a contender as Joan's mother. These offerings made to the king were to act as a guarantee that the monarch would continue to keep to himself what he knew about the supposed relations between de Vaux and the wife of Henry Pinel.[18] Misreadings of the Latin source by some historians and genealogists have likely led to the misinterpretation that it was John himself who had the affair with Clemence Pinel. Given what we know about this king, it is an easy mistake to make.

Later Welsh sources, in particular, often refer to Agatha de Ferrers, one of John's better-known mistresses, as Joan's mother. However, the first recorded instance seems to be in *The Historie of Cambria*, written by Dr David Powell in 1584: 'About this time Lhewelyn prince of Wales tooke to wife Ione the daughter of king Iohn, by Agatha the daughter of Robert Ferrers Earle of Derby, with whom the said king gaue him the lordship of Elsmere in the Marches of Wales'.[19] Elsewhere in his *Historie* Powell confusingly refers to Agatha as 'a ladie named Clemence daughter to the Earle Ferrers', likely making reference to the Tewkesbury entry. Confusion around the identity of Joan's mother is little helped by misstatements and inaccuracies found in primary sources such as these. The latter reference states that Clemence died before her husband Ranulf (earl of Chester), who then married Margaret de Bohun, the famous female constable of England.

Although William de Ferrers, 4th earl of Derby, was another of John's favourites, it seems very unlikely that Agatha was Joan's mother, even if it turns out she had actually been one of John's mistresses. Agatha de Ferrers' mother was Sybil de Braose, the sister of the infamous William de Braose IV, lord of Gower. This is important to note and is one of the larger arguments against Agatha as 'Queen Clemencia' as it would add a concerning dimension to events that took place in Joan's life in 1230. If Agatha had been Joan's mother, Joan's purported affair with the lord of Gower's grandson, William de Braose, (discussed at length in Chapter Eleven) would have meant that Joan and William were directly blood-related as second cousins – they would have shared the same great-grandparents and such a relationship was well-within the prohibited degrees of consanguinity espoused by the Catholic Church. Joan's legitimisation in 1226 by papal decree surely would have meant a future relationship with William would not have been in the cards as it would have further called into question the legitimacy of her own son, Dafydd, and the legitimacy of his successorship to the kingdom of Gwynedd in the eyes of the English government. By definition, this affair would have been incestuous and, if so, would have given further rise to gossip and perhaps used as additional ammunition by Joan's detractors to denigrate her worth and status, never mind ammunition to greatly condemn her character.

Constance, duchess of Brittany (1161–1201), was the daughter of Conan, earl of Richmond and duke of Brittany, and Margaret of Huntingdon of Scottish royalty. She was also, famously, the widow of King John's older brother, Geoffrey, who was killed in a tournament in 1186. She was the mother of ill-fated Arthur and Eleanor, the Fair Maid of Brittany, successors to the English Crown after the death of Richard I in 1189. Constance spent her life pursuing her claims to the duchy of Brittany and her own political ambitions, including her son's successorship to the English throne. Given the power and authority that she rightly fought to wield, especially after Geoffrey's death, Henry II seemed keen to have her married to a magnate he and his family could rely on for enduring support. In theory, his chosen match for her second husband in the guise of Ranulf de Blundville, 6th earl of Chester in early February 1188 should have met all expectations.

Ranulf de Blundeville was a powerful player in Anglo-Norman England and as the most powerful Marcher lord during the late twelfth, early thirteenth centuries, he was one of the leading antagonists to the Welsh, and Llywelyn in particular. Succeeding his father, Hugh de

Kevelioc as a minor, it was under Ranulf's administration that the earldom of Chester enjoyed its apogee. Ranulf was favoured by the Angevins, John in particular, and received his knighthood around the age of 18, the same time as his marriage to Constance was being negotiated. Ranulf, who was referred to by contemporaries as 'prince' – a title he accepted, was one of John's most powerful allies during his lifetime and who strongly supported him during the Baron's Rebellion in 1215. Upon John's untimely death in October 1216, Ranulf acted as one of his executors. The earl of Chester was also a strong supporter of Henry III during the tumultuous time after John's death and the threats of French invasion. Ranulf's lordship holdings were spread far and wide, from Normandy in France to Lincoln and Richmond in England. During his short marriage to the duchess of Brittany, he took to styling himself duke of Brittany.

Unlike her marriage to Geoffrey Plantagenet which is purported to have been a match well made, Constance's marriage to Ranulf was an unhappy one, to say the least. In 1196 Richard I, Constance's former brother-in-law, named the then 9-year-old Arthur as his heir, adopting him because he had no male heir of his own and likely because John was not to be trusted. Accusations of Constance being partisan to the number of rebellions that took place across Brittany in the mid-1190s that favoured her personal ambitions left her estranged from Ranulf. Animosity, perhaps simply dictated by their own conflicting loyalties, at one point, led to her being abducted and imprisoned by the earl of Chester while on her way to finalise a treaty with Richard. Constance was released two years later in 1198 and travelled back to Brittany where it appears that she instigated the annulment of her marriage to Ranulf. That she was a strong and resilient woman not to be contended with, there is very little doubt.

It had been rumoured that Constance and John had an affair, hence her status as one of the entrants for Joan's mother. Nevertheless, it is also well known that there was no love lost between John and Constance (largely concerning successorship to the English throne and Constance's stalwart support of Arthur's rights) and it seems extremely unlikely that any such relation could have ever taken shape. Perhaps, like Agatha de Ferrers, the most important argument against Constance of Brittany being Joan's mother is linked to her relational affinity with John. There is no way either would have been able to subsequently marry without papal approval if they had embarked on any sort of carnal relationship. Canon law would have stopped any such attempts. Besides, if knowledge of a sexual relationship between these two had any basis of fact, it would be astounding if contemporaries, particularly monastic writers, agreed to maintain a collective silence. Again, it would have been incest and for many, it would have been the ultimate (though not only) example of John's complete depravity. If nothing else, parallels with Henry II's notorious relationship with the 'fair' Rosamund Clifford would have been easily made. As no evidence of this is indicated anywhere, the duchess of Brittany can be decisively ruled out.

Constance, however, is not the only one of Ranulf of Chester's wives to be associated with Joan. Clémence de Fougères (d. 1252), whom he married as his second wife in September/October 1199 is the first of the two stronger candidates for Joan's mother. Clémence, the widow of Alan of Dinan, came from Normandy, her father being William de Fougères and her mother Agatha du Hommet. Both her father and brother, Richard, were constables of Normandy. Clémence and Ranulf were married for thirty years and on his death in 1232, she remained a widow for the next twenty years. She was a powerful woman in widowhood, more so than she was as Ranulf's wife, and used her own seal and counterseal as the countess of Chester to issue grants. As Ranulf's wife, she consented to many of his grants, but there is no evidence of her actually witnessing any of his own acta.[20] If she were Joan's mother, Clémence must have died in her late-seventies, early-eighties.

By the time Ranulf went on crusade in 1218 it seems he had become a part of Llywelyn's household, according to the Welsh annals. When he returned two years later, the two men, both referred to as prince (*princeps*) by contemporaries, affirmed their alliance in a move that was unprecedented between any earl of Chester and prince of North Wales. Recent research has shown the interesting conformity in the personal power and interactions between Ranulf and Llywelyn before 1218 that alludes to a more personal connection, in spite of the earlier discord between them.[21] Could part of this intimate connection be related to Clémence de Fougères being Joan's mother? Certainly, the relationship between the two families was solidified in 1222 when Joan and Llywelyn's daughter Elen married Ranulf's nephew and heir, John the Scot. It was a move made to guarantee a long-lasting peace and ensure that the powerful partnership between the two regions continued to transcend beyond the deaths of Llywelyn and Ranulf.

Besides being a move that offered Ranulf significant political power in Brittany and Lincolnshire, perhaps his second marriage to Clémence de

Fougères underscored a more personal and powerful connection between the two *principes* that fostered their most unlikely affinity. It is highly possible that Clémence de Fougères was actually Joan's mother. Indeed, rumours circulated at the time that John had taken such a selfish and amorous interest in Clémence that it nearly ruined her planned nuptials to Ranulf. Such a 'close' connection to John may have ensured Clémence's advantageous marital arrangement, especially if she were Joan's mother.[22] There could have been no better match for Joan than to marry a ruler whose own kingdom bordered the lands where her mother may have dwelled.

Most central to the argument that favours Clémence de Fougères as Joan's mother is the matter of her dower rights. The Buckinghamshire manor of Twyford, by the beginning of the thirteenth century a royal demesne, was the only one of Clémence's dower portions not upheld. Though it had been enjoyed by the de Fougères family in 1086 as it appears in the Domesday Book, it was actually granted to Ranulf by John. This could only have happened if John and Clémence had had some form of familial relationship. This in itself could explain the reference to '*Regina Clementina*' in the Tewkesbury annals written around the same time.

Interestingly, in 1203, a truly defining *annus horbilis* for John that included the desertion of many allies in Normandy, especially after the death of his nephew Arthur whose murder he was accused of, John seems to have been particularly suspicious of Ranulf's loyalty. In April of that year, he accused the earl of Chester of plotting against him with the Bretons, even though by then Ranulf was married to Clémence. In 1204, John levied further accusations against his powerful supporter and denounced him for a supposed allegiance made with Gwenwynwyn ab Owain (d. 1216), the rebel leader and prince of southern Powys in mid-Wales, who was a thorn in John's side. De Blundeville held his own against the king's railings, which ultimately proved to be unjust, and tensions eventually blew over, yet it is curious that it was during this time, specifically April 1203, that the king's suspicious nature overcame the best of him and was directed at the earl of Chester.[23] Is it possible that John did not simply suffer from wild delusions, but that a very personal manner of jealousy was in play concerning Ranulf's relationship to Clémence and, perhaps even Joan herself? After all, 1203 is the same year that, according to records, Joan sailed from Normandy to England. Though her whereabouts once landing on English shores are unknown until 1205, if Clémence were her mother it is entirely possible the king's precious daughter resided in the Chester household.

14

The last of the contenders for Joan's mother is Clemence de Verdun (d. 1231), probably born Clemence le Boteler to Philip le Boteler of Wiltshire, and wife of Nicholas de Verdun. In 1202 Clemence le Boteler married Nicholas, the son of Bertram de Verdun. Originally hailing from Normandy, the Verduns themselves seem to have had close connections the English Crown, including evidence of some of the family spending that fateful Christmas in Caen in 1183 with 'the devil's brood', when Henry II tried with one last attempt to mend the irreconcilable rift in his family. Bertram and Henry seem to have been close. Clemence and Nicholas had one child who was the heiress of the vast Verdun estates spread across England, Ireland and the Welsh March.

How, and if, Clemence met John before her marriage to Nicholas is one of those frustrating basics to Joan's story that will likely remain unearthed. Nevertheless, the strongest evidence we have for anyone being Joan's mother is, indeed, that for Clemence de Verdun. Chancery enrolments tell us that on 28 November 1228 custody of Susanna, Joan and Llywelyn's daughter, was given to Clemence and Nicholas. Susanna was likely handed over as a young, well-kept, diplomatic hostage and part of a peace agreement that Joan herself may have brokered. It would not be the first time Llywelyn would have given up a child as a diplomatic hostage, but at least in this instance it seems there may have been security in knowing Susanna was in relatively safe hands (pun intended).[24]

Another curious connection between Joan and the Verduns concerns the manor of Rothley in Leicestershire. Although Staffordshire was the caput for the de Verdun family estates, they had very significant holdings in Leicestershire. In 1225 the manor of Rothley was gifted to Joan by her half-brother Henry III, though this was confiscated and returned to her on and off as part of the political games between the king of England and Llywelyn. Henry took permanent possession of it in June 1231 and, in the end, gifted all rights to the manor, including the advowson, to the Knights Templar. Perhaps most significant is the confiscation that took place 27 March 1228. Seven days earlier, Nicholas de Verdun received a pardon for payment of an amercement of 15 marks he made to Stephen Seagrave, England's future chief justiciar, while in Leicestershire. Later that year, 8 November, Joan's rights to Rothley were restored and twenty days after that, Susanna was sent to Clemence de Verdun and Nicholas.

It is intriguing that Rothley and the surrounding area played such a role in both Joan's life and those of the de Verduns and in relatively close time frames as exampled above. Although the 1175 Lancashire and Chester Pipe Rolls highlight a connection between Bertrand de Verdun and the royal demesne of Rothley, there is, in fact, a much earlier connection found in the Domesday Book.[25] One must ask, why of all the manors in the royal demesne at Henry's disposal was Rothley granted to Joan in the first place? Leicestershire is a long ways from Wales and is certainly the anomaly when it comes to Joan's other English holdings, all of which surround Shrewsbury and Worcester. Is it because of the strong de Verdun presence in Leicestershire? In 1235 Roesia de Verdun founded the Augustinian priory of Grace Dieu, in Thringstone, Leicestershire, less than thirteen miles away from Rothley. Could Joan's possession of Rothley have allowed for her to spend time with her mother, and perhaps even half-sister in earlier years, while visiting the manor without giving away 'the family secret'? The de Verduns had connections with numerous Marcher barons, including Ranulf of Chester, and it would not have been so terribly peculiar that the wife of the leading Welsh leader would meet with some prominent landholders in the area. Though it should be kept in mind that the de Verduns also had significant holdings in on the March, like in Shropshire, so opportunities to meet there also would have been uncomplicated.

In spite of her mother's unknown identity, Joan was accepted openly and lovingly by her father. She was probably John's first child, though far from the last. In fact, next to Henry I (r. 1100–1135), who had at least twenty-one illegitimate children that we know of, John had the second largest known number of bastards of a medieval English monarch. He may have had as many as eight, and at least five that we know of were probably old enough to have been conceived before and during his first marriage to Isabella of Gloucester, which lasted ten years.[26] Of all his bastard children Joan is the most well-known. Her half-brother Richard of Dover, also known as Richard FitzRoy was the son of Adela (?) de Warenne, the daughter of Hamelin de Warenne. Hamelin himself was related to John, being Henry II's half-brother, making Richard's mother and John cousins.[27] The identities of John's mistresses are historically important.[28] His many secret relationships likely had political repercussions, just as his not-so-secret ones were undoubtedly politically motivated gestures, not least of which affected his most famous illegitimate daughter.

Chapter Two

Gwynedd and the
Rise of Llywelyn ap Iorwerth

Up to the thirteenth century the attitude of the English Crown toward Wales was uncertain. Wales, though beset with strife, was ultimately more important to the Welsh and to the Marcher lords than to the English monarchs. The fact remains that the invasion, domination and subjugation of the 'untamed' and disorderly country was not an objective of the rulers of England. Out of an astounding twenty-one English royal military campaigns undertaken against the Welsh over the course of 200 years, only King John and his son and successor Henry III were to lead the two most successful expeditions into Wales, in 1211 and 1241 respectively. In fact, no English king before Edward I sought to subdue and conquer the Welsh by means of force, though John did come close to achieving this in the early thirteenth century.

The reluctance of the kings of England to enforce their overlordship in Wales before the end of the thirteenth century was determined by a number of factors: royal preoccupation with retaining lands in France, subduing their own civil wars and unrest in England, aristocratic in-fighting and the geographic landscape of Wales, especially the mountainous region of North Wales. The fight for control over Wales was also greatly affected by the powers and ambitions of the Marcher lords. The area surrounding the Welsh-English border, a large swath of land referred to as the Welsh March, was a political anomaly in Britain, stemming from the time of the Norman conquest of England in 1066. Marcher barons were Anglo-Norman gentry who ruled the English-Welsh border as royal agents of the Crown. However, they had enough freedom of rule to pursue their own ambitions, and thus cause problems for both Welsh princes and English kings. Because of the Marcher lords' hold over the Welsh-English border, and their increased incursion into southern Wales especially, the majority of English monarchs were largely satisfied with undertaking occasional military expeditions into Wales as and when events dictated; their desire to ensure English hegemony over the Welsh was not wholly defined by the need for and use of military force. However, concern was not unwarranted.

A determinant in the Crown's interest to bring Wales under its wing was the consistency in which the Welsh political landscape remained unstable throughout the twelfth and thirteenth centuries. The constant bickering and internal warfare that pitted brother against brother, cousin against cousin and dynasty against dynasty directly affected the domestic politics of England. Ongoing conflict meant that the Welsh frontier could not be easily defended or secured if obtained by force. Nevertheless, as a strategic stronghold for control of the Irish Sea, neither could Wales be ignored, for the rulers of England depended on the stability and security of the Irish seaboard for trade and as protection from invasions. During the mid-twelfth century, Henry II was the first king to really engage in Anglo-Welsh relations. He was fearful that Wales would develop into a problem and one that would endanger his newly acquired control and position as supreme ruler over much of the island of Britain. Henry was a king intolerant of disorder, yet he was faced with the fact that Wales and the Welsh frontier lacked internal governments. This made the arrangement of treaties and alliances difficult. Nevertheless, in 1177, after years of struggle, the Angevin king finally succeeded in aggressively attacking Wales and was officially accepted and recognised as overlord of Wales – but not as a conqueror.

Native Wales was made up of a large number of territories, many of which were ruled by lesser princely dynasties. Some dynasties, especially in the south and middle March, mostly remained independent during the twelfth and thirteenth centuries, even while the powers of the three chief kingdoms of Powys in mid-Wales (Mathrafal), Deheubarth (Dinefwr) in the south and Gwynedd (Aberffraw) in the north, in particular, began to rise and pull them under their influences. There were also many dynasties whose status shrank so considerably during this time that their lands and titles were appropriated by the more powerful houses, more or less denigrating them to the level of nobility. The myriad of multiple kingships, ruled by sovereigns who had their own interests and priorities in mind, prolonged political hostilities and prevented the Welsh from unifying under one leader. Gerald of Wales, himself, the medieval scholar, cleric and pernickety Welsh patriot, observed that the Welsh were obstinate in their steadfast refusal to submit to one ruler. The successes of military might by one leader were not guaranteed to extend across generations. In fact, throughout the various Welsh kingdoms, the achievements of one generation were often wiped out by the next. This was exacerbated by the customary practice of partible inheritance. Such insecurities played a large role in defining Llywelyn's reign and his and Joan's status.

The only time a semblance of unification occurred was during the reign of Gruffudd ap Llywelyn of Gwynedd (r. 1055–1063). In 1055, after successfully leading a large army to defend the Welsh border, Gruffudd's status as a sub-king was recognised by the Anglo-Saxon ruler, Edward the Confessor (r. 1042–1066) and during his tenure Gruffudd was the one leader to efficaciously unite Wales. He was adept at forging alliances with both Welsh and central Anglo-Saxon dynasties, himself marrying Eldgyth (*fl. c.* 1057–1066), the granddaughter of the famous Lady Godiva, wife of Leofric, earl of Mercia. Gruffudd was not only recognised by his Welsh compatriots as 'King Gruffudd, sole and pre-eminent ruler of the British', his kingly status was also acknowledged by Continental rulers and those from England and Ireland. In most ways, Gruffudd ap Llywelyn was 'King of Wales'. Although the Welsh enjoyed a shared identity in their culture, such as through their warrior-ruler ethos, oral and bardic traditions, connections to Arthurian lore and history and their laws, the future of a united Wales depended on an effective leader who had the acumen to disentangle princely feuds and assert his authority over his peers. No matter his successes, even Gruffudd was eventually betrayed and killed by his own men and over the course of the following two centuries the future of a united Wales seemed largely dependent on his descendants, the rulers of North Wales, the principality of Gwynedd as a whole being the general forerunner in Welsh politics.

Part of Gwynedd's strength and ability to remain independent from the English Crown up to the late thirteenth century lay in its geographical location. It was a vast area that was less approachable than the other two main Welsh kingdoms of Powys and Deheubarth because of its natural mountainous barriers, river estuaries and the Irish Sea. The seemingly innate rise of Gwynedd's superiority was greatly helped by its terrain; the Snowdonia mountain range at its heart acted as a natural fortress in defence of the kingdom. In his *Journey through Wales*, written in 1194, Gerald of Wales described the favourable landscape of the northern region:

> I must not fail to tell you about the mountains which are called Eryri [eagle] by the Welsh and by the English Snowdon, that is the Snow Mountains. They rise gradually from the land of the sons of Cynan and extend northwards near Degannwy. When looked at from Anglesey they seem to rear their lofty summits right up to the clouds.[1]

The ancient Isle of Môn (Anglesey) was the cradle of agriculture, allowing for Venedotian self-sufficiency, especially when under attack. The river Conwy ran through the kingdom of Gwynedd, dividing it between what was known as Gwynedd Uwch Conwy (Gwynedd above Conwy, to the west) and Gwynedd Is Conwy (Gwynedd below Conwy, to the east). The eastern division of Gwynedd, known as the Perfeddwlad ('The Four Cantrefs')[2] was the most vulnerable to foreign incursion. So much so that the Normans even established a base in Deganwy, at the mouth of the river Conwy, shortly after the Norman Conquest of England in 1066. Thereafter, Anglo-Norman invasions were particularly common to this more exposed geographical area.

On the whole, the natural defences not only helped better protect this great northern kingdom, but also helped make way for the Venedotian rulers to penetrate south Wales in attempts to extend their power. This was much easier than entering northern Wales from the south. Nevertheless, as Llywelyn's biographer Roger Turvey has rightly pointed out, 'Gwynedd's geographical strength may also be considered a source of potential weakness for if it was a difficult kingdom to attack it was equally difficult to control and govern'.[3] This was certainly the case before Llywelyn's reign.

The superlative authority that the princes of Gwynedd possessed was concomitant to their esteemed and legendary lineage. The Venedotian dynasty was tied to the renowned ninth-century ruler Rhodri Mawr, or Rhodri the Great – the first Welsh leader to be given such an epithet. It is a traditional belief that Rhodri's son Anarawd established the House of Aberffraw and became the first king of Gwynedd. The time-honoured court of Aberffraw, itself on the south of the isle of Anglesey, is the location that the native law books describe as the *eisteddfa arbennig* (principal seat) of the dynasty of Gwynedd. As the chief headquarters for the rulers of Gwynedd, Aberffraw was steeped in political and cultural tradition and celebrated as the court of Brân the Blessed, the legendary king of Britain extolled in Welsh mythology. As we will see, by 1230, in order to emphasise his hard earned power, influence and unique status among Welsh rulers, Llywelyn ap Iorwerth wisely adopted the official title 'prince of Aberffraw, lord of Snowdon' (*Lewlinus princeps de Aberfrau, dominus Snaudon*) as a means of legitimising his Wales-wide hegemony. In variations of the Welsh laws written in North Wales during Llywelyn's reign, Welsh lawyers promoted the status of Gwynedd by claiming that the king of Aberffraw was to receive gold from the other Welsh kings as homage, while the king of England was to receive gold from the king of Aberffraw only, a clear indication of the Venedotian king's status in Wales. Llywelyn's amalgamation of the titles 'prince of Aberffraw' and 'lord of Snowdon' was not only a tactic used to further establish his territorial and political authority, but more importantly, it was used to demonstrate his ambitions as the leading Welsh ruler.

The titles and designations used by Welsh rulers seemed to be as changeable as the weather at times. Ultimately, because of the overuse and conflation of the term 'king', *brenhin* (*rex*) by a number of petty or lesser rulers, the more powerful Welsh leaders from the larger kingdoms, namely Deheubarth, Powys and Gwynedd, reverted to the use of other designations that to us seem contrary to the axiomatic nature of establishing authority. The terms 'lord', *arglwydd* (*domius*), and 'prince', *twysog* (*princeps*), were widely adopted throughout the twelfth and thirteenth centuries to imply the nature and breadth of their authority. For these three larger kingdoms in particular change to the use of 'prince' and/or 'lord' often was concomitant with the changes in governmental administration and increased levels of centralised power.[4]

Llywelyn's lauded contemporary the Lord Rhys (r. 1155–1197) of Deheubarth at one point styled himself prince of Deheubarth or South Wales (*proprietarius princeps Deheubarth/Sudwallia*) and as prince of Wales (*Resus Walliarum princeps*), conceivably referring to his own patrimonial rights. Though Lord Rhys was influential in mid-twelfth-century Wales, he never achieved the position that Llywelyn did, regardless of his once used title 'Prince of Wales'. In contrast, the Lord

Rhys' wife, Gwenllian (Gwenllian ferch Madog ap Maredudd of Powys, *fl.* 1184 × 1188) who does not even appear in the Welsh chronicles, is only ever referred to in acta by her name, rather than through either titles or even lifecycles, such as wife or mother.

Just as the terms for establishing kingship were tenuous and often changed with the power, might and ambitions of individual rulers, definitions of queenship remained even more mysterious and highlight a real problem in assessing the power and authority of royal women in Wales. Simply because a ruler was referred to as *brenhin, tywysog* or *argwyledd*, we cannot assume that his consort employed the corresponding designations, especially those of *brenhines* (queen) or *tywysoges* (princess). *Rhian*, also meaning queen (as in the Rhiannon, the famous and mysterious queen in the First and Third Branches of the *Mabinogi*), was used earlier sources, although it eventually evolved over time to mostly refer to a woman as a 'maiden' or 'virgin' rather than to denote the formal status of a ruling consort. Early Welsh culture, based on an oral tradition that is still revered to this day, does make it clear that not only was *brehines* the most formal designation used to identify a consort as 'queen', it was the highest form of designation and intimated that the highest status was being conferred.

In fact, it is astonishing that only one woman in any of the native Welsh sources originating from the twelfth and thirteenth centuries is awarded the title of *brenhines*, that is Angharad ferch Owain ab Edwin (d. 1162), wife of Gruffudd ap Cynan, king of early twelfth-century Gwynedd. In both the Latin and earlier Welsh versions of the *Life of Gruffudd ap Cynan* (*Vita Griffini filii Conani/Historia Gruffudd vab Kenan*), possibly commissioned by Angharad herself sometime after her husband's death in 1137, she is referred to as his queen, but, she is also referred to as his wife: *regina Angharat eius uxor*; *Angharat vrenhines, y wreig briawt ynteu*. The Welsh version in particular also highlights her position as a *gwraig briod*, a wife of the highest status – an important distinction to make as Gruffudd had a number of illegitimate children by a number of concubines.[5] It is a distinction that underlines just how substantial the status of a formal wife was in comparison to lesser wives, or certainly in the context in which a husband had numerous partners who bore him children.[6] Such characterisations are central to understanding her own personal status and that of the office of the Welsh queen. Certainly, Gruffudd's biographer describes Angharad as the king's symbolic equal, his figurative counterpart, as both wife and queen. The amalgamation of these two superlative identifiers reinforce the power of Angharad's own royal standing.[7]

It is through the famous Anglo-Welsh cleric, Gerald of Wales, that we find the second, and only other reference to a very real, historical ruling queen in Welsh sources, namely that of 'the queen of North Wales', which is found in his autobiography, *De rebus a se gestis*. The nature of the reference itself is infuriating as the contents of the chapter, which supposedly discussed a letter written by Gerald to the 'queen of North Wales', have not survived.[8] Because of this, we have no idea to whom he was referring. Most undoubtedly, it was not Joan, but perhaps her aunt and predecessor, Emma of Anjou wife of Llywelyn's uncle, Dafydd ab Owain (r. *c.* 1170–1194). One-time contender to the leadership of the Venedotian domain, by 1202 Dafydd was in English exile and Llywelyn at the helm of power. But, Gerald was ever-so exacting when it came to expressing his opinions that if it were Emma he had written to, use of the title 'queen' was a way of demonstrating his political bias. Saying that, it is also possible that Gerald was referring to another wife of Llywelyn's as it is believed he may have been married before Joan, possibly to a sister of Ranulf, the earl of Chester. Even though we know nothing of Gerald's queen, and perhaps even because of this, it can also be argued that the letter may have been addressed to Tangwystl, Llywelyn's known 'conbubine' (*consobrina*) and mother to his first-born son Gruffudd and probably at least one of his daughters, Gwenllian de Lacy. The one indication that it may have been Joan to whom Gerald wrote revolves around the fact that King John and Gerald clashed, to say the least, and as John pursed Gerald on many an occasion and 'thundered against him with violent threats' it is possible the letter was an appeal to her for help. In the scheme of things, however, it is not necessarily important to know the identity of the woman Gerald wrote to as his use of the title 'queen' was much more about him making note of who he was being deferential to. In this light, his use of 'queen' undoubtedly highlights the important status that a Welsh consort seemed to enjoy.

In the long run, regardless of what actual designation individual rulers and their consorts used to define themselves, it remained understood that that the male leaders encompassed the cultural ideals and expectations of kingship as a whole, i.e. rulership defined by the power of the individual persona, ambition, wealth (both landed and cometary), personal and political connections and, above all, the warrior-ruler ethos that embodied military leadership, strength and success. Llywelyn's own connection to the court of Aberffraw promoted his dynastic rights to govern the lands traditionally associated with this very ancient court and, more importantly, the right to govern the principal seat of Welsh overlordship. In other words, his eventual title 'prince of Aberffraw, lord of Snowdon', referred to both the antediluvian caput of Aberffraw *and* the kingdom of Gwynedd, signifying the two integral aspects of his established authority. The territorial gains he amassed during his reign, his successes in warfare and eventual recognition of his status by the English government firmly established him as a model of Welsh kingship, symbolically and literally. As will be discussed later in this book, Joan's status as Llywelyn's wife and royal-consort, mirrored his ascendency and the change in her own title from 'princess of North Wales' to 'Lady of Wales' (*domina Walliae*) exhibited even further, the Welsh-wide authority of Llywelyn's rule. As Llywelyn's consort, Joan found herself a contemporaneous model of queenship in her own right.

Over time, the political and military undertakings of rulers such as Gruffudd ap Cynan and his son and successor, Owain Gwynedd (r. 1137–1170), Llywelyn's grandfather, arguably established Gwynedd as a fairly stable, prosperous and increasingly expansionist kingdom; advancements that eventually led to it becoming the premiere authority in Wales in the Middle Ages. However, like many other Welsh princely houses, the Venedotian dynasty had its own share of familial in-fighting, which often threatened to destabilise the region. Upon Owain's death in 1170, there was an arduous campaign and fight for power between his sons. Shortly after he died, his first-born, illegitimate son and chosen heir (*edling*), the famous warrior-poet, Hywel, was treacherously murdered in the battle of Pentraeth on Anglesey by his two half-brothers, Rhodri (d. 1195) and Dafydd. Tradition has it that Hywel's murder was plotted by Owain's second wife Cristin (*fl. c.*1161–1170) of Tegeingl so that her sons could rule Gwynedd between them.

Llywelyn's grandfather Owain married Cristin as his second wife. She also happened to be his cousin. In Wales, first cousins often married each other and Welsh royalty were hardly exempt from 'keeping it in the family', so to speak. Marital alliances between close kin was a means of furthering dynastic authority and legitimising power. The Welsh greatly valued 'distinguished birth and noble descent more than anything else

24

in the world', preferring to 'marry into a noble family than into a rich one'.[9] Genealogies were preserved largely by court poets, in both oral and written form, and in the many that have survived, it is clear that descent was an important means of emphasising and defining ancient familial relationships. Maintaining clear blood connections through the marriage of cousins enhanced the promotion of 'good ancestry', but more importantly, rights to sovereign power. Cristin herself was the daughter of Gronw ab Owain ab Edwin, brother to Queen Angharad of Gwynedd.

The marriage of first cousins easily fell within the church's prohibitive realms of consanguinity[10] and the widespread acceptance in Welsh custom of cousins marrying one another was a state of affairs much lamented by the church. The marriage of Owain and Cristin, in particular, was lambasted by the archbishop of Canterbury, Archbishop Theobold of Bec (r. 1139–1161) who claimed that this union was the crowning horror of the plague that riddled Wales.[11] This 'plague' was also in reference to the practice of concubinage and there were a number of ecclesiastical mandates sent to Owain demanding he end his relationship with Cristin. As Owain ignored these, Pope Alexander (r. 1159–1181) wrote to the new Archbishop Thomas Becket of Canterbury (r. 1162–1170) to discuss his punishment. By the time this letter was written in 1169, Owain had dropped the formal title of 'king of Wales' (*rex Walie*) which he had previously adopted, and was using 'prince of Wales' (*Waliarum princeps*) or 'prince of the Welsh' (*Wallensium princeps*). It is impossible to know if this change in Owain's designation was also reflected in a change in those used by his wives, which is disappointing as his decision to make the change himself was likely a result of the rise in his status as a ruler and was singular to his reign.[12] In fact, Cristin is only referred to in sources by her lifecycles, as cousin (*consobrina*), wife (*uxor*) and mother. However, there is some indication in the Becket correspondence that her status as a reigning consort was recognised to some degree. In fact, Becket himself told Owain that although it was demanded that Cristin be cast aside for moral reasons, she was to be provided for financially, according to the needs of a woman of her status (and as his kinswoman). It is apt that this concern for her economic well-being primarily mirrors an understanding and acceptance of her position as queen.[13]

As for the attitudes of her Welsh compatriots, however, concerning her position as queen, and after Owain's death, queen-dowager, these are much harder to discern as she appears in only one native source where she is named.[14] The court poet Perfy ap Cedifor wrote an elegy lamenting the murderous death of Hywel at the hands of his own family and the ruin that befalls a kingdom when bonds of kinship and blood alliances fail.[15] Hywel, himself, happened to be Perfy's foster brother. *Marwnad meibion Cedifor* mourns Hywel's death, specifically calling Dafydd and Rhodri the 'unchristian Cristin's brood' (*anghristiawn O Gristin a'i meibion*).[16] Of course, one of the most obvious interpretations concerning Cristin being portrayed as 'unchristian' can easily be based on traditionally accepted gender ideals and expectations. As such, it can be argued that Cristin was criticised for not conforming to the stereotypical medieval traits of the 'ideal' wife, or mother, or widow who was supposed to gentle, kind and merciful. She was also 'unchristian' for being involved in an incestuous relationship.

An interesting reading of contemporary and native reference to Cristin and the rise to power of her own sons is important as it helps us to understand the undertakings of Welsh queenship in context; and attitudes that would have continued through Joan's reign and affected how she, too, was later perceived. Although on the surface Cristin comes across as the 'wicked' stepmother, the play on words may also reflect not only a recognition of her status and position as a queen dowager, but of the political activities undertaken by her. Because of her long-standing position within the Venedotian court, it has been argued that she understood all too well the governmental and administrative duties of the kingdom, and likely possessed great insight and the political acumen needed to maintain cohesive power, much more so than her stepson and Owain's designated heir, Hywel, who was absent from the kingdom for substantial periods of time.[17] In this light, Cristin's status as a queen, and queen-dowager, closely mirrors that of her aunt Angharad's, previously queen of Gwynedd, particularly as a queen 'knowledgeable in all things'.

Not one to be left out of the moral, and social, commentary on the subject of Cristin's marriage to Owain, Gerald of Wales uses the rise and fall of the family's fortunes in his *Journey through Wales* as a didactic anecdote to warn his readers of the immorality and degeneracy of 'public incest', namely marrying within the prohibited degrees of consanguinity. Perhaps as a means of denigrating her position as a 'wanton woman' he denies Cristin any reference to her status as a royal consort. Although he calls Owain the 'prince of North Wales', he refers to his reigning consort simply as Owain's first cousin (*consobrina*). Gerald denies the legitimacy of Cristin's sons Dafydd and his young brother Rhodri, in large part, due to her perceived immoral sexual nature.[18] And yet, as was so typical of the biased and often sycophantic nature of Gerald, by the time he had edited his *Journey through Wales* for a third time around 1214, Llywelyn was in power. Conveniently, Gerald seems to have forgotten that the Venedotian leader's own parents, Iorwerth ab Owain and Marared ferch Madog ap Maredudd, were also first cousins. He did not dare declare that Llywelyn was 'born in incest', nor could the aged cleric use the prince's life story as a moralistic one to illustrate how the committing of adultery and incest were so displeasing they inevitably incurred the wrath and vengeance of God, mitigating any rights to rule. All of this may have been expressly more pertinent, as, after all, Llywelyn was married to the daughter of the king of England.

Gerald had issues with women who seemed to wield any kind of authority, especially over the fate of men, which is clear in his anecdotes about Gwenllian the queen of Deheubarth, Lord Rhys' wife, who he blames for having been an interference and wielding such power in exercising her 'womanly charms' that she stopped her husband from going on crusade.[19] In doing so, Gwenllian denied her husband his manhood and the prospect of living the life of righteousness. Like many of his religious peers, the pains of marriage (*molestia nuptiarum*) are popular themes found in his writing where women are generally portrayed as 'contentious, prideful, demanding, complaining and foolish … uncontrollable, unstable and insatiable'.[20] Obviously, as a cleric, and one who was particularly misogynistic and bent on religious reform within Wales, his opinions and descriptions of powerful married women, especially royals, are exceptionally acerbic. In Gerald's opinion, society was only able to progress if sexuality was regulated, and more to the point, women removed from the public domain of men – a well-ordered society based on the absence of women was the definitive configuration. Gerald's overall treatment of married women in his writings on Wales is that the usurpers of social order and control. Married women, and in most of his cases royal women, seem to have been a source for what he saw as constant anxiety, social disorder and dissatisfaction.

Obviously, Gerald had his own personal agendas when it came to his writings and expressing his opinions, but his invective against powerful (e.g. royal) wives who were active and independent should be viewed in a constructive and affirming light. Gerald is a great source for native Wales, having intimate knowledge of how society and culture operated, revealing an unrivalled panoply of material concerning cultural and historical realities of his time. In context of Welsh queenship and in attempting to assess the roles of royal women, and attitudes towards them, Gerald, in fact, delivers the goods on many occasions. Examples of uxorial agency in practice found in his Welsh works are not found any other native Welsh source. Because of this, and in spite of his moralistic overtones, his writings reveal some of the very real norms and perceptions related to gender expectations and roles in native Wales. His commentaries are important in the context of Welsh queenship and wifehood overall, as they go hand-in-hand with the illustrations that are found in other native sources in which queenly and uxorial agency are expressed in public, and importantly, political forums.

By his first marriage to Gwladus ferch Llywarch ap Trahaern, Owain Gwynedd's eldest legitimate sons were Iorwerth Drwyndwn (d. *c.* 1174) and Maelgwn (d. after 1173). It is believed that the moniker Trwyndwn, or 'The Flat-Nosed', may be an indication that Iorwerth perhaps had a disability that acted as a barrier to him to taking the gauntlet as leader in Gwynedd. However, there is evidence that this prince was not as much of a minor player as traditionally has been believed.[21] Iorwerth married his own first-cousin, princess Marared, a daughter of the king of Powys, Madog ap Maredudd (d. *c.* 1160), himself the last of his family dynasty to rule over an undivided kingdom. Llywelyn was the couple's only apparent son and it is through his father that Llywelyn had direct claims to the throne to the kingdom of North Wales. When Owain Gwynedd died and his lands partitioned, Iorwerth received the *cantref* of Arfon, in north-west Wales as part of his share. Arfon, itself, was at the heart of the kingdom of Gwynedd, opposite Anglesey on the Menai Straits, extending into the Snowdon mountains, including militarily crucial Llanberis Pass. It is also likely Iorwerth controlled Nant Conwy, a *commote* (*cwmmwd*)[22] that ran along the Lledr, Llugwy and Penmachno valleys, extending from the shores of the Irish Sea deep into the mountains. Nant Conwy was an area that Joan and Llywelyn are noted to have spent much time during their own reign.

Very little is known about Iorwerth himself, yet we find a curious story, unfolded in the pages of *The Legend of Fulk FitzWarin* that provides a surprising and interesting anecdote in which not only Iorwerth and

Llywelyn appear, but so, too, does Joan. The legend regales the activities, victories and defeats of Iorwerth. In complete contrast to the notion that this prince of Gwynedd suffered from a disfigurement that meant men would not follow his lead, Iorwerth's strengths as a warrior were great indeed. According to the anonymous author, Iorwerth at one point assembled over 20,000 Irish, Welsh and Scots to attack the March and on another occasion, he seized,

> the whole of the march from Chester unto Worcester and had dispossessed all the barons of the march. And Sir Fulk, with the host of the King [Henry II], made a fierce assault on Jervard, and in a battle nigh unto Hereford, at Wormeslow, he forced him to flee, and to abandon the field. But ere that came to pass, many were slain on both sides. And for four years fierce and grievous war endured betwixt Sir Fulk and the Prince, until, at the request of the King of France, there was held at Shrewsbury a love-day between the King and Jervard the Prince, and they embraced one another, and were reconciled. And the Prince restored to the barons of the march all the lands which he had taken from them, and to the King he restored Ellesmere, but for no gold would be render up White Town [Whittington] and Maelor. 'Fulk,' said the King, 'since you have lost White Town and Maelor, I give unto you, in place thereof, Alleston, and all the fief that belongs to it, to hold for ever.' And Fulk thanked him with fervor. And to Lewis, the son of Jervard, a child of seven years, King Henry gave the little Joan, his daughter, and for marriage gift he gave unto them Ellesmere, and many other lands, and Lewis he took with him to London. And the Prince Jervard, with his retinue, took leave of the King, and went into Wales.[23]

Of course, if there is any truth to the accounts of Iorwerth in *Fulk* then it would be easy to see where Llywelyn gained first-hand knowledge regarding successful tactical warfare skills and even policy. Nevertheless, this legend is riddled with misrepresentations, mix-ups and inaccuracies (referring to Joan as Henry II's daughter above all). It suits the fanciful nature of such romance legends and it is probable that some of Llywelyn's own exploits were used in the stories concerning his father. Saying that, it does not mean we should entirely dismiss information found in *Fulk* and some matters might just even have a variable level of credibility.

This account is interesting. We know that Ranulf the earl of Chester and Fulk FitzWarin, both young adherents to King John, spent time in the royal household as children. If Llywelyn was another of such an elite to do so, what is the likelihood he met Joan, or at least knew of her, long before the 1201 peace accord? Admittedly, if the account above took place when Llywelyn was only 7, this would mean the narrative is roughly set around 1177 when John himself would have been a mere 11 years old. However, we have no knowledge of Llywelyn in records until 1188, the year Gerald recounts that he began his campaign against his two uncles, Dafydd and Rhodri, for power in Gwynedd, around the age of 14 or 15. Llywelyn makes his first appearance in Welsh chronicles six years later in 1194. We know nothing of Llywelyn's childhood or upbringing, his 'wilderness' as it is often referred to by Welsh historians. For all we know, Llywelyn may have actually spent time in France during his 'wilderness' years and, as such, may have had some sort of minimal contact with the young Joan if she, too, resided at one of the Angevin courts in Normandy. Very young children they were, of course, but experiences and impressions made in childhood are often indelible. Feasibly, beyond Joan's own important role, Llywelyn's political capacity in dealing with the English court once he was a ruler in his own right stemmed from first-hand knowledge he obtained in his younger years.[24]

A more likely scenario is that Llywelyn and his mother Marared spent time in Powys Fadog, after the death of his father sometime around 1174. Llywelyn's maternal uncle, Gruffudd Maelor (d. 1191) was prince of Powys Fadog and married to Angharad ferch Owain Gwynedd (*fl.* mid- to late twelfth century), Iorwerth's sister. Some evidence that gives weight to this theory is that during the early years of Llywelyn's reign, one of his most stalwart supporters was Gruffudd's son, Llywelyn's cousin, Madog (d. 1236). Though it is difficult to verify, it may be that Marared married as her second husband a member of the Marcher Corbet family of Caus in Shropshire (bordering Powys). It may have been here where Llywelyn spent some of his adolescence, honing his understanding of Marcher politics, laying the foundation for his future aptitude for dealing with the March during his rule. Alternatively, one of the more famous antiquarians of Welsh history, Sir John Wynn who inherited the Gwydir estate in the Conwy valley, wrote the *History of the Gwydir Family* in the early-seventeenth century, highlighting the noble lineage of his ancestors. Wynn asserts that Llywelyn was raised in his uncle Rhodri's household at Aberffraw. However, this seems highly improbable given that Llywelyn's status as Iorwerth's son made him a direct threat to Rhodri, whose own authority was untenable given the endless struggles he had with Dafydd over the power of Gwynedd. Llywelyn may have been at Aberffraw, but if anything, it would have been as a prisoner.[25]

Historians are only able to piece together snippets of how Llywelyn actually came to power as the plague of silence looms large across the thirty years between the death of Owain Gwynedd and the rise of Llywelyn 'the Great'. Control over the reins of Gwynedd largely vacillated between Cristin's sons, Dafydd and Rhodri, but it was not necessarily a family feud based purely on personalities. Part of the problem was how kingdoms in Wales were governed. Rights to successorship throughout the Welsh kingdoms were nebulous as primogeniture was not widely practised. In fact, it was not until Llywelyn and Joan's reign that it was adopted in Gwynedd in the early 1200s; a direct result of Llywelyn's real first clash with John as king of England and Joan's first political intervention and act of diplomacy.

Traditionally, partible inheritance was par for the course on the death of a ruler, meaning that, in theory, all sons who had been recognised by their fathers were to receive equal division of lands within a kingdom. This, however, did not necessarily mean fractious division of a kingdom itself. The law codes of native Wales call for an heir-apparent to be designated, rulership to go to a king's designated successor, or *edling*. However, the *edling* was not necessarily the king's first-born son (illegitimate or not) who was considered to be the rightful heir to a kingdom. The *edling* was a kinsman specifically chosen by the king to act as his heir. In other words, the status of the *edling* was directly related to, and not derived from, the status of the king. It seems this is done as a way of safeguarding 'the prerogatives of the reigning king'.[26] It was against the on-going backdrop of fratricide and internecine warfare after the death of Owain Gwynedd that Llywelyn rose to power.

In 1194, at the supposed age of 21, Llywelyn was old enough to claim his rights as his father's (designated?) heir, as well as those of his grandfather Owain Gwynedd's. Records suggest that around this time he fought and defeated Dafydd at the battle of Aberconwy. From this point on, the fledgling ruler spent time and effort consolidating power. He seized his share of land and secured a position in the governmental proceedings of the Perfeddwald, or 'Four Cantrefs', lying between the Norman stronghold of Chester and the Welsh bulwark of Aberconwy, and by 1197 had turned his share of the Perfeddwald into sole rulership. The year year 1199 seems to have marked the crossroad to Llywelyn's career as ruler of Gwynedd. On 28 September, John, recently crowned king of England, confirmed by charter English support for Llywelyn's political gains. In other words, the new English overlord offered Llywelyn protection for the lands he had not only won by this date, but any future lands he was yet to conquer in his quest for rulership of North Wales.

The politics of twelfth- and thirteenth-century Wales and England are intricately woven into a web of extraordinary complexity. Because of the fragility of the political and power structures within Wales itself, interventions by the English Crown often resulted in a turn on the dime for numerous Welsh leaders. Their authority was viewed by English kings as similar to that of English barons; Welsh princely status was closer to English tenants-in-chief rather than as ruling royal equals.[27] English kings perceived Welsh lordship as personal, rather than territorial. As the importance of kinship connections and lineage were two defining factors in Welsh culture, the status and right to rule by an individual was based not on land ownership, but on the birthright and inheritance linked to ancestry – hence Llywelyn's future play on his connection to Aberffraw. Such a structure, combined with partible inheritance, was highly problematic in that it gave nobles and lesser princes independence. Ownership of their own lands meant they had no reason to conform to the will of a more powerful ruler, or single monarch, as a means of maintaining their position and power in society. Consequently, John, the first English ruler to pay so much close attention to Wales, likely expected that he would naturally obtain homage and fealty from the strongest of the Welsh princes.[28]

John's overall tactic was to play Welsh rulers against one another, with an 'aim to divide and disintegrate' the power and authority of the more formidable leaders.[29] It was a game that was highly advantageous to the English Crown, if a king found himself adept at playing it. Conversely, the weak periods of rule and foreign distractions faced by the kings of England themselves overall also allowed the more enterprising of Welsh leaders to carve out their own power-wielding political maps of Wales and this is exactly what Llywelyn did throughout his reign. No matter how cowed he appeared to be to the English eye, the Welsh prince took advantage of the difficulties faced by both John and Henry to advance his own agenda of expanding and reinforcing his position within Wales.

Llywelyn's celebrated status was imbued with the mythical and legendary associations of King Arthur, as Merlin's 'son of prophecy' (*mab darogan*), by his court bard, Llywarch ab Llywelyn, also known as Prydydd y Moch. As a descendant of the eagles of Snowdon, Llywelyn was the long-awaited ruler who finally would rescue Wales from centuries of foreign invasion and restore Wales to its proper glory.[30] With the vision of his grandfather's accomplishments in mind, throughout his life, Llywelyn himself made clear his intentions to his people that he would become a leader of great calibre, one who promised to restore an undivided sovereignty over all of Gwynedd. This he did in a startling short amount of time, between the years 1199 and 1203. Llywelyn's warlike prowess and exploits have been celebrated enough throughout history to earn him the eponymous epithet 'Llywelyn Fawr', or 'Llywelyn the Great'.

As was the duty of his trade, the poet epitomised the feelings of admiration and fondness Llywelyn aroused in Welsh men and women alike; feelings that still linger today. Over his forty-year reign, Llywelyn became the beating heart of Wales. The fact that he was so successful in establishing, and moreover maintaining, his Wales-wide power is a testament to his individual character and ambitions. This is especially apropos in the knowledge that after his death in 1240 much of what he achieved vanished under the governance of his chosen successor Dafydd, his legitimate son by Joan.

Llywelyn was, and still is, renowned for his political acumen, and he knew one way to establish and maintain his power as a leading ruler was to continue the practice of his Venedotian forebears of recognising English suzerainty. This is exactly what he did in July 1201 when he came 'into the king's service' – and along with many of his powerful men, swore fealty to John in an act of peace. This new relationship established by *fidelitas* and *servitium* was reinforced by Llywelyn's agreement to pay homage.[31] This is one of the reasons why the 1201 treaty signed with John was so important and Llywelyn's marriage to Joan shortly thereafter was a crucial step in solidifying this move.

Chapter Three

Marriage, Queenship and the Roles of Women in Wales

Marriage was a powerful tool and in the Middle Ages, political needs and ambitions defined the marital relationships of royals and members of the aristocracy and nobility. For those in the top tiers of society, marriage served as the all-encompassing means to create and cement a powerful network of alliances, to promote public relations and the positions of families within their immediate and even more widespread communities. Although not to be entirely discounted, love was a cursory reason for marriage and if a couple happened to feel affection for one another, it was considered a windfall. Saying that, though marriages were contractually based, efforts were made often to ensure that matches were as compatible as possible; the longer a marriage lasted, the longer family agendas remained intact. Rulers and heads of households, both men and women, sought to consolidate long-term family interests, which included the need to preserve ancestral dignity and familial reputation. As such, thoughts of future inheritance and successorship carried significant weight in the creation of many a marital alliance.

The kind of power that was transferred through marriage, in other words land, meant that women were a strong link to legitimating Welsh dynastic rule. Welsh genealogical tracts and pedigrees are a great source of information that indicate how women were viewed in society. On the whole, they are identified first and foremost as wives, then as daughters. This is similar in fashion to how women are labelled and identified in Welsh chronicles as well. In fact, the important connotations of a woman's association with her husband as a marker of status suggests much older origins where the importance of women was unambiguously linked to land and where the king married the lady of sovereignty in a symbolic ritual to claim power. Literary sources, like

34

the Welsh Triads and stories from the *Mabinogion* which themselves are based on a much more ancient, oral tradition, define women by their lifecycles as wives and daughters directly distinguishing them as the figureheads of Sovereignty.

Traditionally, before the advancement and settlement of the Norman lords in the south of Wales at the end of the eleventh century, the pursuit of orchestrating alliances between native dynasties through the guise of marriage was the principle tactic for many Welsh rulers. When it became clear that Norman lords were lured by promises of profit and land in the west of Britain, and were becoming firmly entrenched on the Welsh borders and within south Wales especially, the marital strategies among the Welsh leaders began to change.

The Normans also used marriage as a tool to gain legitimacy in the areas they occupied in Wales and on the Welsh March. They used marriage to eradicate other's claims to power and lands by effectively 'inheriting' them through marital alliances, not long after 1066. This policy was recognised by the Welsh who, along with the Marcher barons, put it into practice during the colonisation of south Wales. In many ways it was used as a source of contact more convivial than down and out warfare. Going against traditions of the house of Deheubarth, which customarily sought marriages for their sons and daughters with the dynasties of Gwynedd and Powys, the Lord Rhys became the first prominent Welsh ruler to fully use the marriage of his children to extend his dynasty eastwards and infiltrate the Anglo-Norman aristocracy; it was a constructive means to bind his Marcher neighbours closer to him.

Marriages beyond Wales made it much easier for rulers such as Llywelyn to integrate their dynasties into the wider circles of the Anglo-Norman nobility. As Llywelyn himself proved through his own policy of intermarrying his children by Joan to powerful Anglo-Norman dynasties, intermarriages between the Welsh and Anglo-Normans were used as the principal means of assuring amity by the middle of the thirteenth century. They offered power and the possibility of more long-term security. Technically, such marriages helped Welsh leaders like Llywelyn a greater semblance of peace of peace than through straightforward political negotiations. This appears to have been his strategy when marrying his daughters by Joan, Gwladus, Marared and Elen, and his son Dafydd, off to prominent Marcher families, specifically de Braoses, Mortimers and to the heir of Chester.

Nevertheless, the political significance behind such intimate Welsh-Welsh and Welsh-Norman connections is not always obvious as strong political partnerships were not always offered through marital alliances. Arguably, the bigger importance lies in the political, economic, social and oftentimes dynastic motives behind the creation of alliances through marriage, as opposed to the political results. The late-thirteenth-century marriage of Ada de Hastings and Rhys ap Maredudd of the Dinefwr dynasty in southern Wales acts as a model example of the ultimate motivation behind marital alliances. Native sources record that their union was to end 'the major enmities and mortal wars between the kinsmen and ancestors' of both families.[1] Of course, the reasoning behind this union was nothing new. Records pertaining to the 1175 marriage of Llywelyn's uncle Dafydd ab Owain Gwyendd to Emma of Anjou a century earlier emphatically stress the fundamental purpose of their marriage which was to maintain peace between the kingdom of Gwynedd and England. The chronicles claim, 'That same Dafydd then married the king's sister – Emma was her name – because he thought that he could hold his territory in peace thereby.'[2] Gerald of Wales also commented that Dafydd's political strength against his own brothers as they wrestled for control of Gwynedd was due to the fact that he was married to Emma and because she was the king's sister. Dafydd alone received support from the English Crown.[3]

International brides such as Emma, and later Joan, were often afforded a greater sense of influence and power because of their unique backgrounds and origins stemming from the Continent which enhanced their cultural perspectives. There was a distinct expectation that they would intervene in political concerns if needed. The court poet Llywarch ap Llywelyn, stresses Emma of Anjou's royal status and international position in one of his praise poems (*mawl*) by defining her as Dafydd's wife and mother of his heir.[4] It was often through the exploitations of kinship ties that noble, aristocratic and royal women were able to further their family's political power, never mind their own in a number of instances. Thus, in terms of the intimate relationships between women and men, frequently wives were the conduit through which men in power were able to develop their spheres of influences, over both land and kin.

Within the Welsh kinship system, the positions of women were multifaceted and it is a mistake to simply assume that Welsh marital customs followed the 'natural' suit of the older and more established Roman custom in which a woman left the *potestas* of her parents and organically transitioned to that of her husband's. Legally, there was no clear delineation as to which family wives inherently belonged. This limbo-status centred around two fronts. First, once married a woman was never completely assimilated into her husband's family. Second, although married, a woman was never fully alienated from her own natal family or kinship group. This was primarily due to the fact that married women were the leading links between dynastic kin-groups (*gwelyau*) and, as such, legally, they did not fully belong to either kindred.[5] Their position was viewed as the knot that tied two families together in an act of solidarity and alliance. It was an unmarried woman's paternal lineage upon which her legal status greatly depended. If she had a brother, her status was dependent on his. After marriage, it goes without saying that her status was defined by that of her husband.

Ultimately, the position of women overall was defined by their sexuality, loosely related to their ability to bear children. In fact, marriage – intrinsically viewed as a loss of virginity – and menopause, were the two distinct demarcations in a woman's life; her transition from young to old. For men, their lifecycles were demarcated by social movements and involvement in public life, including one: acquiring land, and two: becoming the head of the household once married.

Because of the ambiguity in women's status, it is easy to assume that they were deemed objects, and it has often been believed that they never enjoyed complete juridical power or freedom, regardless of the socially eminent role they may have played in the functioning of society as wives. Yet it was through certain activities undertaken by married women, such as jointly or independently supervising the distribution and transmission of family lands for following generations, frequently through the making of marital arrangements themselves for their own children, that helped enhance the power and prestige of their own dynasty.

This is similar to our understanding of places like Anglo-Saxon England for instance where, although women seem to have been faced with few barriers in their acquisition to power, real exercise of female agency primarily came through conjugal families, and women's necessary involvement in familial and kinship networks. A married woman could derive much power by effectively exploiting her family's own long-term, and often elevated ambitions. Through this system which has been loosely defined as 'predatory kinship',[6] a married woman was able to establish and greatly expand her own career; doing so was seen as crucial to the enduring prosperity of her family. This is distinctly obvious in the business of some of Joan's female forbears in Wales who were, in essence, queens.

Joan's predecessor and aunt, Emma of Anjou provides the perfect example. Charter evidence suggests that, like Joan after her, Emma was 'a prominent and influential consort in Welsh polity'.[7] Also like Joan, Emma's membership within the Angevin dynasty was initially a springboard to her activities being valued by both her husband, Dafydd, and half-brother Henry II. Circumstances also dictated her participation in events, especially in terms in lordship administration, where she acted as the sole representative for her husband and her own family. Between 1180–1203 Emma is found consenting, sometimes along with her son Owain, to grants of lands in Stockett and Crickett in Shropshire, part of the Ellesmere estate, to Haughmond Abbey.

During her reign, she also issued her own grant to the monks of Haughmond, not only with the assent of Dafydd, but independently. Emma obviously enjoyed a strong element of noble authority as her charters were affixed with her own seal, and even some of the witnesses found on charters issued by both her and Dafydd separately contain the names of some of the same men, including Bishop Reiner of St Asaph (Denbighshire). Interestingly, the wording of Emma's grant issued mirrors an earlier grant issued by her husband with her consent, which may indicate Dafydd's need to obtain her consent to grant any lands from Ellesmere, which was her marriage portion. It should be noted that one of her grants issued in 1194 was later confirmed by her nephew, Richard I.[8] Henry II granted Ellesmere to her in May 1177 and it was eventually to become Joan and Llywelyn's gift of marriage in 1205. Emma continued to manage these lordship estates while Dafydd was a Welsh political prisoner during the years 1197–98.

That one of Emma's bequests concludes that the monks of Haughmond shall not be troubled by anyone concerning her grant indicates that she likely enjoyed an officially recognised level of lordship agency and unhindered authority, at least on certain matters. Her combined use of lifecycles and titles to identify herself in her grants also highlights her independent authority, status and position. The lifecycles are used in a specific way that draws attention to her relationship to the powerful men to whom she was connected. This is hardly unusual and, for wives in particular, is a common occurrence found in Welsh sources, especially in acta and chronicles. Importantly, Emma identifies herself by her title first, Lady (*Domina Emma*), followed by her connection to Henry II (*soror Henrici regis*), then her uxorial position as Dafydd's consort (*uxor David filii Owini principis Norwallie*).

In general, the labels Emma uses in her acta mirror Dafydd's own as he identifies himself through both his status as the prince of North Wales and his patronymic. All of these identifiers underscore her social status, as well as the gendered authority and influence in both personal and political capacities. The use of her seal further highlights the elements of power she enjoyed, certainly during the times the charters were issued. Interestingly, in charters where she only identifies herself as Dafydd's wife and not *domina*, and/or that have no sealing clauses, likely reflects the change in her own status within Wales itself while Dafydd was imprisoned, either through her own perception or those of the document scribes themselves.

Indeed, Emma may have only issued acta in her name while Dafydd was in captivity because he was unable to do so himself. Nevertheless, neither his absence nor presence within the family lordship likely affected Emma's capacity to issue gifts by her own right, or the freedom to do so, certainly as far as Ellesmere was concerned. What is important to remember is that, collectively, the charters issued by her, Dafydd and their son Owain, as a family unit or independently, show how a family acted as a collective pool of patrons and partook in the administration of the wider family lordship as a means of further securing authority and hegemony through patronages, most certainly during times of political insecurity.

Ultimately, marriages were matters of arrangements between families who sought control over the movement and transference of land, property and wealth, and potential bridegrooms sought wives who were the daughters of men whose lands, power and prestige they coveted. Llywelyn was no exception. He may have been married at least once before his betrothal to Joan because two women that we know of appeared in his trajectory in the late 1190s, early 1200s. It seems that Llywelyn may have married a sister of the prominent Ranulf, earl of Chester and stalwart supporter of the English Crown around 1192.[9] This is an interesting association between Llywelyn and Ranulf, who were supposedly enemies in the late-twelfth century, but which may be the fundamental reason for the supposed marriage, on point. This is, indeed, a more interesting and curious connection if Clémence de Fougères, Ranulf's second wife whom he married in 1200, was actually Joan's own mother.

Llywelyn's marriage to Ranulf's sister seems to have come after his attempts to marry a daughter of the king of Man were stymied when her father delayed her travels to Wales. However, not only is there no concrete evidence to back up the union with Ranulf's sister, we do not know the woman's name or her fate. If she were married to Llywelyn, it is assumed she died shortly afterwards as Llywelyn continued to pursue marriage with the princess of Man until it became clear that a viable marriage to a daughter of the king of England, albeit illegitimate, would tie him directly to the English Crown.

The constant threat to England resided in the potential alliance between, and support of, an ambitious Marcher baron and a warring Welsh prince acting in defiance against the Crown. When John Lackland claimed the throne for himself after the death of his brother in 1199 he had the advantage of already being familiar with Welsh politics having been a border baron himself for ten years. He was overtly aware of the unscrupulous private interests of the Marcher lords, and even though he was continuously preoccupied with events on the Continent, he kept a close eye on the prevailing Welsh rivalry and attempted to maintain relations with parties on both side while iniquitously playing them against one another for his own means. According to the famous Welsh historian, J.E. Lloyd, in order to sustain any influential power over Wales, John should have continued to play the princes against one another.[10]

Much to his folly, and one of John's biggest errors early on in his reign was to misjudge the aspirations of the Venedotian prince. Thus, although aware of Llywelyn's increased influence throughout his native Wales, in 1201 John openly and formally recognised the prince's unique supremacy. In turn for Llywelyn's homage, the Angevin ruler acknowledged his tenured rights to lands he acquired while campaigning in Wales and made him subject to fair, legal proceedings in England and Wales. This is the first ever recorded Anglo-Welsh treaty. In order to maintain a policy of friendship, John offered the hand of his illegitimate daughter, Joan, in marriage. Likely assuming that such an offer, hot on the heels of an unprecedented recognition of Welsh authority, would keep Llywelyn in check, John would soon find his presumption a grave mistake; the consequences of which embroiled his daughter in a tug-of-war of emotions and loyalty, effectively for the rest of her life.

Chapter Four

Princess to Queen

Princess: Journey to England

It is perhaps not a coincidence that we are given our first glimpse of Joan in records for 1203. In Wales, Llywelyn's uncle Dafydd died in English exile, being survived by his wife Emma of Anjou and heir, Owain, by at least another eleven years. And, although Owain never seems to have been a contender for Venedotian rule, it may have been because of his father's demise that Joan and Llywelyn's marriage was truly set in motion. Occurrences overseas, however, may also have triggered the need for Joan's journey to England at this time. King John had a lot on his plate in 1203 and little of it was palatable. War with France had broken out the year before and his control over Normandy teetered on the edge. His nephew Arthur mysteriously disappeared and rumours swirled that John had murdered him. Numerous allies jumped ship. By now in her early eighties, his seemingly all-powerful mother, who had recently offered her support in opposition to Arthur's claims for the throne, became gradually more ill. That John seems to have fled France by the end of this year indicates his precarious position there and it is possible that he saw this as the time to ensure that Joan was safe from harm's way, in a land 'securely' under his control. And so, in this year, under the king's writ and at the king's expense, his daughter sailed on a certain vessel from Normandy to England.[1]

Though confusion and ambiguity surround Joan's maternity, there is evidence that provides a small snapshot into her possible upbringing, namely in the person of Robert Vieuxpont. Vieuxpont was in the royal service of King John in Normandy, being in charge of troops and military works, and was the man ordered to oversee Joan's journey. He had already proven his worth to the king and was highly trusted by him because previously John had placed two other children close to him

41

in his care: his own illegitimate son – and Joan's brother – Richard, and his niece – Arthur's sister – Eleanor, the Fair Maid of Brittany. Clearly, at some point, Joan, too, was Vieuxpont's ward as he organised 'the daughter of the king's' journey to England. Whether she was a long-term ward, or simply under his guardianship for the voyage to her new life, it is impossible to say. Nevertheless, that John assigned his bastard son Richard and his niece Eleanor to be raised in Robert's household during certain points in their lives, certainly makes the case more credible that Joan maybe spent longer in Robert's custody than the time it took sail across the Channel and be settled somewhere in Britain after landing.

Another theory as to Joan's upbringing may reside in a curious grant that the king of England made in February 1203, which should perhaps also give us pause for thought. Originally founded by Robert de Beaumont, 3rd earl of Leicester (a man who actively participated in Richard I's coronation in 1189 as a ceremonial sword-bearer), John granted alms to a Cistercian order of nuns for the building of their abbey, Fontaine Guérard.[2] Set in the lush Andelle valley, on the outskirts of Lyon's forest, the abbey is situated not more than thirteen miles from Rouen, where John spent most of 1203. Is it possible that Joan was originally raised and educated by the nuns of Our Lady of Fontaine Guérard, and that John's grant to them was a gift of thanks? The lack of information in the charter does not necessarily mean this was not the case.

For royal, noble and aristocratic girls in the Middle Ages, education was important and the two types of institutions that offered this were nunnery schools and great households. Receiving an education in a nunnery was certainly not uncommon. Contrary to popular belief, nunneries were not places where young girls simply acquired spiritual edification, or an education in 'good manners', or how to craft textiles traditionally associated with women, like spinning, embroidery and weaving. Some nunneries, in fact, provided what we now consider a 'liberal arts' education, delivering important intellectual stimulation, from teaching girls to read and/or write Latin (the two were not necessarily complementary), to lessons in religion and music, medicine, astronomy, arithmetic and geometry. Some even provided education in law, dialectics and rhetoric – nuns themselves producing treatises on the like. Spirituality aside, and arguably the most important education girls received from nunneries was an understanding and appreciation of the types of very public power women could wield as nuns owned and managed vast portions of land. Indeed, many enjoyed a power unmatched by other contemporary women. In reality, nunneries provided many young girls with excellent models for exercising female agency.

Land management and lordship administration were crucial skills for young aristocratic girls to learn and besides nunneries, many did so under fosterage in great households. Fosterage was a common practice where children were raised and educated by other families. For girls, much of their education in these great households was fashioned for them to 'shine in society'.[3] This included a combination of learning practical skills that they would need as wives. Administrative and household management skills were especially important for those girls destined to marry into vast lordship estates. They were also educated in more refined accomplishments, such as the art of playing chess, verbal repartee and music, skills which helped girls learn how to conform to idealistic gender constructs that women of the upper echelons of society in particular faced; constructs, by this time, dictated by the popular and social and cultural phenomenon of courtly love – a genre notably at its apex during Joan's lifetime. Girls were also cultivated to be good at sports, especially hawking, which was a common and favourite pastime for many aristocratic women. Joan was undoubtedly adept at hawking and perhaps even spent much of her time as a new bride getting to know her new adoptive country while hawking and learning the lay of the land herself. A few short years after their marriage, Joan and Llywelyn received falcons as gifts from John and there is little doubt Joan would have enjoyed spending time in the wilds of Wales undertaking the sport.[4]

The idea of training a woman to be the 'good wife' was a pragmatic one that was also defined by its vocational nature. Numerous didactic treaties from the Middle Ages abound regarding the need for the woman as a wife to know how to meet the needs of her husband, her family and the family lordship. Whether Joan was raised in a nunnery or in a greater household, or even as part of the English queen-consort's household, her education would have been an important part of her upbringing, even as an illegitimate child. Bastard or no, she carried royal blood and her social position afforded her more opportunities for movement up the political and social ladder than her illegitimate brothers. She was betrothed to royalty after all and, wherever she was raised, she was most certainly given instruction as to her main role as an international bride and taught the fundamentals of familial and political diplomacy.

On this last matter, it is possible that Joan was reared in one of John's own households in Normandy.[5] Certainly, if she were raised as part of the queen's own household, her education in diplomatic skills would have been significantly furthered. However, given that the queen of England, who by 1200 was Isabella of Angoulême (r. 1200–1216) and roughly the same age as Joan, it seems unlikely that Isabella would have had that particular command. Nonetheless, and perhaps more enlightening, it was while the queen was sojourning at Caen in 1203 that Robert Vieuxpont was paid back for organising Joan's travels, disbursements made from the queen herself 'for the hire of a certain vessel to carry the daughter of the King and the equipage of the King to England 18 li. 13s. 3d.'. This by no means proves Joan was an integral part of the queen's household, but indicates that she was probably there at this time. It may even be that once the treaty with Llywelyn was signed in 1201 John began making plans to ensure that Joan received the education befitting a daughter of royal blood, and one who was destined for a royal marriage. Perhaps, then, the similarity in age between his queen and his beloved natural daughter was thought to be more of an appealing advantage than a cause for animosity.

In early December 1203, John landed at Portsmouth on the southern English coast, after spending much of the year holding court at Rouen, Caen and Bonneville-sur-Touques, among a number of other places in Normandy. Regardless of where she was raised, surely during this time the king saw and spent some time with the young, teenage Joan as their relationship after her marriage indicates they were, indeed, close. In spite of his sometimes venal performances and behaviour, John is known for having been a loving father and it would have been somewhat out of character for him not to have met with his daughter at least once before her journey to offer fatherly love and support, and to waylay her concerns and apprehensions pertaining to such a major life change.

In fact, John might not have simply given her a hug and offered words of comfort before her move to a foreign land as a young bride-to-be, but in reality, may have personally escorted her to England. He and Robert Vieuxpont sailed from Barfleur together and landed in Portsmouth on 7 December 1203 and it is almost certain that Joan was with her father and travelled with him to Southwick, Hampshire on landing.

It is probable that she would have stayed with John's retinue at least until after Christmas, spending the day itself with him in Canterbury. Had Joan been Robert Vieuxpont's ward, perhaps after a brief sojourn with her father over the winter season, she journeyed to one of Robert's English holdings and remained there until her nuptials.[6]

There are, of course, numerous other possibilities. She could have spent time in bustling London, at Whitehall palace or perhaps even stayed at the Tower of London, or down in Windsor. Depending on who her mother was, she could have been housed in Chester with Ranulf and his wife, Clémence de Fougères, or spent time in Staffordshire at the Verdun caput with Clemence de Verdun. Perhaps she spent time in a nunnery preparing for her marriage to Llywelyn. Another possibility is that she stayed at Ellesmere with her aunt Emma of Anjou, getting to know both her and the manor that would soon be under Joan's own control. Ellesmere, having been held by Emma in marriage to Dafydd, was a prominent location near the border towns of Shrewsbury and Oswestry and its proximity to the earldom of Chester made it an important asset to Welsh leaders. As we will see, it seems that Ellesmere and the Shrewsbury area were important strongholds for Joan and it is perhaps here, under Emma's tutelage, that she advanced her knowledge of not only lordship administration, but also Marcher politics, Welsh history and the rules of Welsh queenship, and her own future career as an envoy.

Surprisingly, not only do we not know where Joan stayed on her arrival to England, we also do not know exactly when or where she and Llywelyn were married. Even pinpointing the date of their marriage is tricky. Nonetheless, it is possible to narrow the scope. The Chester annals and royal letters close record they were betrothed sometime before 15 October 1204. The Worcester annals give the year 1206.[7] It is most likely that they were married between February and March 1205. In February, Llywelyn withdrew his request for a papal dispensation to marry an unnamed daughter of Reginald, the king of Man (r. 1187–1229). Curiously, it is believed that she was already known to Llywelyn, apparently having been the wife of his uncle Rhodri (or at least betrothed to him). As such, papal approval would have been a necessary measure since the couple would have been related by bonds of consanguinity; Llywelyn's move to obtain the dispensation indicates that Rhodri, indeed, had married the princess of Man first.[8] It seems as if the young Welsh prince was (rightfully) wary of trusting that the English king would make good on his promise that his daughter's hand in marriage would reinforce the 1201 English-Welsh alliance and looked to garner himself another political association as back-up. Papal confirmation that Llywelyn's request to marry the Manx princess was given the go-ahead in April 1203 may have been another factor in Joan setting sail for England that year. It follows that, in spite of the two-year negotiation process, Llywelyn withdrew his original request to marry the princess of Man in February 1205 when the promise that the more prosperous union with the king of England's daughter was to be made good on. To make sure that his planned marriage to Reginald's daughter would be dropped without question, the Welsh prince manipulated canon law to suit his change in fortune. He provided witnesses who swore that Rhodri and the Manx princess had consummated their union, leaving Innocent III (r. 1198–1216) little choice but to rule that Llywelyn could not marry her after all. In March 1205, Joan and Llywelyn received the manor of Ellesmere as a marriage portion.

As for the location of their marriage, there is not one mention of it to be found in records unearthed, so far. As with so much of Joan's life, this, too, is likely to remain a great mystery. Chester has seemed to be one of the more obvious choices and the original cathedral of St John would have been the venue because it has had links to northern Welsh leaders both before and after Llywelyn and Joan's reign. Yet given the existing animosity between Llywelyn and Ranulf, the earl of Chester at this time, the marriage of the Welsh prince in a hostile territory would have surely given him cause for concern – even if Clémence de Fougères were Joan's mother, and Ranulf one of John's strongest supporters, both factors which, in theory, would have offered more assurances of safety than would have otherwise been expected.

Worcester, in fact, may have been the more likely location, especially given King John's own ties to the cathedral, the surrounding area and the fact he was there in March 1205.[9] Is it a coincidence that on 17–19 March the king was at Kenilworth, one of Robert of Vieuxpont's holdings, and from there travelled to Worcestershire, where he stayed a full week? In fact, according to John's itinerary, at no time between 7 December 1203 and 17 March 1205 did he visit Kenilworth. Moreover, he did not visit Kenilworth again until July 1209.

Some of the king's favourite hunting lodges were to be found at Kinver and Feckenham in Worcestershire and his itinerary shows that he did spend some time on 19 March 1205 at his royal manor in Feckenham. From there he spent 20 and 21 March in Worcester itself, and then 22–24 March at Woolward. Though speculative, there is enough evidence to suggest that John may have indeed attended Joan's wedding to Llywelyn and that it took place in Worcester – conceivably even escorting her himself from Kenilworth. Maybe this is why the marriage between Llywelyn and Joan was recorded in the first place in English records. Worcester also happens to be the place that Eleanor de Montfort (r. 1278–1282) and Llywelyn ap Gruffudd, Llywelyn's grandson and last prince of Wales, were married in 1278 – the wedding paid for by the Edward I, king of England, who himself gave the bride away. The long-term connection between Worcester, the kings of England and the north Walian leaders may have run deep, indeed.

Queen: Journey Through Wales

We have no record of Joan from the time she was married until the political crisis that occurred six years later in 1211. But we can presume that upon returning to Wales with Llywelyn, integration into her new life would have consisted of a fast and furious education – both how to be a queen, including customary practices, and wifely expectations. Indeed, it would have been vital for Joan to have learned the customs and ways expected of the queen in the Venedotian court as quickly as she could. As a foreigner, and moreover as King John's daughter, her position among her peers would not have been so easily secured, appreciated or even liked, simply because she was Llywelyn's new and legal wife.

In the very least, she attended court to entertain visitors, both when Llywelyn was in attendance and while he was away. Welsh would have been the primary language in the royal court, though Llywelyn, himself, seems to have a background in Norman French, Joan's own language. Given the expectations of the queen to host and maintain her own circuit, Joan must have learned Welsh over her thirty-plus years as reigning queen of Gwynedd. Native Welsh sources provide a litany of illustrations of the queen partaking in an official position within the royal household, often centred around the highly treasured custom of Welsh hospitality.[10] Gerald of Wales claimed that 'Welsh generosity and hospitality' were 'the greats of all virtues', and that the host and hostess had important obligations when entertaining. His own experiences in the court of Emma of Anjou and Dafydd ab Owain seem to have been particularly pleasing to him during his travels through Wales in the late twelfth century.[11] The twelfth-century acclaimed court poet, Cynddelw, applauded the Welsh court as a dwelling place of hospitality where all were made welcome. He specifically lauded the hospitality of the late twelfth-century princes, Owain Cyfeiliog of Powys and Cadwallon ap Madog ab Inerth, but he was also court poet for Madog ap Maredudd of Powys, and Owain Gwynedd and his son Dafydd.[12] So important was hospitality among the Welsh that Walter Map, an English royal clerk, tells a story of a wife's breach in the hospitality code that resulted in an all-out family feud.[13] The Welsh royal *llys* (court) was the model example of how a household should be managed. The royal couple was the exemplary representation of how married couples should conduct themselves, especially when entertaining. As such, the rules of Welsh hospitality unquestionably pertained to the princely courts above all and there is no doubt Joan became accomplished in all the manners and expectations of her rank.

Native sources provide illustrations that hint at the prominence of the queen in the royal *llys*, especially as applied to the apparent responsibilities assigned to her. Examples are found in the twelfth-century biography of Gruffudd ap Cynan, king of Gwynedd. The Welsh vernacular and later Latin version have discernible differences in the ways that Queen Angharad is described and the implied duties ascribed to her. Besides intimating the queen's presence in the court, certainly when providing alms to the poor, the Welsh version specifically refers to her responsibilities concerning hospitality within the *llys*.[14] Numerous examples of royal women entertaining in the king's court also appear in the many tales of the *Mabinogion* and are often reminiscent of the traditional trope of the lady with the mead cup.

The image of a queen holding out a drink or cup of peace is one that prevails from the Middle Ages. It is important to remember that this was not just a fanciful illustration, but one based on the very real duty of queens acting as intercessors, or mediators. From the Anglo-Saxon *Beowulf* and Norse and Icelandic paintings to the Irish legend of *Táin Bó Cúailnge* found in the Ulster Cycle, the portrayal of queens offering chalices of mead are symbolic representations of very real offerings of peace. The 'lady with the mead cup' is linked with the role of the queen in many early medieval societies and, in turn, the queen is linked to the Sovereignty goddess figure whose power lay in offering libation to a man chosen to be king, symbolically marrying him to the land he was to rule. It is no accident that Queen Medb of Connacht's name means 'she who intoxicates', Medb being etymologically associated with the Celtic word for 'mead'.

In medieval Wales, too, the image of the queen, or the lady with the mead cup, also prevailed – Queen Gwenhwyfar is the most notable figure to be in possession of a chalice of wine within the public realms of the royal *llys*, as is found in the native tale 'Peredur'. The offering of a drink of mead or wine in native Welsh society was an act of conferring honour upon the recipient. As a public act it was also likely associated with bridging a peace and cementing alliances and friendships.[15] The concurrence between Queen Angharad's duties in the Life of Gruffudd ap Cynan being defined both as a hostess and a counsel-woman, *cyngorwreic*, should neither be overlooked nor underestimated. Joan would have learned the history of her predecessors and the place of the queen in Welsh culture.

The later fifteenth-century series of verses, or songs dedicated to the officers of the Welsh court, *Canu i Swyddogion Llys y Brenin* (*A Song to the Officers of the King's Court*), provides the most overt example of the Welsh queen in her role as a cup-bearer, gift-giver and her important function in the *llys*. Addressing the queen, the poet says:

> In the palaces of Britain
> And fair splendour
> … dwelling
> And others unsightly
> lying out flat.
>
> I saw honour
> … feast and hand-maidens
> The colour of bright seagulls
> … which they brought,
> drinks without ceasing (?)
> with a silver cup in hand …
>
> the noble-faced queen.
> It is she who brings to me
> it is …

Fair is she who brings
to me gifts every day.

Y mordai Prydain
a cain arderced
... aned
ag eraill heb ued
yn eu hir orued.

Gwelias anryded
...wled
a laufornynion
liu guylain gwynion
... a dygant,
wirodau d[ ] gwant
a ffiol ariant
yn adaf.

Although much later than the time frame under discussion, *Canu i Swyddogion Llys y Brenin* is important to understanding the longevity of the image of the Welsh queen as an intercessor, or symbolic cup-bearer. In fact, it may be a long-established remnant of a centuries older tradition attributed to Taliesin, the famous sixth-century bard.[16] Joan surely would have been made to understand the magnitude of the queen performing such a function, especially as she was one of the three top-ranking members of the royal household, between the king and *edling*.

Interestingly, the importance in the status of the Welsh queen as a hostess, cup-bearer and gift-giver in *Canu i Swyddogion Llys y Brenin* is tempered by imagery of the king dispensing the gift of wine in a very clear manner: 'The wine is dispensed in the hand of the king not ... of the queen' (*Diwalau y gwin| yn lau y brenin | na [ ] brenhines*).[17] This is not to say, however, that the gift of drink was provided by either the king or the queen. In fact, it was likely both in practice, the couple working together as a cohesive symbol of royal authority. It should also be taken into account that mead itself was one of the more common food-renders and payments of exchange were made between the king, or his (local) officers, and townships. With this in mind, it is likely that in practice the act of honorary gift-giving (especially through the offer of libation) was divided into two different forms: the *rhoddi*, a transfer of ownership of the gift, and *estyn*, the physical act of handing the gift over. If anything the queen's role was probably the latter (that is not to say, however, she did not also undertake the former) as the *estyn* may provide a metaphor for mediation.

Some versions of the Welsh laws emphasise that it was the queen who gave a hornful of mead to the *penteulu*, the captain of the king's household, a close relative of the king who was not necessarily related to the queen herself (perhaps a son or nephew). The chief groom (*pengwastrawd*) and the chief huntsman (*pencynydd*) were also bestowed privileges of drink, all three officers receiving three hornfuls of mead, the first two from the king and queen. As the laws imply that it was during festive occasions when these particular acts of gift-giving occurred, occasions when both the queen and king were to be present, it seems unlikely that queen would have carried out her function as a cup-bearer in the more private sphere of the royal chambers. Nevertheless, if in fact, the queen was located in her chamber, sending drinks to the hall instead of offering them herself, it is vital to understand that the royal Welsh chamber was not synonymous with domestic disconnectedness, or, indeed, female isolation. Of course the queen, and likely often the king, dined in her chambers on many an occasion, but it is clear from the myriad of native literary sources that the royal chamber was the hub of political and social activities, including entertaining political elites.[18] Sources indicate that, overall, the Welsh court was a domain in which both the king and queen had hospitable responsibilities, such as in the form of gift-giving, conversation and consultation; whether these duties were undertaken in the chamber or the great hall, it is clear they were responsibilities that complemented one another and signified the strength of authority.

Presenting a united front between queen and king as rulers was crucial to the success of a kingdom and Joan would have been taught that such a partnership manifested in other ways, beyond public displays symbolic gestures. In the first instance, it is important to consider the practicalities of managing a vast, and at times unstable kingdom, especially while a leader was often away for long swathes of time, which Llywelyn clearly was. A necessary division of households and responsibilities would have been made. As part of her household responsibility, it was crucial for the queen to act as the visible face and authority of the king, whether she was on circuit or stationary at one of the royal palaces. Some of the main royal residences that Joan would have spent much time at include, but are certainly not limited to Aber, Caernarfon, Rhosyr, Cemais, Llanfaes, Trefriw, Beddgelert and Castell Hen Blas.

There was a level of shared responsibility between the royal couple, especially as they often held separate courts. As the heart of the king's domain, and especially a warring king, the royal household warranted a management style that distributed the load of administrative duties among separate sections of the household; different officers had the authority to represent the king, giving the king an advantage by ensuring that he was able to spread his powers further afield. Of all the king's officers, it was the queen who was symbolically, and arguably in practice, the most important.

Welsh sources paint a collaborative picture of the queen's obligations to go on circuit. The queen's circuit even having its own idiom, *rhieinglych*. Various interesting references surface in Welsh literary sources that provide clues as to perceptions of, and attitudes towards, the queen's authority while on circuit in the king's lands. Apparently the men of late twelfth-century Powys had concerns as to the far-reaching excesses and powers of the royal woman, claiming that the queen's own 'oppressive' circuit was 'a second tyranny' they had to endure:

> A joint-custom of the warriors, gift-distributors to poets,
> Splended champions, splendidly does it succeed,
> Battle-leaders resisted shame a second time,
> A second tyranny, [the] oppressive circuit of the queen.

> *Cynneddf i'r cedwyr, ced ysgain – i feirdd,*
> *Cedweilch heirdd, hardd yd fain,*
> *Eilwaith gwarth gwrthodes cynrain,*
> *Ail gormail, gormesgylch rhiain.*[19]

A later Welsh proverb teasingly provides a similar impression of the queen's authority veering on autocratic tendencies. Although not the only interpretation, a reading of '*Gwala gwedw; gwreic vnbenn*' suggests that due to the tyrant royal wife, plenty of prayers were needed.[20]

It likely that when the king campaigned beyond his kingdom, the queen's household undertook circuits around the royal demesne. The peripatetic nature of Llywelyn's court overall meant that the running of the *llys y brenin* (the court of the king) itself had to be fluid and adaptive.

It meant that in order for the administration to function at full capacity, collaboration was needed in order to successfully manage both a mobile and static household. Again, a number of native sources provide examples of queens working in collaboration with their husbands as kings. The couple shared royal responsibilities, similar to other more widespread European practices and expectations associated with royal status. Queens, such as Rieingulid, in the Life of St Illtud, and Rhiannon in the First Branch of the *Mabinogi* accompanied their husbands on circuit. In fact, it is said of Rhiannon and her husband Pwyll that '*They* [my emphasis] ruled the land successfully that year, and the next' (*Gweledychu y wlat a wnaethont yn llwydannus y ulwydyn honno, a'r eil*).[21] 'And I will take you as my wife ... and give you authority over my kingdom', so said King Math to Goewin upon learning that she was raped by his nephew and was no longer able to protect him as his virgin footholder.[22] This example from the Fourth Branch of the *Mabinogi* is one of several throughout sources that strongly suggest the office of the queen was one of recognised authority.

Normative examples of political leadership in the Four Branches of the *Mabinogi*, in particular, are so explicit that the stories probably had a much deeper didactic purpose – to provide models of kingship and educate rulers on native expectations; a Welsh version of a 'mirror of princes' (*speculum principum*).[23] As such, in terms of how queens are portrayed, too, likely provided mirrors for reflection. In fact, the varied depiction of queenly agency found in the different kinds of sources, written by different kinds of authors, may possibly reflect wider norms, or even reality, and may have been patronised by leading royal women themselves. Perhaps even Joan.

Importantly, it is key to think about the patronage practices of royal women like Joan and the portrayal of fictionalised queens. Even though little to nothing is known or understood about female patronage in Wales, their influences on the production of stories in how queens were portrayed must have been considerable.[24] Although there were moralistic functions to many works, like the Lives of Saints, where queens are lauded for their modesty and submissiveness, in the exact same works, queens are also portrayed as central courtly figures, hosting and going on circuit. Although many images in literature in which the Welsh queen is exalted may have simply been a means of flattery aimed at the ruler's wife, as both a form of entertainment and, often, spiritual edification, they also had a deeper, more practical functionality.

Thus, upon entering Wales in 1205, Joan would have begun her education in the expectations of Welsh queenship and, equally as crucial, the norms and expectations of her status as Llywelyn's wife. This type of education would have happened through the sharing of knowledge, not just from her Welsh peers, but also from the oral and literary culture that was so pervasive. Expectations Joan faced as a queen, beyond the practicalities of being on circuit and, as will be discussed later, being involved in matters of policy as an advisor, or counsellor, were more superficial on the surface, but equally as challenging to circumnavigate, as they were embedded deep in culture and history, and often contradictory. Medieval literature from all over Europe is paradoxical as far as the portrayal of women are concerned, particularly as attitudes and expectations of all women were predicated on two prototypes that encompassed all the goods and ills of the entire female species, Eve and the Virgin Mary. Religious attitudes towards women aside, the literature of the Middle Ages can be a fruitful and illuminating source concerning gender dichotomies, ideals and expectations in the areas in which it originated. This is especially important for an area like Wales where records of practice are limited. In terms of the persona of the queen in native and normative Welsh sources, she enjoyed the highest status available among her contemporaries.

Her position within the royal *llys* shown in native laws and her activities, roles and use of agency found in literary examples across the board all demonstrate that a woman like Joan was expected to operate in a sphere of influence and in an environment where her presence was unquestionable and anticipated. Of course, using literary sources and a focus on fictional characters as a means of trying to understand the roles, status and activities of real royal women in Welsh society can be problematic for obvious reasons, but they are valuable nonetheless as they illustrate cultural ideals and perceptions, attitudes and expectations that were, themselves, very real in society. The depiction of a Welsh ruler and his consort working in tandem, and in the public eye, in various forms of governance is an image that materialises in a number and variety of sources. Joan's later activities, in the most overt ways, personify these ideals. Joan adeptly learned what was expected of her in her role and, in time, became a clear model of Welsh queenship in practice as the year 1211 was to show.

Chapter Five

Winds of Change

In the beginning, relations between the two kingdoms and the two leaders of Gwynedd and England were favourable and both acknowledged that their ties of affinity were advantageous to having their needs met. While at Bristol on Christmas day in 1208, King John wrote to Llywelyn in response to the prince's concerns about his adversary Gwenwynwyn of Powys, and promised to treat the Welsh leader as 'a good son once more', but only if Llywelyn acquiesced to carrying out promises that John wanted him to make. It is unknown what the terms of the letter were, nor exactly what is meant by reference to 'once more', which, in itself, is curious. Did they fall out behind the scenes at some point, relying early on Joan to mend some sort of rift? Whatever the occasion, it seems as if amicable terms between the two generally remained as 29 January 1209 the king issued safe-conduct to Llywelyn and they may have met in Shrewsbury. A couple months later, on 16 March, Llywelyn was once again promised safe-conduct to meet with the king at Northampton. Joan could have accompanied Llywelyn, and maybe would have been expected to, on either or both journeys. Evidence of Llywelyn's continued loyalty to John had been established with the Welsh involvement in a joint campaign with the English against the Scots in the summer of 1209. It was the only time in Welsh history that a native prince of Gwynedd joined a military expedition outside Wales led by English forces. It is highly unlikely that Joan accompanied her husband and father to Scotland. If nothing else, it is probably around this time that she found she was pregnant with her third child.

Between 1205–10 Joan gave birth to the first three of at least five children that we know about: Gwladus Ddu (Gwladus the Dark, a reference to her dark looks), Marared (assuming she was named after Llywelyn's own mother) and Elen (who was later accused by the chronicler Matthew Paris of poisoning her first husband,

John the Scot, so that she could marry Roger de Quincy). Though there has been debate in the past as to who Gwladus Ddu's mother was, there is really now no doubt that it was Joan. In the least, *Fundationis et Fundatorum Historia* a chronicle written by a canon of Wigmore Abbey, refers to her specifically as Joan's daughter. Gwladus' second husband was Roger Mortimer and it was their descendants in the later Middle Ages who claimed a connection to Joan to verify themselves as rightful claimants to the English throne.[1] As Gwladus married first in 1215, she must have been their first-born child – at least the first of their children to survive and be recorded. Because she and her first husband Reginald de Braose had no offspring together, it seems like Gwladus was perhaps even under-age when betrothed. Thus, the very earliest she could have been born would have been December 1205. Marared must have been Joan's second daughter and born very soon after Gwladus, as she, too, was married to the de Braose clan in 1219. Assuming she was married as soon as she had come of age (12), she was probably born around 1207. Elen married the earl of Chester's nephew and heir in 1222, just at the time when she would have come of age. As such, she may have been born between 1209 and 1210.

Even if Joan were pregnant with Elen in 1209, and it is not recorded, it is important in the context of understanding the more complex nature of the history of medieval Wales when women are included in the narrative, that she may have been present at the royal palace of Woodstock for the truly momentous occasion in October 1209 when Llywelyn publicly repeated his homage to King John, just after the Scottish expedition. In the words of Roger of Wendover: 'And, what had never been heard of in times past, the Welsh came to the king at Woodstock and there did homage to him, although it was burdensome to rich as well as poor.'[2] Llywelyn's actions were not only surprising, but perhaps stupefying to those who understood him to be a man proud of his Welsh sovereignty. To the Welsh, whom Gerald of Wales described as a prideful and obstinate people who refused to conform to the ways of other nations and unite under the rule and dominion of one, Llywelyn's public submission could have verged on being scandalous.

How far his relationship with Joan had to do with his public alliance with the English king is speculative to say the least. She perhaps had a hand in encouraging her husband to remain on her father's good side and not just for personal reasons. Politically it was a move in which

Llywelyn, as the leading Welsh ruler, could greatly benefit from. On the surface, and tactically in line with his marriage to Joan four years earlier, paying homage to the English king underscored a special relationship that distinguished the power of the kingdom of Gwynedd above all other Welsh kingdoms – a relationship that, if not superficially, was to provide the Venedotian leader with a sense of security by proffering him possible English military support if needed.

Llywelyn, the ever-calculating statesman, took advantage early on of the king's favour and of his new status in European politics. This particular public performance of allying himself with the English king was another move that helped to elevate his standing in the larger European sphere. Indeed, it would not be long before Llywelyn's eagerness to befriend other powerful sovereigns of Europe took hold – namely Philip Augustus, King of France (r. 1180–1223) and, arguably the most powerful of all medieval popes, Innocent III. In his eventual, and inevitable, fight with John, which started less than a year after Llywelyn's performance of homage, the Welsh prince gained the support and powerful backing of both rulers. Such alliances challenged and even insulted the English king, who remained at odds with them. Within months of the prince's homage, it became clear to the English king that the prince of North Wales remained unremittent in his opposition of the English government's policies towards the Welsh. It was a conflict that eventually culminated in Joan's intervention.

Even though in January 1210 John gifted Joan and Llywelyn a set of falcons – evidence of good will and fatherly devotion – the once amicable relations were shattered come the summer. The break in the relationship has perplexed historians, leading many to assume the theory that John's continued paranoia, coupled with Llywelyn's ambitions, sparked the embers that fuelled the fire that would remain ever-smouldering, when not roaring; unquestionably, it was a fire that was never entirely extinguished during Joan's lifetime.

It was during this time that another example of the character trait that so defined John's reign played a crucial role in directly affecting the political environment of Wales and the Welsh March, which may have played a role in the eventual clash between Llywelyn and John. It was in 1210 that John famously turned on one of his most powerful barons and supporters, William de Braose, the 4th lord of Bramber. Once a court favourite, the power William wielded in South Wales, as the lord of Gower, Abergavenny,

Brycheiniog, Radnor, Kington and Glamorgan, was a threat to John. The notorious actions of the de Braose family in the late twelfth and early thirteenth centuries left them hated among the Welsh and untrusted among the Marcher lords. Notwithstanding the power and infamy William and his clan enjoyed, the more enduring threat to the English king was personal.

William was a close friend of John's and it is more than likely he was privy to the facts behind the death of John's nephew, prince Arthur in 1203. The young claimant to the throne had mysteriously disappeared and it was widely believed he had been murdered by John's own hands while under the guard of de Braose. Chronicles tell us that in the year 1210 Matilda de Braose,[3] William's wife, made public utterances implicating John in the young boy's death. The wrath that closed in is well known. John hunted the de Braose family across Wales, Ireland and eventually Scotland, where Matilda and her and William's eldest son, also William, were captured. From there they were taken to either Corfe or Windsor castle, and thrown in the dungeon where they literally starved to death. The shock of Matilda and her son's gruesome deaths resulted in clause 39 in the Magna Carta whereby 'No man shall be taken, imprisoned, outlawed, banished or in any way destroyed', nor prosecuted, 'except by the lawful judgement of his peers or by the law of the land'. William the elder eventually died in France in exile the following year. It is thought that Llywelyn and Joan helped the de Broase family in some way during their escape from John's wrath – perhaps either providing them funds or safe refuge at some point.

The position that Joan found herself in from 1210 until the death of John was an unfair and largely unkind one. Joan knew of Matilda, but it is more than likely that Joan and Matilda's paths crossed on more than one occasion, especially given Llywelyn and de Broase's ostensible coalition in 1210. What Joan thought of the de Braose family being so ruthlessly pursued by her own, beloved father, never mind the horrific deaths of Matilda and her first-born son at his hands – including the claims that Matilda may have cannibalised her son in order to survive – is something that we cannot remotely presume to know, and it is hardly something we can ever truly come to grips with or understand.

Up to this point, Joan's time in Wales had been relatively peaceful, at least as far as relations with England were concerned. The de Braose lynching, her husband's rebellion and her father's two counter-offensives over the next year would have put the political reality of her situation sharply into focus if it had not been simmering underneath already. As far as England was concerned, Joan knew her own fate to be secure. Unless she overtly rebelled against the Crown, on Llywelyn's own untimely death, she would have been looked after and, if the time came and prospect arose, offered another prominent marriage. The safeguarded fate of her children by Llywelyn, however, was perhaps not so certain. Her daughters either would have been married off to men below their royal status who were easily controlled by the Crown, So as to not provide ammunition and support for any future Welsh rebellions, or sent to nunneries where they would spend their lives in seclusion. This latter option is exactly what happened in 1282, when Gwenllian, the only child to Llywelyn ap Gruffudd and Eleanor de Montfort (Edward I's close cousin) was sent to Sempringham nunnery in England after the deaths of her parents in 1282. There she spent the entire fifty-four years of her life in en forced confinement.

Although in 1210 Joan was not even yet pregnant with their only son, Dafydd, thoughts concerning the fate of any son she bore to Llywelyn must of loomed large at this time. If Llywelyn died before a hypothetical son reached adulthood, there were simply no guarantees of survival, let alone prosperity. In all likelihood, a lifetime of imprisonment by either the Welsh or the English would have been on offer. Llywelyn already had a first-born son who was seen as the legitimate and legal heir to the Venedotian dynasty and any son of Joan's would have been 'tainted' with alien Angevin blood, a trait most likely to have been detrimental to procuring widespread support for her son's right to rule in Wales. For the English, any son by a formidable, and arguably popular, rebellious Welsh ruler would have been a serious, long-term threat. Ultimately, imprisonment or death would have been the only two options for a son by Joan if providence were to prove to be anything other than divine.

Though her fate at the hands of the English rulers may have promised relative security, Joan probably viewed her fate in Wales, under the Welsh, in a very different light. If Llywelyn suddenly died, where would that leave Joan, the daughter of a much maligned king? Would she have been allowed to return to her family or to one of her English manors? Emma of Anjou found safety and security at Ellesmere when she and Dafydd ab Owain were exiled more than a decade earlier. But, that had been a very different situation, least of all as neither Henry II nor Richard I were nearly as reviled by both the Welsh and Marcher lords as John was during his reign. Neither did Dafydd have the level of power and authority that

Llywelyn enjoyed by 1210; Joan's own standing largely surpassed that of her aunt's. The probability of her capture and imprisonment, and even execution, were all potential realities she would have contemplated at the beginning of the 1210s. With such heart-heavy scenarios to confront was Joan even able to compartmentalise her emotions in order to prepare herself to step into her future role as a mediator? Surely by this time, with the realistic awareness that her father was much despised by the country-folk of her adopted homeland, and with good reason, it was becoming clear that as events unfolded throughout 1210–11 so, too, did the need for her openly and actively participate in Anglo-Welsh relations – for her, both political affairs and affairs of the heart.

Certainly Llywelyn, being the politician he was understood the perks of taking advantage of the king's distraction with the de Braose family, especially while pursuing them in Ireland where he was also involved in quelling a rebellion. The *Brut* records that in the year 1210 'Llywelyn ap Iorwerth made fierce attacks against the Saxons. And because of that, King John was angered, and he planned to dispossess Llywelyn completely of his territory. And he gathered a mighty host against Gwynedd with the intent of destroying it all.'[4] As rumours spread of a Welsh insurgency thought to have been backed, if not led, by Llywelyn himself, the reality of such an uprising threatened to undermine John's strength throughout Britain and his newly acquired authority over Ireland and Scotland. As such, it may have been Llywelyn's expansionist ambitions that eventually warranted enough provocation for the king to take action and demonstrate English might against the Welsh.

First, John mustered a host led by Ranulf of Chester in the spring of 1210. Other important men included in the army were the king's justiciar, Geoffrey FitzPeter, and the bishop of Winchester, Peter des Roches. The army marched from Chester and made their way to Conwy, where they were faced with rebuilding the recently destroyed castle of Deganwy, which Llywelyn had levelled 'for fear of the king'.[5] Llywelyn and his followers persistently attacked the invading English, carrying out raids stretching from Conwy back to Chester, using the protected shelter of the Welsh wilderness as cover.

Not to be defeated, John used additional methods to try to weaken Llywelyn's status and authority. Playing the rulers against one another was an approach that had worked in John's favour in the past and by 1211, his tactic was to isolate Llywelyn politically and physically from other

Welsh rulers. He did this primarily by supporting other Welsh leaders in their own political and military endeavours, and even reinstated Gwenwynwyn as the prince of southern Powys. Nevertheless, Llywelyn seemed undeterred in his fight against John.

As such, his power increasingly threatened and his composure crumbling, John led not one, but two royal campaigns into Wales in May and August of 1211. The first full-scale royal campaign into Wales since Henry II's attempts in 1165, was a complete failure, the events of which were dramatised by David Powell in the sixteenth century:

> The next yeare ensuing king Iohn had manie complaints made vnto him by the Marchers, vpon prince Lhewelyn, how he entering their countrie burned and spoiled all as he went, and slew their men. Wherefore the king gathered a great armie through all England and called him such lords and princes of Wales as held of him, as Howl ap Gruffyth ap Conan ap Owen Gwyneth, whom Lhewelyn had banished: Madoc ap Gruffyth Maylor lord of Bromfield, Chirke and Yale: Meredyth ap Rotpert lord of Cydewen: Gwenwynwyn lord of Powys, Maelgon and Rees Vachan the sonnes of prince Rees, rulers of Southwales. With this great armie he entered into Northwales by Chester, minding to destroie all that had life within that coutnrie. Then the prince hearing of all this preparation against him, as well of his owne countrymen as others, commanded all such as inhabited the Inland or Midle countrie (which is now part of Denbigh and Flyntshire) to remooue all their goods and cattels to Snowden hills for a time. And so the king came along the sea coast to Ruthlan, and so passed ouer the riuer Clwyd, and came to the castell of Teganwy, and there remained a while: but Lhewelyn cut off his victuals behind him, so that he could haue none from England, and there cold not a man scatter from the skirmishes vnfought withal: where the Northwales men always, both for the aduantage of the straits and knowledge of the places, had the vpper hand. At the last the English souldiours were glad to tast horse flesh for pure neede. Then when the king saw no remedie, he returned hom in a great rage, leauing the countrie full of dead bodies.[6]

Frustration at his defeat, and the humiliation of his soldiers being reduced to eating horse flesh, only fuelled the fires of King John's rage, and in August his troops marched into the Marcher border town of Oswestry to launch another attack. From there, the king and his army made their way as far north-west as the cathedral town of Bangor, lying on the Menai Straits, between the great island of Anglesey and the Snowdon mountain range. John burned Bangor to the ground and took the bishop as a prisoner, ransoming the churchman for 200 hawks:

> In August next ensuing he returned againe with a great armie, and the lords before named with him, and entred into Wales, at Blanchmonasterie now Oswestree, whereof Iohn the sonne of William Fitzalan was lord. At this time the king passing the riuer of Conwey, encamped there by the riuer side, and sent part of his armie with guides of the countrie to burne Bangor: who did so, taking Rotpert the bishop prisoner, who was afterward ransomed for 200 hawkes. Then the prince seeing all England and Wales against him, and a great part of his land won from him, thought it best to entrate with the king. And thervpon he sent Ione his wife the kings daughter to hir father to make a peace, who (being a discreet woman) found the meanes that vpon pledges giuen for safeconduct the prince came to the king, and made peace with him, and did him homage. Then giuing him pledges, he promised vnto him towards his charges 20,000 heads of cattell and fortie horses. Moreouer he granted to the king the Iland for euer: wherevpon the king returned to England with great triumph, after that he had brought all Wales vnder his subiection.

The end result of the second royal campaign was John's victory. Llywelyn was forced to capitulate and submit to the English king as his overlord. This is the first and only recorded episode of Joan's role as a political mediary found in the thirteenth-century Welsh chronicles.

Where Joan and her family remained hidden during the initial military incursions is unknown, though they would have been in a location that was highly secured and protected by the natural terrain. Remaining at one of the royal palaces on Anglesey, Aberffraw or Rhosyr, would have offered a quick escape route via the sea.[7] Other possibilities could have been deep in the mountains at Dolwyddelan castle overlooking the Lledr valley. It is also probable Joan and her children sought refuge in or near a monastery, like Beddgelert near Moel Hebog mountain, where they also had a manor.

The Welsh annals tell us that upon the August invasion, Llywelyn (and presumably Joan) retreated to the Eryri mountains for protection and that the conflict was resolved when the king received a handsome payment of costs 'on behalf of Llywelyn'.[8] The entry is tantalising in that it verifies another account found in the Welsh chronicles that Joan was the diplomat who oversaw peace proceedings. The context to the reference 'on behalf of Llywelyn' in the Welsh annals relates to her intervention, which is confirmed by the explanation of her position as Llywelyn's wife and King John's daughter (*Annam filiam suam in uxorem dederat* – Annam likely referring to Joannam). What the entry also reveals is that in this important labelling of Joan through the use of her lifecycles as wife and daughter is the well-placed status that these positions afforded both sides. It must be remembered that Joan was not the first wife of a Welsh ruler whose Angevin origins promised political value and diplomacy. Emma of Anjou probably played a similar role. As mentioned, Gerald of Wales and the Welsh chronicles both stress the importance of her political marriage to Llywelyn's uncle, and, moreover, her own ability to wield the diplomatic power that both her status and position as a member of the Angevin dynasty and wife of a Welsh ruler ensured.

The Welsh chronicles, *Brut y Tywysogion* and *Brenhinedd y Saesson*, not only provide a more informative account of the events, they confirm that Joan, indeed, was the political envoy sent to parlay for peace:

> And then Llywelyn, being unable to suffer the king's rage, sent his wife, the king's daughter, to him by the counsel of his leading men to seek to make peace with the king on whatever terms he could. And after Llywelyn had accepted safe conduct to go to the king and to come away from him free, he went to the king and was reconciled to him on condition of his giving the king hostages from among the leading men of the land, and of his binding himself to give the king twenty thousand cattle and forty steeds.[9]

The exacting requirements for peace meant that Llywelyn not only had to surrender the Perfeddwlad in north-east Wales and to pay substantial levy in cattle, he was also forced to recognise the English king once again as overlord, but this time as a humiliating obligation rather than an independent choice. The ultimate salt in Llywelyn's wound, however, must have been the demand that he hand over his own first-born son, Gruffudd (by Tangwystl, his previous consort) as one of the twenty-eight hostages. All in all, however, this was a small price to pay when imprisonment or death were the other alternatives. According to Roger of Wendover, John was satisfied with his subjection of 'all the princes and nobles without opposition', and the receipt of such noteworthy hostages, which was assumed to ensure Welsh 'submission for the future'.[10]

The success of Joan's enterprise and her abilities to achieve peace have long been recognised. Yet her actual involvement in the events, especially in terms of influence, is often consigned to the margins of history, credit conferred to the wisdom of Llywelyn and ministerial elite for making the decision to send her to meet with her father.[11] It seems impossible that Joan herself sat quietly on the sidelines while talks of further tactics and the possibility of relenting to a truce reverberated throughout the prince's domain. Traditionally in medieval Europe, there was an expectation that the wife, and queen-consort, would play the role of emissary if family disputes required. Joan was not only obviously aware of such a role she would likely play after her marriage, it is also very likely that she was educated and prepared, to some degree, in how to undertake such a responsibility. Regardless of where her upbringing took place, from 1201 onwards she would have been educated in the art of political diplomacy. Further, expectation of the Welsh queen to be present within the ruler's court, even as a hostess, means that it should be expected that Joan's appearance and presence during discussions 1211 was inevitable, and likely widely accepted among Llywelyn's ministerial elite.

After being married to Llywelyn for six years, Joan also would have been well-versed in the ways of the Welsh court and the expectations of the queen. Native literary and narrative sources collectively tell us that the Welsh queen was prized for her knowledge, kindness and, most importantly, her status as an advisor, a counsellor or wise woman. In Welsh, *cyngorwreic*. Joan's predecessor Queen Angharad is lauded by her husband's biographer for being a *cyngorwreic*, counsel-woman and knowledgeable in all things. Literary sources, like the *Mabinogion* and the Lives of Welsh Saints, also applaud the counsel and wisdom of the wives of rulers. In any event, Joan understood the imperative nature of the task at hand and it is practical to assume that she was directly involved in counselling Llywelyn, acting as one of his leading advisors in this particular instance. Her relationship with her father was beyond advantageous, especially since there seems to have been real affection between the two. It is significant that the subsequent peace treaty was written and signed by both parties only after Joan had pleaded with her father and secured the safety of her husband.

As for the treaty itself, although there is no recorded mention of her participation in its codification, she was surely present. Furthermore, it is worth taking into serious consideration that she actively participated in negotiating some of the terms that are laid out and some may even have been initiated by her. The most noteworthy indication of this is found in the article that stipulates if Llywelyn died without a legitimate heir by Joan, his kingdom would escheat to the English Crown. Why would Llywelyn acquiesce to such dire terms? According to Welsh custom and law, he already had a legitimate successor in the guise of Gruffudd. Although technically illegitimate by birth, his illegitimate status did not bar him from ruling if he were openly recognised as his father's *edling*, or heir.

Evidence that can be pieced together suggests that in the late summer of 1211 Joan was probably pregnant with her first-born son, Dafydd, whom she most likely gave birth to at Castell Hen Blas in Coleshill (Bagillt), Flintshire in the spring of 1212.[12] Anticipation that this fourth child may be a son must have had some bearing on how the treaty was laid out. This surely played a part in Llywelyn's acceptance and willingness to deny Gruffudd his patrimony – a decision that paved the way for an unstable future and proved to be the undoing of Llywelyn's legacy after his death in 1240.[13] For Joan, her influence over such a directive makes sense as it ensured her own child's future as Llywelyn's legitimate heir, side-lining her stepson.

In 1854 T.J. Llywelyn Prichard wrote a scathing report of Joan's involvement in 1211:

Joan soon became the mother of a prince who was named David. It is not known how early after his birth that she

> began to play the part of the harsh stepmother towards
> Griffith, Llywelyn's eldest son, but in course of a few years
> afterwards it is certain that she had succeeded in her grand
> aim of alienating the affections of his father from him, and
> of transferring them to his second son, the young prince of
> whom we are treating, with her own child.[14]

Hardly an unbiased assessment, it is one that is easily challenged. Ensuring that a future male child with Joan was designated his heir may have also been a tactic of Llywelyn's, and one that supported his own aspiring policies. Joan's interactions and relations with her father's Angevin court unarguably allowed Llywelyn intimate access to the king and provided him with a more profound understanding of the workings and policies of the English Crown, and of his father-in-law as a person. This intimacy would have caused such an astute man as Llywelyn is purported to have been to assess the types of strategies required to ensure his own personal success, that of his progeny and, more importantly, that of his kingdom. In many ways, the prince of Gwynedd desired of Gwynedd desired to bring Welsh policies and the way of rule more in line with western European traditions and he willingly embraced elements of European acculturation that he perceived as useful to elevating Gwynedd's status on the wider European stage. Accepting the practice of primogeniture was a most decisive step in that direction.

Thus, by adhering to the required changes in Welsh customs of succession by openly accepting the traditional European practice of primogeniture, Llywelyn moved the management of Gwynedd more in line with European standards. Ensuring a direct blood-connection between the Venedotian and Angevin dynasties was a move that certainly elevated Gwynedd's status over the other Welsh kingdoms. Acquiescing to such a dictate suggests this was Llywelyn's means of preserving Welsh autonomy, but also may bear evidence of Joan's own designs.

There is evidence that points to Llywelyn taking a number of steps throughout his reign to safeguard Dafydd as his chosen successor. Nine years after his submission to King John, Henry III recognised Dafydd as Llywelyn's legitimate heir, at the expense of Gruffudd's own customary rights. The royal statute deliberately emphasised Dafydd's maternal line, thus highlighting his formal status via his blood connections to the English Crown. In other words, his rights through Joan. Throughout the statute Joan is identified by her gendered status as wife, mother and sister –

labels, all of which, duly emphasised her own royal lineage. The 1220 statute that Henry signed also carried the signatures of Stephen Langton, archbishop of Canterbury (r. 1207–1228), and Pandulf, the British the papal legate.[15] Six years later, in 1222, Llywelyn sought confirmation of Dafydd's legitimacy as successor from the pope. Sometime in April or May 1226, the prince sent a petition to Honorius III asking him to sanction the earlier statute that declared Dafydd's legitimacy. In the petition, Llywelyn proclaimed that Dafydd was to succeed him by hereditary right through Joan, his legitimate wife, daughter of the late king of England. The prince went further in establishing Dayfdd's birthright by declaring that he had actually abolished the 'detestable' Welsh custom of recognising illegitimate children as legal heirs.

Llywelyn was not alone in petitioning the king in 1226. That same year, another petition from Wales reached Rome. The appeal, likely from Joan herself, concerned requests for papal dispensation regarding her own illegitimate status. She was granted legitimacy (a move backed by Henry III) and with the success of her quest for legitimacy, Dafydd's claims to his father's patrimony were further secured. Back in the spring of 1205 the young, Welsh-born, Gruffudd would have been right to have doubts about his future and security upon meeting Joan for the very first time when she arrived in Wales as Llywelyn's new bride and his new stepmother. Securing Dafydd's successorship does not mean that Joan was the 'wicked stepmother' or that she had a horrible relationship with her stepson, or any of her stepchildren for that matter. The sheer political weight of this move suggests it was a dogmatic approach aimed at safeguarding the future of Welsh independence as far as could be made possible.

For Llywelyn to recognise Dafydd as his heir was a way to avoid the type of civil strife that Gwynedd experienced after the death of Owain Gwynedd in 1170, in which the powerful kingdom ended up virtually in tatters. For Gwynedd to lose its strength after being united under one ruler was a certain death blow to Welsh independence as a whole. As it was, the ensuing battle between Dafydd and Gruffudd after Llywelyn's death landed Gruffudd prison. First in Wales at the hands of his half-brother, then at the Tower of London as a prisoner of Henry III. It is the Tower of London where Llywelyn's eldest son, and many say rightful claimant to the Venedotian throne, met his demise. Both Gruffudd and his eldest son Owain, also a prisoner, fell to their deaths after linens they tied together to shimmy their way down from their prison cell unravelled. This 'fortunate' situation for Dafydd, nevertheless, did little to quell the growing dissent between him and the king of England. Even after receiving Dafydd's homage in 1240 and recognising him as Llywelyn's heir by placing a golden cornet on the Welsh prince at Gloucester cathedral, within a year, Henry invaded Gwynedd and up to his premature death in 1246, Dafydd, who chroniclers referred to as 'the shield of Wales' (*tarian Cymru*) spent the rest of his life fighting off the eventual and, arguably unavoidable, loss of Welsh independence.

Llywelyn became a principal supporter of the Barons' rebellion and with the signing of the Magna Carta on the fields of Runnymede in June of 1215, the interests of the Welsh prince(s) were secured. The three Welsh clauses in the Magna Carta include the king's agreement to return the Welsh hostages taken in 1211, meaning Gruffudd above all, land that Llywelyn had been forced to surrender under the same treaty and, importantly, recognition that the Welsh had rights to follow their own legal customs. Certainly the former two clauses are directly related to the treaty that Llywelyn had been forced to submit to four years earlier, the nature of which not only hints at the extent to which John was willing to compromise to ensure a lasting resolution with the Welsh, but also to Joan's influence. The question remains as to why John was willing to be so conciliatory. In the years leading up to the great baronial rebellion and the Magna Carta, it was obvious that the English king had made concessions in his dealings with Wales, despite his desire to bring the country to its knees. It is unquestionable that some of his accommodating behaviour was brought about by the fact that Llywelyn's chief counsellor was his own daughter.

The agreement of 1211 had many implications, not least of which was the bearing it had on Joan's own political status; arguably, a status that was raised because of the significance of her maternity.[16] The wording used in the agreement defines her gendered and social responsibilities. In contrast to the use of *princeps Norwalli(ie)* to describe Llywelyn's position and status, Joan is strictly labelled by her lifecycle positions as the king's daughter and the prince's wife.[17] Such use of terminology strongly implies a number of things. First, it does underscore her position as a 'peace-weaver', through the bonds of marriage agreed upon by the two rulers. Second, that her positions within the two courts, as wife and daughter, allowed her a certain freedom and intimacy not allotted to the consorts of other Welsh rulers. Third, such a position allowed her to act with authority as Llywelyn's representative. Although these factors suggest a great deal as to the kind of agency Joan could have enjoyed as a political agent, it is important to remember that the wording of the treaty makes it clear that her sole responsibility was to ensure that she produce a legitimate male heir for the house of Gwynedd. The effect of this was two-fold: one, to better secure dynastic legacy by ensuring the succession rights of legitimate heirs, which aimed to lessen contentious claims to the Welsh 'crown'. Two, to help further elevate the status of Gwynedd, and by arguable extension Wales, within wider European politics. In terms of Joan and Llywelyn's children, and specifically their son Dafydd, recognised legitimisation promoted direct Venedotian links to the Angevin dynasty, thereby legitimising Gwynedd's hegemony in Wales. On all these fronts, Joan was successful.

To label a woman a 'daughter' or 'wife' and presume her direct involvement was only because of her familial and marital positions – that she simply fulfilled the traditional obligation of a woman of her status as a 'peace-weaver' – negates the individuality and intelligence of Joan as a woman who was deeply and immersed in the situation. Sure, her initial involvement in 1211 may have been predicated on the fact that she was the king's daughter and Llywelyn's wife, but she demonstrated clear capabilities as a political diplomat; an expertise that was recognised, utilised and honed over the years. Evidence suggests that her status as a competent emissary continued to grow throughout her reign.

Travelling, perhaps even fleeing, from Normandy to England in 1203 under her father's protection was the beginning of lifetime defined by both uncertainty and certitude. Joan's early years up to 1211 were a mixture of the peaceful and the turbulent, to say the least. As a young daughter, wife, and mother, she faced real uncertainty in years marked by war, peace, marriage, motherhood, rebellions, invasions and subordination. Yet, these such circumstances also provided an invaluable platform of personal and public growth for Joan. By 1211 her time to enter centre-stage arrived; it was the year in which medieval chroniclers recorded that a woman of great notability had the opportunity to influence two powerful, feuding monarchs and used her position to ensure peace between hostile kingdoms. It is the first year in which it is suggested that Joan embraced her duties as *cyngorwreic*.

Assuming a character of strength and determination, Joan intervened as intermediary officer, acting as an agent between the lord of England and the lord of North Wales, she had a significant impact on both parties. Llywelyn was able to maintain the foundations of his realm, while King John had the satisfaction of securing homage from, never mind utter humiliation of, the most powerful Welsh prince. The following years would prove to be more turbulent for the whole of Britain, and a time that must have been especially trying for a woman who, like so many of her status, had to constantly juggle divided loyalties. Yet, the following years proved that for Llywelyn Joan was his 'best friend and faithful supporter'.[18]

Chapter Six

A Letter of Warning

After the formal resolution of the violent and chaotic events of 1211, there was undoubtedly incentive for both parties to reassume and maintain a cordial relationship, even if only on a personal level. It is clear that some amends were made on that front, for in the Spring of 1212 Joan and Llywelyn spent Easter in Cambridge with John. It was a long distance to travel for the royal Welsh couple in what could have been potentially hostile territory – John, of course, being infamous for acting out on suspicious whims. Moreover, Joan was probably heavily pregnant at this time with Dafydd, which would have made the journey to the other side of Britain and back an even more arduous one for her physically and mentally. It is doubtful that their entourage would have covered more than ten miles a day in either direction. Ultimately, the fact that Joan and Llywelyn covered at least 450 miles round-trip to spend time with her father, perhaps with at least two, or even all three, of his young granddaughters in tow, is not only a testament to the effort that both sides put in to making their relationship work, but a testament of genuine affection between the king of England and his first-born daughter.

It may have been during their time at Cambridge that some of the more stringent affairs from the previous year were further ironed out. John, in particular, needed to make attempts to ensure that Wales was secure enough to leave him the space required to focus on his planned attack on France. Nevertheless, as J.E. Lloyd put it, Joan and Llywelyn's 'visit to the English court can hardly have failed to disclose ... the crazy foundations on which rested the imposing superstructure of the king's power'.[1] Discontent over the king's seemingly lawless reign rumbled throughout the kingdom and it was not to be long before open revolt by John's most powerful subjects would rear its head. As for the Welsh prince, it was clear that in spite of his humiliating defeat at the hands of his father-in-law and his acquiescence to what seemed to be hugely debilitating terms, by the summer of 1212 he had reclaimed much of his former power and had absolutely no intention of remaining subservient to a foreign overlord.

It was probably on their return from Cambridge that Joan finally gave birth to Dafydd at the royal manor of Castell Hen Blas in Tegeingl in north-east Wales. The political situation of Tegeingl at this time is unclear and it generally has been believed that John maintained occupancy over the area, and Castell Hen Blas, as a result of events in 1211. As Easter celebrations at Cambridge, in fact, may have included talks between Joan, Llywelyn and John about the king relaxing some of the harsher provisions in the 1211 agreement, this may have resulted in the *cantref* of Tegeingl being passed back into the couple's hands.[2] Or maybe even Joan's own hands.

It has recently been proposed that Dafydd's birth at Castell Hen Blas could have been an overt political manoeuvre by Llywelyn to declare his reclaimed power and authority over north-east Wales – similar to Edward I's decision to have his first-born son, Edward (II, r. 1307–1327) born at Caernarfon castle as a means of stamping English authority over a newly conquered Wales in 1284. While this is more than plausible, and conceivably the correct interpretation, there are further possibilities to consider. Castell Hen Blas could have been one of Joan's Welsh holdings, given to her in dower. The fact that it is located in an area fraught with political tension between Wales and England adds a level of weight to this as there are other examples of Welsh rulers endowing their wives politically sensitive lands.

As very few records survive from early thirteenth-century Wales, it makes it difficult to paint a clear picture of events and practices concerning land alienation and occupation in Wales, especially as far as women were concerned, but there are a handful of examples that show women could easily find themselves at the heart of various matters pertaining to the management of family lordships and, for royal women, the realm. Llywelyn and Joan themselves both expected that their daughter Elen's future husband, John the Scot, give her a dower made up of 100 librates of land on their marriage in 1222.[3] The marital agreement itself being an important document to Welsh history as it is the only surviving piece of evidence that gives insight into just how important gifts of marriage portions and dowers were to Welsh rulers, Llywelyn at least, in the creation of kinship alliances through marriage.

This particular marital agreement is also important in terms of trying to assess the expanse of features that informed the tenets of Welsh queenship in practice. The agreement makes it clear that Joan held lands in her own right that she was willing to pass on to her daughter. In addition, other evidence shows that not only was Joan a land holder, she actively managed some (if not all) of her manorial lordships. Though the only surviving evidence we have are of Joan's English holdings, there is little doubt she held lands in Wales as well as Llywelyn's wife and reigning queen. A range of examples from all over Wales during the twelfth and thirteenth centuries of the wives of Welsh rulers being given lands in dower exists – many lands that were even contentious and aggressively fought over, especially between the Welsh and Marcher lords. Some of the duties and responsibilities of these women as *arglwyddesau*, or lords, included appointing governmental officials and jointly rewarded loyal subjects for their services. Such women also had oversight on agricultural renders, services, putures, dues and amercements, exclusive rights and privileges and court revenues.[4] As the chief queen of Wales, Joan would have been expected to undertake such responsibilities; lest we forget that Llywelyn was often away on campaign and his trust in her as his confidant, consort and queen has stood the test of time.

As such, it makes sense that Castell Hen Blas may have been more associated with Joan than Llywelyn. If not her own manor, it was part of her *agweddi* with Llywelyn, the 'common pool' of marital property, given they had been married for seven years by 1212. A strategic point for both Llywelyn and John, and later Henry III, it would have been a sagacious move for both parties to ensure that someone who was partial to both sides and more personally invested in outcomes than some other appointed official have control over the Castell Hen Blas, if not Coleshill or even the whole *cantref* of Tegeingl. The argument that 'a prince of Llywelyn's standing would hardly have allowed his wife to be brought to bed so near the English border if he had any apprehensions that she and the much awaited heir would be in danger of seizure as hostages by the English king' is largely an outmoded one, as if nothing else, it paints Joan as a completely passive figure in events.[5] This she was not. Arguably, her safety, and that of her husband's successor and heir, would have been far more secure if her own rights to the manor had been acknowledged by her father. Joan's aptitude for mediation, and her position as the wife of a Welsh ruler and daughter of the English king, likely meant she had more of a voice, and one that was adhered to, than has previously been recognised.

Dafydd's birth in the spring of 1212 at Castell Hen Blas, may, indeed, have been a political statement made by Llywelyn, but Joan was hardly a passive performer. A woman carrying a child to (almost?) full-term after travelling an enormous and uncomfortable distance, and someone of her apparent fortitude, would hardly have been reluctant to voice her opinion about her needs concerning childbirth. Later records indicate that other children also may have been born there, further suggesting the manor had special significance to Joan. At Dafydd's birth a chapel was built at Castell Hen Blas in celebration and it was a celebration indeed. Llywelyn finally had the heir required of him in the 1211 agreement and just at a time after he had rapidly regained traction and re-established much of lost authority from the year before. Both seemed to be factors that spurred Llywelyn forward in his attempt to eliminate English rule over Wales.

While John was in the north of England preparing his army for an invasion of France that summer, Llywelyn's displeasure with the English garrisons who had been stationed in North Wales by the king after his defeat in 1211 increased. Llywelyn's frustration was such that he appealed to the leading Welsh princes, friends and foes alike, to appear at his court to discuss the miserable state of affairs. Well aware of his father-in-law's increased desire to grasp a firm hold over Wales, coupled with his own political ambitions of a Wales-wide hegemony, Llywelyn sought recruits for a rebellion. His staunchest supporters, like Maelgwn ap Rhys of Deheubarth, Madog ap Gruffudd Maelor from Bromfield in Powys and Meredudd ap Rhobert of Cedewain were in attendance, as was his most formidable rival, Gwenwynwyn of Powys. The positive response to the Venedotian prince's call to arms is hardly surprising. Llywelyn's thrashing by the English king and unconditional surrender to such harsh terms in 1211 essentially stunned the Welsh into action; the action seen as an attempt of unification.

Llywelyn is recounted as rousing the princely assembly with the call for unification, urging his fellow leaders to recognise that the Welsh should 'have a prince of their owne nation' rather than being subjugated by a foreign 'stranger' – a state of affairs, of course, largely created by the Welsh themselves being unable to unite under the solid leadership of one ruler. Llywelyn's declaration that they needed to unify and agree to defend 'their ancient estate' was met with pledges of fealty to him as the prince of Gwynedd by the attending, lesser princes.[6] It is believed that Llywelyn not only had the support of these rulers, but that he had a powerful backer for the rebellion in the guise of Philip Augustus who may have had agents urge Llywelyn to break his pledge to John and form a Welsh alliance. The pope, too, blatantly supported Llywelyn and two of his greater supporters, Gwenwynwyn and Maelgwn, by lifting the interdict on their lands – an interdict that Innocent had placed on John three years before. More importantly, the pope released Llywelyn, Gwenweynwyn and Maelgwn of their obligations to King John, nullifying their previous oaths of loyalty.

By this time, the English king's landed power in Wales was at an all new and unprecedented height, extending south from Gwynedd Is Conwy in northern Wales, down the Welsh March, which included the confiscated territories once held by the Braose and Lacy families. John and his adherents also embarked on a tactical castle-building exercise in places such as Aberystwyth on the west coast and Mathrafal in Powys, near Welshpool, in the east. It was such an alarming display of power that the Welsh rose against the king in defiance. With such powerful European figureheads as the pope and the king of France behind him, Llywelyn seemed to have little to lose.

Seeking to rectify the insults done by the king's men, Llywelyn's host was bent on reclaiming lands and cutting down the English posts on the frontier. He recovered the Perfeddwlad and marched towards Rhuddlan and Deganwy (though he failed to take these). During the uprising, Swansea in South Wales was burnt, while Llywelyn himself, with the help of Gwenwynwyn, moved into to Powys with the aim of laying siege on Mathrafal castle. The newly constructed Mathrafal was held by none other than Robert Vieuxpont – the very same lord charged with the responsibility in overseeing Joan's passage to England in 1203 who was, by this time, the king's lieutenant in Powys. King John was informed of the renewed Welsh insurgency and, in fury, levied his own army to relieve Robert Vieuxpont and razed Mathrafal castle to the ground. Under the false assumption that the Welsh problem was relatively in hand, he returned to England where he had greater issues to face. The perceived misuse of his royal authority and the mismanagement of his kingdom by his frustrated barons was beginning to mount to real and troublesome discontent.

How wrong the king was. With the determination to reverse their fortunes, the Welsh continued to take advantage of the strife and discontent that engaged him in England. Within a year of his submission to the king, Llywelyn not only had repaired a great deal of the damage that was done to him, he continued to greatly extend his authority – and with success. It was during this time he struck a formidable alliance with Philip Augustus, and although nothing came of their coalition, the fact that they both agreed to not even parlay with England, let alone make peace, shows the extent of Llywelyn's intensified influence and authority. The king learned that in his absence the Welsh relentlessly ravaged the Marches and by August, John was determined to solve the problem of the Welsh once and for all. He rerouted the army he gathered to invade France, which consisted of his entire northern army, to Chester. Contemporaries commented that no person in living memory remembered seeing such an array of military might or the sheer number of soldiers. The king's seemingly sole goal was to make the Welsh face the brunt of his anger by bringing them under complete and direct control of the English Crown. In the words of the contemporary chronicler, Roger of Wendover:

> When these events became known to the English king, he was very indignant, and collected a numerous army of horse and foot soldiers, determining to ravage Welsh territories, and to exterminate the inhabitants.[7]

Sources claim that in utter rage upon hearing the news of Welsh insurrection and the alliance with France, John condemned all twenty-eight of the Welsh hostages he had received the year before as part of the peace bargain negotiated by Joan to be hanged – as a point of further cruelty, two of the hostages, the sons of Deheubarth's Maelgwn ap Rhys, were castrated before hanging. Robert Vieuxpont followed similar suit and hanged Maelgwn's youngest son, who was only 7 years old, in the Welsh-Marcher border town of Shrewsbury. Shock at the king's vicious act reverberated throughout Britain. The outrage expressed at the cruelty of punishing the innocent for the sins of their fathers is visceral in contemporary sources. Episodes such as this reared periodically during John's reign, often believed to reflect his infamous Angevin temperament and rage, have left lasting scars on his character and which have defined his reign as malicious, vindictive, spiteful and brutal. The inability to escape such negatives, until very recently, have marred more objective approaches to understanding his political abilities and acumen; they have shadowed the positive attributes and activities, which he certainly did have. Perhaps a small argument in his favour relates to the fact that he spared Llywelyn's illegitimate son, Gruffudd, who had also been handed over as a hostage, from the same fate. Hanging Gruffudd would have given Llywelyn cause for all-out war, a fact that did not escape the king when he gave the execution orders. Additionally, it seems likely Joan would never have forgiven him for harming her husband's young son and that such an act would have damaged their relationship irrevocably.

Certainly, cruel actions such as these helped unite the Welsh further and it is evident that there were plans underway to thwart the English king's hold over Wales once and for all. Some sources say that it was while the king was in Nottingham making final preparations for his attack on his mutinous son-in-law and followers that he received shocking news, foiling his vengeful ambitions. A few days following the mass hanging, and before the invasion, John received two letters, independently verifying each other's reports, that there was a plot to dethrone him and put someone else in his place. The chronicler Matthew Paris narrates that:

> When the king was preparing to go on a military expedition, and to invade the Welch [*sic*], a report was suddenly spread abroad that the earls and barons of Chester had conspired against him; on which account he returned, as if thunderstruck ... he was greatly agitated at the circumstances.[8]

Roger of Wendover's account is much more melodramatic, having events reach their culmination in Nottingham after the hanging of the Welsh hostages:

> On his arriving with his army at Nottingham, before he either ate or drank, he ordered 28 youths, whom he had received the year before as hostages from the Welsh, to be hung on the gibbet, in revenge ... While he was, after this, sitting at the table eating and drinking, there came a messenger from the king of Scotland, who delivered letters,

77

warning him of premeditated treachery against him; soon
after which there came another messenger from the daughter
of the same king, the wife of Leolin king of Wales.[9]

The first letter is said to have arrived from William, king of Scotland. The
very same king that John, joined by Llywelyn, marched against and defeated
in 1209. More importantly, the second letter was from Joan. According to
Wendover and other chroniclers, although both of these letters,

> came from different countries, [they] were to one and the
> same effect … if the king persisted in the war which he
> had begun, he would either be slain by his own nobles, or
> delivered to his enemies for destruction … the king was
> alarmed on learning this … [and] put more faith in truth
> of the letters; therefore wisely changing his intention, he
> ordered his army to return home.

There is no contemporary Welsh report of this event, although a later
account is found in the first complete history of Wales claims that:

> In the meane whiel that the king remained at Notingham,
> he receiued letters from the princesse of Northwales his
> daughter, declaring that his nobles had conspired with the
> French king against him, and for proofe thereof she alledged,
> that Robert Fitzwalter, Eustace de Vescy, and Stephan Ridell
> were secretelie fled into France, and that the French king
> prepared an armie to come to England, vnder the colour that
> the king was a rebell from the church, for that he would not
> condescend to the bishop of Rome's requests.[10]

Unfortunately, there are no other sources known that corroborate
Wendover's, and by extension Paris' story, nor Powell's later elaboration.[11]
Interestingly enough, there is no account in Welsh records of this event
and the silence on the matter is extremely curious.

Surely, if it were widely known that Joan intervened as her father's
adherent, the foreignness of a wife of a powerful Welsh ruler, who also
happened to be the daughter of their most hated and fearsome enemy,
would be cause serious backlash to those who doubted her loyalties.

Was it recognised that Joan not only knew of plans, but supported them as a matter of governing policy that protected the interests of her own family? As impossible as it is to determine whether Joan presided at court with Llywelyn and attended the original assembly of princes, it is a notion not to be dismissed out of hand – even if she had recently given birth. Having already acted as the primary diplomat and negotiator in the preceding year and having first-hand, intimate knowledge of details involving the arbitration, it certainly seems likely that Joan's input would have been necessary, if not simply sought after. In fact, given Welsh customs of the royal court and the overall intimation that the queen had opportunities and even, at times, expectations to partake in counsel, Joan not only had a firm understanding of the situation, it is not inconceivable that she was present during discussions. Even if she was not present during council, there can be no doubt that she was still privy to details of the discussions that took place and her opinions and counsel expressed privately to Llywelyn.

So, why did Joan send the letter? What were her motives? First and foremost, we simply cannot rule out human emotions and the likelihood that Joan had real, genuine concern over her father being in grave danger. It seems only natural that upon learning of such a plot her instinct would be to raise the red flag. However, speculation as to how she learned of the information leads to calls for a deeper examination of possible Welsh tactics involved, especially as there are more political nuances to the letter Joan sent her father than meets the eye.

It is important to remember that having the English invasion called off would have been greatly advantageous to the Welsh. Conceivably, as in 1211, Llywelyn's council, including Joan, made a joint decision for her to intervene, using her relationship with her father as the bait. A noteworthy political tactic if it was one, but perhaps not entirely unique to Llywelyn's way of governing. Other actions taken by the prince during his reign caused similar consternation leading many to conclude that more subversive political intentions underlay certain behaviours.

Joan is also at the heart of one of the leading examples. Theories abound as to the real intent behind the hanging of Llywelyn's greatest enemy, William de Braose, in the spring of 1230, after he and Joan were apparently found in Llywelyn's chamber carrying out an affair. That Joan was quietly imprisoned for a year – knowledge we have from one English source only; Welsh sources, again, remaining interestingly silent – but then resumed her political career immediately after release certainly bears the hallmarks of a joint plot to firmly establish Llywelyn's hegemony in Wales, which was, indeed, the end result.[12]

A comparable example of Joan sending a secret political letter is found in the contemporary *Legend of Fulk FitzWarin*. The story tells us that the hero, Fulk, a Welsh Marcher lord who erred on the wrong side of King John (in this instance, being married to a woman John lusted after), received a letter from Joan at some point during his clash with the king. She warned Fulk that Llywelyn had received a letter from John, seeking terms of peace:

> And when the King could in nowise avenge himself of Fulk, nor put the lady [Fulk's wife] to shame nor seize her, then he sent a letter to Prince Lewis, who had wedded Joan, his sister [*sic*], and prayed of him that of his love he would banish from his household his mortal enemy and felon, (that which was Fulk) and he would restore unto him all the lands which ever his ancestors had taken from his seigniory, on condition that he should possess him of the body of Fulk. The prince called into his chamber Johane, his wife, and showed her the letter which the king ... had sent him. When the lady had heard the letter, she sent the entire import of it to sir Fulk, and that the king wished to come to terms with her husband.[13]

One needs to ask, what Llywelyn's motives were in sharing a letter such as this with Joan and either, or both of them, passing the information on as a warning to FitzWarin? If this, indeed, did happen, there may have been yet another personal motivation on Joan's part as the same source claims that Joan and Fulk's wife Matilda le Vavasour were friends. If Joan spent much time at her manor of Ellesmere, which she likely did over the years given the numerous occasions she went to Shrewsbury on diplomatic matters, it makes sense that the two women would have met and become friends. Whittington was only a mere five miles away.[14] Again, however, there may be more to things. Assuming the story in *Fulk FitzWarin* is based on some semblance of fact, indeed, Joan's friendship with Matilda may have been a catalyst for the head's up. An alternative suggestion, beyond Joan simply taking initiative and sending the letter of her own volition, is that the women's friendship was used to camouflage the fact that the news was being sent from Llywelyn directly. Could this, too, have been the case in 1212? Was Llywelyn being subversive and calculating in his tactics to save Wales from another royal invasion? Either way, Joan would have had to be a willing participant.

In his biography of King John, W.L. Warren surmises that if John's plans had played out in 1212, it seems likely that he, and not his grandson, Edward I, would have been acclaimed as the conqueror of Wales. Edward only recruited half as many men for his invasion of Wales than John had planned to use. The faith that John had in his daughter and the credibility that she established as a political emissary were both weighty determinants in the king's decision to call of the massive expedition. Joan's intervention in 1212 – with or without Llywelyn's prodding – was just as unprecedented and influential as it had been the year before.

It is, of course, impossible to say how Joan felt about the harshness of her situation and her struggle with such divided loyalties. Certainly, she had a close relationship with her father, who is known for being attentive and lavishing towards his children. That he secured for her, a bastard, a notably royal marriage is not to be shrugged at. And, during their lifetimes, they seem to have spent many occasions together. It should not be overlooked that in August of 1212 it was Llywelyn's entire family that received safe-conduct to meet with the king at Chester before all plans were aborted. Again, it was a venture that called for Joan's political agency. But it was likely also a personal venture as well. One which would have likely allowed the king a chance to meet his grandson for the first time and dote on his granddaughters.

As Llywelyn's wife, Joan was a great supporter and confidant in his time of need. She was an incredible asset to Llywelyn in his dangerous plight. The prince had been hard pressed by her father, yet the surprisingly lenient terms to which he submitted, can only be attributed to Joan's political diplomacy. There is an agreement between the chroniclers of history, both then and now, that if it had not been for Joan's intervention in the 1211, the prince of Wales would have had to pay a much higher price for his act of defiance against the king. Joan's intervention prevented King John from taking advantage of Llywelyn's sudden fall from power to weaken the latter's position absolutely. In 1212, her intervention offered the exact same results on the swing side of the pendulum.

Chapter Seven

To Worcester

After the turbulent events of 1212, the following three years offered no relief. While John was faced with the outright rebellion of his most powerful barons and the invasion of Louis of France (r. 1223–1226), Philip Augustus' son, Llywelyn wasted no time in 1213 resuming and expanding his authority in Wales. The Welsh chronicles tell us that:

> strife spread so much that all the leading men of England and the princes of Wales made a pact together against the king that no one of them, without the consent of all the others, would make peace or agreement or truce with the king until ... there should be restored to each one of them their laws and their power and their castles, which he had taken from them without law or truth or justice.[1]

After claiming the crucial castles of Deganwy and Rhuddlan and reclaiming the whole of the Perfeddwlad, Llywelyn headed south, eventually retaking Ceredigion, Camarthen and Gower. It was also during this time that he aligned himself with the English baronial rebellion that eventually resulted the signing of the historic Magna Carta.

After mounting pressure, seemingly from all sides in retribution for his governing style, John began to yield, at least in confrontations that caused him the most harm. Thus, in late Spring 1213 the king conceded to the pope's power and agreed to become his papal vassal, allowing England to become a papal fief. Beyond recognising the appointment of Stephen Langton as the archbishop of Canterbury,[2] one of the results of the king's act of contrition towards the papacy was that the papal legate Pandulf brokered a truce between Llywelyn and John. For Llywelyn, agreeing to the armistice meant forfeiting his earlier alliance with the king of France, though there seems to have been no repercussions in doing so.

In July 1214 John had to face his defeat against the French in Bouvines while attempting to recapture Normandy. This trouncing led to greater baronial discontent and conspiracies in England. As such, John attempted to amend his alliance with Llywelyn and tried to woo him into offering support during the progressively worrisome situation he found himself in. The king had his work cut out. By December 1215, Llywelyn's rulership had expanded to larger portions of greater Wales and with great speed – authority of which he continued to advance with various continued campaigns into mid- and south Wales where he successfully captured a number of crucial strongholds including Cydweli and Cilgerran, to name just a couple. There was little reason for the Welsh ruler to comply with any acts of appeasement that his father-in-law offered. John had proven himself to be untrustworthy regardless of the fact that the much-loved Joan was the unifying force between the two men.

Between the years 1214 and 1215, Joan continued to demonstrate her political agency and diplomatic skills and wield the power of her position within both courts. Actively supporting her husband – and perhaps encouraged by him to take advantage of the upper hand he then enjoyed – she successfully petitioned the English Crown for the release of at least six remaining Welsh hostages handed over in 1211. On 18 December 1214, the sheriff of Gloucester, Engelard de Cigogné, received a letters patent from the king, who was at Monmouth, calling for the release of five of Llywelyn's men. These men were to be handed over to Llywelyn's envoy 'at the petition of our daughter, the wife of Llyewlyn'. Later, on 7 January 1215, King John ordered the release of a sixth hostage, Gwyn ap Iorwerth, again having been petitioned by his 'beloved daughter'.[3]

Undertakings such as petitioning for clemency would have been an integral part to Joan's role as the royal consort a Welsh ruler. Petitioning was likely a reflection in practice of a form of offering protection, or *nawdd*. *Nawdd* refers to the temporary power that one was accorded over another to safeguard legal immunity, although it also could have related to physical protection. Similar to customs of hospitality, the concept of *nawdd* was important in medieval Wales and the variation in powers are according to the variation in rank of the 'protector'.[4] Even though the protection of the king was the highest on offer in native law, the protections granted by the queen are noteworthy. Different redactions of the Welsh laws have underlying threads featuring the level of the Welsh queen's authority and her legal power to offer protection from pursuit and prosecution. That the queen's scope of protection was geographically defined as being 'over the boundary of the country' is a strong indicator as to the remit of the queen's accepted authority throughout the king's territories and, importantly, beyond.[5] The scope of her *nawdd* certainly indicates her privileged status, if not her institutional one.

The customs of *nawdd*, and similarly the *rhieinglych*, advocate the high level of authority and administrative powers that Joan likely had the right to exercise and are illustrated in her royal petitions. Whether she executed her own orders, or simply acted under the directive Llywelyn, almost remains a moot point. The important issue is that she was endowed with opportunities to exercise agency at the highest levels of government, and she did. Furthermore, she was rewarded by it. The Welsh laws highlight how the queen's own officers had administrative duties associated with the use of her patent seal and coffers, implying that her duties were, at times, very real, very public, and often political. The laws conferring upon the queen the rights of *nawdd* further augment this idea. Moreover, the queen's intimate access to the king would have made her privy to 'state' secrets, helping her acquire the knowledge and wisdom of counsel that was so valued in a Welsh queen and needed for the successful administration of lordships and the wider realm. The concept and practice of *nawdd* lends further credence to the idea that Tegeingl may have been under Joan's protection.

It has been accepted that Joan was Llywelyn's confidant and such demonstrations of agency like petitioning indubitably hint to the idea that her actions were indeed defined by her office as queen. Mediation in various formal arrangements was a skill she honed throughout her life, as twenty years later, Joan was still politically active and still successful in her petitions. In November 1235 King Henry, her brother, acquiesced to her request that he pardon a man by the name of Robert, son of Reginald.[6]

No evidence survives indicating that any of Joan's requests were sent in writing, but looking at the official styles used in royal documents to identify her, they most likely were.[7] The fact that she had her own scribe, and there is evidence that she shared a scribe with Llywelyn, and the survival of one letter written by her to Henry in the 1230s support this. It should be acknowledged that lack of written evidence as far as Joan or any royal woman from Wales is concerned does not negate the importance of their activities and duties of office – or in the least, opportunities given to individual consorts to perform in matters of realm when needed. Formal, political communication and demonstrations of royal power were not just conducted in writing and the spoken word was not any less important. Some of Llywelyn's own acta state that information the prince wished to share with the king of England, be it John or Henry, was not always issued in writing, but orally.[8]

Regardless of John's overtures and attempts at mediation, of which Joan may have be partisan, the Welsh ruler ultimately placed his bet with the dissenting barons against the king. It was during these events, and as a result of them, that Joan and Llywelyn's daughter Gwladus Dda was wed to Reginald de Braose in 1215. Llywelyn seemed to have maintained a relationship with the de Braose family even after the deaths of Matilda and William in 1210 and 1211 respectively. It is believed that Giles de Braose, the exiled bishop of Hereford, may have been a key player in establishing the 1212 alliance between Llywelyn and Philip Augustus. Reginald, Giles' brother, returned to Wales at his brother's insistence to join the Welsh resistance in an attempt to re-establish the caput of the de Braose lordship in southern Wales.

The prudent tactician, Llywelyn actively fomented the inter-marriages of his own children to Marcher families as a cogent strategy to better secure his own governing authority. By no means was he the first prince to do so, nor was he the first to establish and manipulate a relationship with the notorious de Braose clan. In 1189 the renowned Lord Rhys of Deheubarth married his first-born legitimate son and eventual successor, Gruffudd (d. 1201) (by his wife Gwenllian ferch Madog ap Maredudd) to Margaret de Braose (d. 1210), Reginald's sister. According to the Annals of Dunstable, it was through the help of his father-in-law, Llywelyn 'king of Wales', that Reginald was able to regain much of the de Braose authority in Wales. As Llywelyn and Joan seem to have been wont to do with their daughters, Gwladus was provided with a significant dowry for her marriage to Reginald, which included a great number of lands in Powys, namely the *commote* of Ceri and the *cantref* of Cedewain.

Where the couple were married is unknown, but the Welsh chronicles themselves adhere to the utmost importance of the alliance simply by recording it. It is possible that Joan was involved in marital negotiations as a woman of her status often was, though given the nature of the partnership and the context in which it was agreed upon, it does seem that the formal proposition would have come from Llywelyn himself. Nonetheless, there can be little doubt that Joan attended the ceremony. Gwladus, after all, would have been no more than 10 years old and it would have been difficult for any mother to see one of her own children married off at such a tender age. It may even have transpired that Gwladus stayed in her mother's care at least for another two years, until she had reached the age of maturity. It was probably after Reginald received the de Braose estates back from John in May 1216, thus making him the lord of Brecon, Abergavenny and Buellt, that Gwladus took up residence in his household as a young lady.

The year 1215 is infamous in British history, and the signing of the Magna Carta arguably the most transformative occasion. Welsh chronicles tell us that as London was taken from the king by his barons, Llywelyn led the Welsh in sacking Shrewsbury and that 'the town and the castle were surrendered to them without resistance'.[9] As Llywelyn's biographer Roger Turvey points out, 'The taking of Shrewsbury was a significant act on the part of a Welsh prince and must not be underestimated, for Shrewsbury, along with Chester and Hereford, symbolised English power on the border.'[10] Ellesmere would have been used by Llywelyn as a staging-post, being little over seventeen miles away, and it may be that Joan herself resided there at the time. However, with such a crucial campaign, and one that kept Llywelyn away from his own kingdom for long durations, it seems more likely that Joan would have remained in Gwynedd maintaining her roles and responsibilities as consort, being left with a number of duties as overseer to the family estates, if not in some official capacity the remaining figurehead of Venedotian power, and caring for her young children.

Even though Magna Carta contains clauses specific to the Welsh cause – explicitly the return of Welsh lands and liberties taken by the king, the return of hostages (and importantly to Llywelyn, his young son Gruffudd, who had remained John's prisoner for four years), the annulment of extortions carried out against the Welsh princes as a result of 1211, and the right to adhere to Welsh, Marcher or English law in trial based on the status and location of lands – neither Joan nor Llywelyn were on the fields of Runnymede on 15 June in witness to John's humiliation. Because Llywelyn was not there, as the leading Welsh ruler, he and a number of his princely peers met the king at Oxford at the end of July so that the Welsh terms could be ratified.

Llywelyn had been granted safe-conduct to attend and was escorted by the archbishop of Canterbury who led the mediation.

It has been argued that it was down to the success of Archbishop Langton, who was in charge of supervising the Welsh discussions at Oxford, that Llywelyn, in particular, received further allowances from the king 'as if to emphasise [his] status and standing in Wales'.[11] In particular, Llywelyn received two manors, Bidford in Warwickshire and Suckley in Worcestershire. It is far more likely that this was Joan's doing and that the success in garnering these manors, and thus further recognition of Llywelyn's status (and hers) from her father, should be attributed to her. The examination of later records intimate Bidford and Suckley were in Joan's hands, and even overseen by her, and these gifts in July 1215 seem to mark the beginning of a trend whereby Joan was rewarded by the Crown for her diplomatic endeavours and achievements with English manors. At such a crucial event in both Welsh and English history, and for the two most important men in her life, it would be most surprising to find that Joan did not travel to Oxford with her husband to see her father on this important occasion. Further, given her past achievements in mediation, it would be equally surprising if her skills were neither called nor relied upon, even as back up in an unofficial capacity.

Regardless of the positive resolutions that took place in the summer of 1215, by September, all hell had broken loose and the English barons revolted once again, this time openly inviting Louis of France to take John's place as England's king. Though Llywelyn was probably not party to these intentions, he did take advantage of the disturbances. During this time he continued to establish his authority further into South Wales and captured the principal strongholds of Carmarthen and Cardigan. It was the first occasion in which Llywelyn led 'the whole chieftaincy of Wales to battle, his first appearance as a war leader in South Wales. He won such victories as secured to him the unquestioned primacy of his race until the end of his life'.[12]

Again, Joan probably held down the fort, so to speak, in Gwynedd, while Llywelyn continued with his rare winter campaign, having begun his operation in early December. Unlikely for Llywelyn to have made it back in time (or even seen any importance to do so), Joan would have been busy in sole supervision of court preparations for Christmas festivities. Along with Easter and Whitsun, Christmas was one of the three most important festivals according to Welsh law and, similar to many royal courts across Europe, it was a time when networking and diplomacy were carried out in the Venedotian court.

The laws imply that it was during such occasions that offers of peace and gestures of alliances were carried out in the form of gift-giving, including offers of wine and mead. It was an opportunity for sovereigns to demonstrate their power and for the lesser and lower nobility to petition and air complaints or concerns in a friendly and congenial environment. As Llywelyn's queen, Joan, at the very least, would have commandeered organisation of celebrations and took part in them. It would have been doubly important for her to do so at a time when Llywelyn was so close to fulfilling his ambition and establishing uncontested rule throughout much of Wales. Perhaps at no other Christmas would it have been more important for Joan to publicly act as the benevolent representative of Venedotian rule than in the winter of 1215.

Llywelyn's supremacy was effectively recognised a few months later at the Council of Aberdyfi in 1216. Having summoned the Welsh princes to attend, it was here that the prince of North Wales acted as the leading arbitrator concerning the territorial claimants of the lesser native rulers in return for their public homage and pledge of allegiance. The main objective was to end the civil strife that beleaguered the kingdom of Deheubarth. Incisive politician that Llywelyn was, with the consent of the other princes, he formally divided the principality of Deheubarth among the heirs of the great Lord Rhys who had been at war since Rhys' death in 1197. Llywelyn granted partitions of the Welsh districts, taking nothing for himself, but was transparent in his bid to be the overseer and regulator of the arrangement. By doing this, the prince of Gwynedd won the affection and homage of the warring princes and validated his status as a powerful overlord.[13]

J.E. Lloyd referred to this event as effectively being the first Welsh parliament. Although this claim is hyperbolic, the import should not be underestimated as it was at Aberdyfi that Llywelyn was recognised as the de facto ruler of Wales – a position he held until the end of his life. Though it was many years later when Llywelyn's change in title reflected this supremacy, by the end of 1216, he had consolidated a level of power within Wales that had not been witnessed since the reign of Gruffudd ap Llywelyn, 'king of Wales', as far back as the eleventh century.

By association, Llywelyn's rise in status and authority after Aberdyfi meant that Joan's, too, ascended unparalleled heights and the designation she claimed in later years as the 'Lady of Wales' reflects this. This does not mean that her activities or duties increased, or that she suddenly enjoyed new levels of autonomous, regnal authority. However, it should be accepted that she became an even more important figurehead than she previously had been, whether or not she enjoyed associated powers in practice.

Like almost every event that occurred in her life, we have no idea if she was in attendance at Aberdyfi. And again, as is the case for so many of these important episodes, it is essential to simply consider that she may have been there. Indeed, it may have been an event where not just the Welsh princes were present, but that some of their wives joined them. And why not? It was a great gathering of Welsh royalty and would have offered an ideal setting for older alliances to be reconfirmed and new ones better established through the involvement of royal wives themselves, even if it occurred in a different setting while the council itself took place. If Llywelyn hosted the council, is it worth considering that Joan may have also been there to host ancillary meetings, or perhaps even to act as Llywelyn's joint host at court during meals? Undoubtedly, her presence would have helped portray the image of a united front and face of Welsh premiere rulership. It is an appealing idea, and at the root, it makes sense that at a crucial time for Llywelyn to illustrate the depth of his power, his wife – the daughter of the English king no less – and mother to his chosen heir, would be at his side. It would have made for a strong visual display, not only of dynastic authority, but also of Llywelyn's wider European reputation and recognition of status.

For Joan, however, the year 1216 was not one defined by great elation and joy. It was also defined by great sorrow and mourning. Soon after Aberdyfi, John implored Llywelyn, and his powerful son-in-law Reginald de Braose, to aid him in his fight against Prince Louis, whose army had landed in Kent early that summer and marched to London where they were greeted with open arms. In fact, the English king 'begged' for reconciliation 'in every way' possible.[14] Unsurprisingly, however, Joan's father's pleas for help were ignored by both her husband and son-in-law, and John died suddenly at Newark on 19 October, not long before his fiftieth birthday. How the news reached his daughter is unknown, but we can assume it arrived quickly. The death of a king was no paltry gossip.

Given their close relationship, the heaviness at the loss of her father must have been immeasurable – furthered by regrets of the soured relationship between him and her husband. The ignoble last few years of John's reign also must have weighed heavily with her.

Llywelyn, on the other hand, though empathetic to his wife's grief, understood that John's 'death created an entirely new situation, which was for the Welsh leader a hopeful and auspicious one'.[15] In all reality, the might of the English Crown would not be strong again for many years to come, allowing the Welsh leader respite and the opportunity to extend his own authority in Wales. As such, the prince of North Wales made the decision to wait out the tail-end of England's civil war, 'confident that, whatever its issue, he would be able at its close to dictate his own terms of peace'.[16]

Although John was buried at Worcester cathedral, Joan would not have been present at his interment. Indeed, it would have been odd for her to attend the funeral of the late king in Worcester and skip out on the coronation of his successor, her younger half-brother, at Gloucester soon after, which is exactly what the royal Welsh couple did when the 9-year-old Henry succeeded as heir to the English throne. Not only did they not attend Henry's coronation, Llywelyn had earlier rebuffed the request that he partake in the election of England's new king. Llywelyn's ambitions were to continue to expand his dominance and maintain his newly established status as the nominal prince of Wales. It was in Wales he and his queen stayed.

This was probably the reason Llywelyn remained aloof to requests to be involved in English affairs. It was important for him to maintain distinguished independence from Henry and not be seen to lessen his own authority by essentially conceding to the notion that the English king was his overlord, which would have been the case if he had allowed himself to be embroiled in the political dynamics of England at this time. Further, the boy-king, even if he were being guided by the legendary William Marshal, earl of Pembroke, as acting regent was not a particular threat to Llywelyn or the other Welsh princes during his minority.

Eight months after Henry III was crowned king of England, Llywelyn and Joan received shocking news. In 1217, Gwladus' husband, Reginald, had finally succumbed to English efforts to win him over to their side and on 23 June, he formally submitted to the English in return for restoration of all the de Braose lands which had been confiscated almost a decade before. The signing of the Treaty of Kingston and the desertion of their son-in-law caused much consternation. Llywelyn spent that summer invading Reginald's lands in the south, including Brycheiniog and Gower and while on campaign, he received hostages and monetary payments by many of those he subjugated, getting them to agree to his rule. Such submission was eventually offered by Reginald himself at Swansea when he was finally faced with Llywelyn's fury.[17]

The whereabouts or plight of Gwladus at this time are unknown, though she may still have been in North Wales with her other siblings, all likely in their mother's care. As elsewhere in Europe, fostering was popular in Wales, however, it seems a dangerous and problematic convention for the prince and princess of North Wales to have indulged in themselves – especially while Llywelyn was on his trajectory to power. Allowing even allies to foster their own children offered no recourse to peace of mind that their children, and heirs, would be safe in a society that was beset with strife and the constant reversal of fortunes and allegiances.

Gwladus would have been a noteworthy and vulnerable hostage if taken. Indeed, she was perhaps 12 years old at the most in 1217 and although technically of legal age to take her place at her husband's side, with the instability that southern Wales especially faced, she would have been far safer remaining in her homeland until she was a few years older. It seems unlikely that Llywelyn would have put either the safety of his daughter or his power-hold at risk by inadvertently putting Gwladus in danger of becoming a hostage, either by her native Welsh or the English. Arguably, with Joan as his wife, it was safer for his children, like Gruffudd and perhaps even Susanna further down the road, to be internees in English hands because Joan's royal status and position with the Angevin dynasty offered a semblance of security.

Upon Llywelyn's return to Gwynedd after dealing with Reginald, discussions between Joan and Llywelyn likely took place regarding the marriage of their (second?) daughter Marared, who was close to marital age. Though still too young to marry at the age of 10 (the age she would have been at the least), and in many ways even at the legal age of 12 (the age she would have been at the most), it was important to Llywelyn's agenda to create strong alliances through the marriage of his children. Because of Reginald's bold insurgence, which not only laid bare Reginald's untrustworthy nature, but Llywelyn's weakness in southern Wales, the prince took active measures to counteract any further insurrections by his son-in-law. Llywelyn switched his own alliances concerning the Braose lordship by supporting Reginald's nephew, John, as claimant to the family estates – John being the eldest son of William de Braose and Matilda (Maud) de Clare, daughter of the earl of Hertford.

John's father William died of starvation, along with his grandmother Maud de St Valéry, in the dungeon of Corfe or Windsor castle, at the hands of King John. This sore fact is what earned John the Welsh nickname Tadody ('fatherless'). He himself spent his formative years in hiding in the family lordship of Gower, being viewed as a continued threat to the Crown as a successor to the de Braose estates. Eventually he and his brother Philip were captured and imprisoned by King John and only released in 1218 by Henry. It was after his release that the subject of a marriage between John and Marared warranted negotiation. Llywelyn wanted to punish Reginald for his defection and John wanted to oust his uncle and take the title to the family estates for himself. The Welsh chronicles tell us that a year later, in 1219, Marared and John married. Upon their marriage, they received Gower as a marriage portion.[18] John and his mother Matilda sued Reginald for their rights in 1220 and in years to come, it would indeed be John who would finally have the satisfaction of re-establishing the senior branch of the de Braose dynasty, saving it from virtual distinction.

The fact that both Marared's and Gwladus' marriages are recorded in native chronicles attests to the sheer importance of the affinity between Venedotian and de Braose dynasties in its ability to shape the political structure of both *Pura Wallia* and *Marchia Walliae*. Mostly, these chronicle entries highlight Llywelyn's political dominance. It was a dominance that was finally and formally recognised by the Crown in the early spring of 1218 with the signing of the all-important Treaty of Worcester.

A year-and-a-half earlier, England's civil war had come to an end with the signing of the Treaty of Lambeth in September 1217. The remainder of the rebelling barons were brought to heel, the French Prince Louis conceded he had no right to the throne and returned to France and the Scottish warband retreated back to Scotland. It seemed a momentous opportunity to parlay for peace with Wales at this time as well. As it was, the Welsh found the terms of the treaty entirely dissatisfactory.

Chiefly, it was mandated they yield the significant gains they had made in expanding their territory. The Welsh, meaning Llywelyn of course, shunned the deal and continued to harass his opponents on the March in the south of Wales – especially Reginald after his defection to England that year. The prince's rejection of the deal may in part be the reason why, a month later, the young King Henry III ordered that the sheriff of Worcestershire seize the manor of Suckley from Joan and Llywelyn and restore the seisin to one Roger of Clifford, who held it at least until March 1218. By October of that year, it had been restored back to the Welsh royal couple, along with the manor of Bidford, which had also previously been reappropriated by the king.[19] Yet, with Bidford, there is some indication that Joan and Llywelyn retained some rights to their manor, as in April a royal charter was granted allowing Bidford to hold a weekly market.[20]

In February 1218 the king and royal council, threatened by Llywelyn's sustained campaign in south Wales, his successes and, crucially, his unremitting display of independence and authority, requested that the prince of Gwynedd meet in Worcester to discuss terms of peace. Llywelyn received a royal letter in which he was instructed to appear 'with his adherents to do homage to Henry at Worcester on 11 March' and was given safe-conduct to attend.[21]

After a series of talks, agreements were made, eventually culminating in a recognition of peace made at Worcester, where Llywelyn's superlative position in Wales was formally recognised. He agreed to receive no enemy of England and promised that the Welsh would pay customary homage and fealty to the English king. In fact, it was the prince himself who was to pay homage the English king as his overlord and pledge that as the most prominent Welsh ruler, he would encourage the other lesser Welsh princes to follow his lead. He also acknowledged that Wales was not a principality where the magnates swore homage to him; however, over the next few years he advanced his claims to this right. In return for the Crown's acknowledgement of his status, Llywelyn surrendered control over the territories of Cardigan, Montgomery and Carmarthen and received them back to hold as an English castellan. On 15 March, Llywelyn received another promise of safe-conduct for him to appear at Worcester once again, on 22 April, in order to do homage and pay fealty to Henry as promised.

Realistically, the peace made at Worcester was a humiliation for the English Crown, because it only affirmed 'status quo', yet abandoned the substance of it. Llywelyn exploited the power bestowed upon him by the treaty, but at the same time was aware of the imminent importance of his relationship with the Crown. He needed English support to be trusted as an agent of royal polices and to help him deal with the other Welsh princes. By the end of the year 1218, there was relative peace and harmony between Wales and England and though many conflicts continued and issues flared up on a number of occasions, the peace of Worcester marked a turning point in Llywelyn's career. His recognised status was one that he retained throughout the remainder of his reign. In the words of J.E. Lloyd:

> The year 1218 closed in profounder peace between English and Welsh than had been seen for many a long year, and yet the struggle had not exhausted the energy of Llywelyn, who had merely completed the first stage in his victorious career, the period of growth, of youthful triumph, of ascendancy achieved. He had still before him many years of strenuous and successful work of assured supremacy, of good fortune which scarcely knew rebuff.[22]

Although after 1215 records remain silent up to the early 1220s as regards to Joan specifically, the constant toing and froing that took place between Llywelyn, his other advisors, and the kings of England between Shrewsbury and Worcester compellingly suggests that she, too, may have made appearances at many of the important gatherings, even if she did not actively participate in much, or any, of the political lobbying. In terms of Henry, with the king being so young, both sides, including Joan herself, may have seized opportunities for her to engage with him on a more personal level, in the least providing him support and encouragement in learning how to make his own informed decisions. She may have wanted to see him succeed as her little brother and ensure trust remained between them as king and vassal, in spite of any future political wrangling between him and her husband.[23] Like with her father, there appears to have been genuine affection between Joan and Henry either in spite or because of the almost twenty-year age difference. Events and interactions between the two over the next seventeen years attests to this.

Joan may have been one of Llywelyn's 'adherents' who attended the summit in Worcester, if not in March for the settling of peace, then in April to witness Llywelyn pay homage to Henry. If in attendance, she would have been Llywelyn's regal consort,[24] and it would have been recognised that she had already proven her worth as the Welsh leader's most valuable and successful diplomat to the English Crown. Surely, such a firm and overt display of peace between the two countries would not have taken place without the central figure that united the two together. Both men played on their personal relationships in letters to each other over the years, and the fact that Joan was their uniting force is often forgotten or overlooked; so too the agency she wielded on occasion, stemming from this very position. Given their perceived loving relationship, the opportunity to witness confirmation of her husband's authority would not likely have been passed over. By extension, the recognition of Llywelyn's newly claimed status was a recognition of her own as his reigning consort. Though gone unobserved by historians, this would not have been overlooked by her contemporaries and may, in part, be one of the reasons that the following decades saw a rise in her political activities. In the 1220s, especially, Joan's actions may have increased as per expectations of her royal duties as queen-consort.

By 1219, around the age of 31, Joan was already first-hand witness to a lifetime's worth of experience, adventure, drama, joy and sorrow and had been faced with the precarious and precious nature of life at every turn. She was involved in the meteoric rise of her ambitious husband, shocked at the sudden demise of her beloved father, and beheld the establishment of her young brother's rule as king of England. As the first two decades of the thirteenth-century came to a close, the princess of North Wales had been married over thirteen years and bore at least four, probably five, children. Gwladus was established in the de Braose lordship with Reginald by this time, being a young teenager and thus considered an adult. Marared, who was very close in age to Gwladus and being a young teenager herself, may also have been ensconced in her marital home in Bramber in Kent with her de Braose husband John by 1219. Elen and Dafydd, between the ages of 12 and 8 years old respectively, still would have remained in their parents care, and the royal couple presumably had another tumbling toddler in their household at this time, as their youngest daughter Susanna must have been born no earlier than 1217, and no later than 1219.

From the time of her marriage to Llywelyn, Joan became adept in successfully operating in the traditional role of the married woman as the 'peace-weaver', whether as an envoy, a petitioner or as an instigator in events. Certainly, her career as an intercessor throughout the early thirteenth-century was innately linked to her lifecycles as a wife of a Welsh ruler and as a direct member of the Angevin dynasty. Nevertheless, from the first few years of her reign alone, there is enough evidence to support the argument that her political successes were more a combination of her position as Llywelyn's wife and the activities that her status and role as a 'queen' required. She used both as bargaining chips, as powerful means to achieve some of the very real political objectives flowing from the Venedotian court and Llywelyn's own ambitions. Perhaps it is not a coincidence that Joan's name is absent in sources between the years 1216 and 1222, the era in which Llywelyn reached an ascendency in Wales, having successfully reclaimed both his authority and the lands he lost in 1211. Although Henry III was in his minority during those years, by the mid-1220s he had reached maturity. It is no surprise to find that upon his declaration of adulthood that Joan once again took centre-stage in the tempestuous Anglo-Welsh affairs.

Chapter Eight

Royal Female Authority

The 1220s were a decade that seem to have been most prolific for Joan as a 'career politician', if she were ever to receive such an accolade. Although it may be that it just happens to have been the decade in which a number of her movements were tracked, it does not seem to be a coincidence that she is recorded as being at her most active during a very tumultuous era for Britain.

The year 1220 itself started out as an eventful one for Joan and Llywelyn. In early January a date had been fixed for Llywelyn to travel once again to Shrewsbury to meet with a border council, but the prince requested the meeting be delayed by a month. It transpired that the meeting was delayed a further four months to May due to the lack of availability of the new legate, Pandulf, to attend before then. By 1220, Henry III had been king for four years and was the ripe age of 13, relatively close in age to at least three of his Welsh nieces, Gwladus, Marared and Elen. Verging on being a legal adult, Henry began taking some measures in asserting his authority as king over that of his regents. As threats to the young king's authority naturally existed both in and around Britain and from France, acts of homage to the English Crown were actively sought. Llywelyn, himself, caused much concern after 1218 with his continued general harrying of the March and south Wales and the annexation of important territories during that time, in spite of what had taken place in Worcester. As such, one of the reasons for the spring meeting was to form an amicable agreement between Llywelyn and the new earl of Pembroke, William Marshal, who was bent on recovering the lands he had recently lost to the prince. Hence, it was in May 1220 the Welsh royal family likely travelled together to Shrewsbury to convene with the king.

Although Llywelyn and Marshal agreed to a temporary truce, more significant undertakings occurred.[1] Here, under the watchful eye of the archbishop of Canterbury, Stephen Langton; papal legate, Pandulf; and justiciar, Hubert de Burgh, Llywelyn agreed to surrender the homage of his nobles to the king. It was a perspicuous move; the peace agreed to at Worcester made it clear that the homage of the Welsh prince belonged to the king. This act of conciliation was not one-sided, however. This was an interchange that seemed to also benefit the Welsh royal family.

At Worcester, Llywelyn had agreed not to raise the question of the princedom of Wales until the king was of age. This meeting in early May proved the ripe time to do so because plans were underway for Henry to be coronated a second time. Though the king was still under age, the coronation which took place at Westminster cathedral twelve days after his meeting with Joan and Llywelyn was an event that, among other reasons, helped convey his monarchical power. Thus, by the time he declared himself of age seven years later, in 1227, his authority was already established. In this light, the meeting at Shrewsbury seems to have been an opportune for the Welsh family to address the future of their Venedotian leadership.

Llywelyn's uncontested power in Wales was reaffirmed by Henry's public and formal recognition that his son by Joan was to be the rightful heir and successor to Gwynedd – a crucial move in securing Llywelyn's hegemony. Importantly, it was stressed that Dafydd was not only Llywelyn's acknowledged successor, but that he was his legitimate descendant – this, too, was a crucial move and one that recognised the esteemed status of the current and future Venedotian dynasty because of Joan's own royal status. Henry was not the only superior to recognise Dafydd's successorship. Two years later, in 1222, it was also acknowledged by the pope. A further four years later, with Joan's own legitimation process, Dafydd's position was cemented.

Three months after the decisive conference in Shrewsbury in May 1220, it is expected that Joan would have travelled to Chester with Llywelyn to meet with earl Ranulf, where the two leaders reaffirmed the friendly pact they made in 1218, when Ranulf had returned from crusade.[2] The somewhat startling alliance between the most powerful Marcher lord, and once adversary, with the most powerful Welsh ruler was an alarming turn of events for England. In fact, the alliance became a major factor in Welsh and English politics in the proceeding years. For Llywelyn in particular, the alliance allowed him the freedom to focus on extending his authority in Wales without having to worry about an English invasion from the north, such as those that John oversaw ten years earlier. Having the northern border secured by such a prominent adherent meant the kingdom of Gwynedd remained strong and secure, itself. It was during this visit that affirmation of this firm new friendship was sealed with the agreement that Joan and Llywelyn's teenage daughter, Elen, marry Ranulf's nephew and heir, John the Scot.

Joan's presence in Chester would not have been unexpected, by any means, especially if, as parents, she and Llywelyn had previously discussed suggesting the marital alliance to Ranulf. As such, Elen would have made the journey to the border with her parents in anticipation of meeting the young man proposed to be her future groom, if she had not been acquainted with him already. It is most probable that Joan would have been involved in organising the wedding festivities, which were held in Chester, for her young daughter. It is hard not to imagine that Elen's wedding celebrations would have been designed to be larger than those of her sisters, Gwladus and Marared, who married into the de Braose clan years earlier. The relationship between Llywelyn and Ranulf was a special one and the act of cementing their alliance through such intimate means was easily a call for great celebration when the nuptials took place two years later. An additional celebration, and one which may have fostered even more of an allure for Joan to travel to Chester late that summer, would have been the prospect of spending time with her mother, if indeed Ranulf's wife Clemence de Fougeres was that woman.

In July 1221 Llywelyn was called to appear before Henry once again at Shrewsbury, this time to answer for his conduct concerning Rhys Ieuanc, prince of Deheubarth. Rhys, angry with Llywelyn's treatment of him because, among other issues, he had not been given custody of Cardigan castle, had sought a threatening alliance with William Marshal, the new earl of Pembroke. In retaliation upon hearing the news, Llywelyn quickly took Aberystwyth castle from him and disposed the prince of Deheubarth of all his lands, forcing the young man to turn to the Crown for assistance. Llywelyn did, indeed, attend Shrewsbury in person and conceded that he had not been fair in his dealings with Rhys and conferred Cardigan and Aberystwyth on him.[3] This meeting in 1221 was witness to the politically sagacious moves Llywelyn was known for; he often knew when to fight fire with fire, and when to dampen the flames, especially when it came to his best interests when the Crown was involved.

Nevertheless, 1221 was the year that saw a renewal in conflict with Llywelyn and Joan's son-in-law, Reginald de Braose.[4] This particular encounter ostensibly resulted in an inevitable broader clash between the Welsh prince and the king of England as Henry's forces came to Reginald's defence of Buellt, which Llywelyn had laid under siege. Reginald's alliance with England meant the loss of Llywelyn's support for his claims to the de Broase family lands in Wales. As such, it was during this time that Llywelyn decided to support the efforts of his other de Braose son-in-law, Marared's husband John, instead.

Although unrecorded, such royal sojourns to Shrewsbury in July 1221, and various occasions to Worcester, likely meant the prince was accompanied by Joan on many an occasion. Of the manors gifted to her over the years, the majority of them surrounded close proximity to Shrewsbury in three cardinal directions (Ellesmere, not thirty miles to the north; Wellington, less that twenty-five miles to the east; and Condover, five miles to the south). Further, two of her other manors were in close proximity to Worcester: Suckley, only eighteen miles to the west, and Bidford, thirty-five miles east.[5] Accordingly, visits to Shropshire and Worcestershire would have provided opportunities for Joan to stop over, or even stay for lengthy periods of time, at her manors to assess the management of her lands and oversee administration of her lordships first hand. In fact, the 1220s was an active decade in terms of Joan's English manors, with many being granted to her during this time, taken away and regranted on numerous occasions, which always seems to fall in line with political events of the time. It was around the 1221 congress in Shrewsbury that the manor of Ellesmere, which had been taken from Joan and Llywelyn in 1211, was fully restored to them and a grant for a market given. They also received other royal gifts. The return of Ellesmere – effectively Joan and Llywelyn's most important English manor – may have been the outcome of Llywelyn's conciliatory arrangements he made with Rhys Ieuanc.

As for other manors, there is considerable evidence to suggest Joan played a direct role in both procuring and managing them to an extent. For example, by Michaelmas 1220 it appears that Suckley, the manor resting in the Malvern Hills in Worcestershire, granted to Joan and Llywelyn by John in the summer of 1215, was firmly back in the couple's possession. Henry had seized it in 1217, allowing Roger of Clifford to manage it until October 1218, when it was likely returned to Joan and Llywelyn in conjunction with Bidford manor in Warwickshire as gifts in recognition of the success that took place at Worcester in 1218. As far as these manors are concerned, although livery was not attained until 1218, Bidford was a part of Joan's original dowry and later evidence by Llywelyn suggests that Suckley was as well.[6]

Between October 1221 and February 1222, the protection of and developments in Suckley, in particular, was one of Joan's manors that warranted some concern for the royal Welsh couple. Llywelyn himself wrote to Henry asking for protection for the men of the manorial estate who suffered from 'unjust molestation' related to the debt previously incurred by Roger of Clifford, the former appointed custodian. Having 'no advocate or patron in England other than the king' to hear the plea, Llywelyn asked Henry to issue an order for royal justices to provide protection.[7]

Although the Welsh prince had heard that the king had previously 'ordered all manors held by his father to be seized into the king's hand', Llywelyn was confident that no one else would have the authority to make a claim regarding 'any of the tenements which the king's father gave in free marriage'. Interestingly, Llywelyn suggested in his letter that if the king wished to 'hold any investigation regarding the aforesaid manor or other manors given to Llywelyn in free marriage by the king's father of blessed memory', the bearer of the letter had permission not only to act on Llywelyn's behalf, but relay 'to the king of other matters orally'. How far should we reflect on Joan's involvement in either instructing how the letter should be dictated, or the delivery of the actual letter itself, Joan being the one to act on Llywelyn's half? The manor was partly under her authority, after all. It is important to remember that Joan was actively involved on various occasions, issuing letters and sending envoys herself to both John and Henry and that the invisibility of women's names in medieval charters does not necessarily preclude inactivity, lack of responsibility or even their presence when charters were drawn up.

After September 1221, however, Henry ordered that all royal manors once held by his father, which had either been previously granted out by John or seized from him at the beginning of baronial rebellion, were returned to the king's hands and made part of the royal domain once again. Henry took serious measures in doing this, issuing writs to all his sheriffs and ensuring that between two to four coadjutors for each county oversaw that this royal command was obeyed.[8] But for Joan and Llywelyn, they found themselves back in possession of both Suckley and Bidford within five months after Henry's instructions for confiscation had been given. Beginning on 10 October 1221, a royal mandate of restoration of both Suckley and Bidford states that the manors had indeed been given in free marriage; by January 1222 Joan and Llywelyn were 'specially protected [to] the enjoyment' of both manors, and by 4 February, orders were given for full seisin to be restored them.[9] Perhaps the imminent wedding of Henry's niece Elen to John the Scot, earl of Huntington, and heir to the earldom of Chester, was a motivating factor in the quick reversal of fortune regarding these manors as at this time Llywelyn was 'still treated by the crown as its best friend'.[10]

Sometime between February and August 1222 Elen and John were married, sealing the most powerful Marcher-Welsh alliance of its time. The only source of information we have concerning Joan's participation in any of her children's marriages resides in the 1222 marital agreement for Elen and John. More importantly, it is a source that is critical to understanding two extremely important facets of her triple-role as wife, mother and queen. First, it helps to illuminate the intimacy of her family relationships and is, in fact, a small glimpse through the keyhole to her family life. As a mother, in this instance it is clear that Joan was actively involved in providing security for her daughter and her future. On their marriages, both Gwladus and Marared received lands that seem to have been in Joan's possession and they, like Elen, may have profited from her mother's financial support.

The marital agreement that was sealed by Llywelyn and Ranulf states that it was to be followed by a charter from 'Lady Joan', who was to independently confirm the gifts of lands granted to Elen and John. The implications are such that Joan did indeed possess rights to these lands – and by extension, oversight of their management and administration – and that her authorisation, or approval, was necessary before they could be formally granted to the newlyweds. In fact, the wording of the 1222 marriage agreement intimates that Joan was directly involved in not only making the decision to gift manors to Elen and her new husband, but that she also had an individual stake in the running of the manors themselves. The lands that Elen and John received were Bidford and Suckley respectively, the same manorial holdings that Joan and Llywelyn received in *liberum maritagium* by King John. They also received Wellington in Shropshire. Reference to Joan issuing her own subsequent charter implies, in the least, that she possessed rights of land.

It was not just the marriages of his children by Joan that Llywelyn used to create strong alliances with Marcher lords, or endow gifts of land. Sometime between 1222 and 1223 the marriage of Gwenllian (d. 1283), his daughter by Tangwystl (and Gruffudd's sister), to William de Lacy took place. William, was the half-brother of Hugh de Lacy, earl of Ulster, his parents being Hugh de Lacy and Rose O'Connor of Connacht. Like Elen and Marared, Gwenllian received lands from her father in free marriage, which included four manors in Dyffryn Clwyd and Rhufoniog. His natural daughter Angharad (d. before 1260), who married Maelgwn Fychan of Deheubarth, also received a dowry, presumably of lands in Ceredigion. The 1222 marital agreement concerning Elen dictates that Joan and Llywelyn expected John to provide Elen with a dower, no less than 100 librates of land. Presumably, expectation that all his daughters received dowers was part of all these marital arrangements.[11]

This particular agreement is important in terms of providing evidence that women, and royal consorts especially, were involved in the arrangement of marriages for their children. There is additional proof to suggest Elen's marriage was not the only one that Joan was involved in negotiating contracts for. The biggest confirmation of this, among other smaller and more introspect examples such as lands being passed down from Joan through her female line, is that upon Gwladus' second marriage to the Marcher lord Ralph Mortimer in 1230, the couple received lands in the manors of Knighton and Norton, both in Shropshire. Though it is hard to pin down the timeframe in which these lands were gifted, sometime between mid-June 1230 and Llywelyn's own death 11 April 1240, it is notable that these were also lands given to Joan and Llywelyn, again as part of their own maritagium, or in free marriage.

In terms of assessing levels of Joan's own agency this agreement is informative. These were English lands, which meant that by English law, it was not necessary for Llywelyn to obtain her consent to divide and gift any part of their maritaigum. Yet, this agreement, which is the only real example of Joan issuing her own acta, confirms the idea that she worked with Llywelyn as a wife on some level of lordship administration, likely as and when the need arose, but also on her own accord. Earlier examples can be found with the Lord Rhys of Deheubarth and his queen Gwenllian, who also consented and assented to the alienation of lands from the dynastic lordship.[12] Closer to home, Emma of Anjou too consented and assented to the alienation lands made as grants to Haughmond Abbey during times when her husband was both free and in captivity. In 1222 Joan was active in participating in determining how and when to alienate marital lands, thus relinquishing some of their landed power as a couple. This notion is also much more illuminating on a grander scale.

The sheer importance of the 1222 agreement in terms of understanding the inner-workings of Welsh polity should not be underestimated. This agreement highlights a number of important facets related to Joan's status and position as ruling queen: her independence as a land holder, the facility to issue her own acta, her participation in alienating marital lands and her involvement in the arrangement of political marital alliances for her own children. Thus, to an extent, it elucidates the institution of 'monarchy' as practiced by Llywelyn and reveals a significant element of Welsh socio-cultural practices that have been long overlooked, which likely included the participation of the queen in helping to establish political arrangements and alliances on occasion. Momentously, it is, in fact, the only extant document in which Joan and Llywelyn appear together in the guise of a ruling couple.

The marriage was probably cause to further celebrate another commemorative event that took place around the same time. Between April and 26 May 1222, the pope formally recognised Dafydd as Llywelyn's heir. A son by his legitimate wife Joan, daughter of the late king of England, Dafydd was to succeeded Llywelyn by hereditary right in all his possessions – though without recourse to the English throne. Llywelyn wasted no time in seeking confirmation of the statute by apostolic authority.

It was crucial that Dafydd, in other words Llywelyn and Joan by extension, have the backing of both the English Crown and the pope in attesting to his legitimate right to successorship. Dafydd, himself, was only still a young child, around the age of 5 or 6 at the time and Gruffudd, Llywelyn's first-born son, was a man in his early twenties. By Welsh custom, law and practice, Gruffudd's rights to the crown of Gwynedd were arguably more legitimate than Dafydd's, who was only half-Welsh. Given the animosity of the Welsh towards their invading neighbours, Gruffudd had strong backing among his countrywomen and men as their next leader by right. Dafydd had the blood of the spawn of the devil in him, his mother being from the Angevin line.

After Llywelyn's failed uprising in 1211, Gruffudd was sent as a hostage to England and spent a significant portion of his adolescent years as a prisoner. In fact, the princeling spent a significant portion of his life overall as a prisoner. As a hostage of King John, Gruffudd may have lost much of his childhood innocence after possibly having been witness to the hanging of the twenty-eight Welsh hostages, his own compatriots, by his Angevin captor at Nottingham in 1211. The four years he remained in captivity likely did little to quell his frustration and anger at being forsaken by his father in such a painful and humiliating, never mind terrifying way. Indeed, the four years he remained in captivity were formative, and understandably must have stoked much resentment which, perhaps, fuelled his rebellion against his father in the 1220s – a rightful protest against Llywelyn's election of Dafydd as his *edling*.

By the time of Gruffudd's release from English internment in 1215, Joan was the mother of at least three of Gruffudd's half-sisters, Gwladus, Marared and Elen. More importantly for Gruffudd, Joan was also the mother of his new half-brother, Dafydd, who had been born in the spring of 1212. Upon his return to the Welsh court, Gruffudd may have been welcomed with open arms by his father and his sisters, Gwenllian and Angharad. Perhaps even his mother Tangwystl was still somewhere in the picture and was able to provide the young teenage Gruffudd comfort. As for a welcoming by Joan, this, too, can only be speculated. Perhaps an effort would have been made on her part to help integrate Gruffudd back into courtly life. This would have been especially true if the affection that Joan and Llywelyn purportedly felt for one another was, indeed, genuine. Nevertheless, Gruffudd's response to having to face the daughter of his tormentor as a stalwart member of his family, whether he lived with them at court or not, could not have been easy, even if Joan were kind to him. Perhaps a small, yet rather suggestive insight into how Joan and her children were perceived by Llywelyn's natural-born children resides in the English chancery enrolments from the early 1240s. Gwenllian, the long-term widow of William de Lacy, sued her half-brother Dafydd – who was by this time reigning prince of Wales – for her lands in Denbighshire, given to her in dower by Llywelyn over twenty years previously.

Gruffudd may have been free from physical imprisonment for a time after 1215, but the knowledge that his ascendency was likely to be overshadowed by the squalling babe in his foreign stepmother's arms was a psychological custodial sentence he likely never broke free from, especially as various steps were taken over the next six years to secure Dafydd's position as Llywelyn's successor. In 1222 Llywelyn wrote to Honorious III with a petition informing him that he had taken steps to abolish the Welsh practice of recognising illegitimate children as equal heirs, essentially barring them – explicitly, though unspoken, Gruffudd – from their due inheritance. The pope gladly granted and confirmed Llywelyn's petition, commending the prince for cleansing Wales of the tradition that was viewed as utterly abhorrent in the eyes of the church; referring to it, in fact, as a most 'lamentable custom'. Four years later, in 1226, Joan took a momentous step and requested her own legitimation – an act that not only safeguarded Dafydd's position, but one that also enhanced her own status, elevating her and her progeny as irrefutable members of the most powerful royal dynasty of the thirteenth century.

Understandably, the relationship between Llywelyn and Gruffudd was fraught and inconsistent. Throughout the 1220s and 1230s, while Llywelyn worked to ensure Dafydd's succession, he also tried to temper Gruffudd's resentment. He was often compensated and rewarded with lands and authority for his loyalty to Llywelyn. In the early 1220s Gruffudd was given control over substantial lordships in North Wales, including the *cantref* of Meirionnydd and the historically important *commote* of Ardudwy, both in north-west Wales. Ardudwy was an important staple to the kingdom of Gwynedd. Like Aberffraw, it was steeped in legend and lore largely associated with the Four Branches of the *Mabinogi*; an area of Wales most greatly associated with Bendigeidfran, or the legendary Brân the Blessed. That Llywelyn granted Gruffudd these lordships was a testament to Gruffudd's standing in his father's eyes. It may have been an attempt to lessen the blow of being cast aside as successor, Llywelyn endeavouring to provide his son with power and profit in ways other than attaining the crown. Nevertheless, Gruffudd's access to these lands was soon revoked, largely due to his uncooperative nature. Loyalty and trust between the father and his first-born son fluctuated back and forth during the 1220s; although Gruffudd headed the skirmish against William Marshal in 1223 on Llywelyn's behalf, had been given the lordship of Llŷn and the appanage of Upper Powys, by 1228 he found himself his father's prisoner in Deganwy where he remained for six whole years, not being released until 1234.

All told, it became clear that the olive branches that Llywelyn continually offered his natural son (many undoubtedly born of personal guilt) quickly withered and eventually decayed. Thus, the fraternal rot between Gruffudd and Dafydd that was stewed by events at Shrewsbury in May 1220 fermented for twenty years. Soon before, or just after,

- ● Venedotian courts linked to Joan
- ● Joan's place of burial
- ▲ English manors linked to Joan

Llanfaes
Aberffraw
Rhosyr
Aber (?)
Castell Hen Blas
■ Chester
▲ Ellesmere
Rothley ▲
Shrewsbury
▲ Knighton
Condover ▲
▲ Wellington
Norton
Worcester
Suckley ▲
■ ▲ Bidford

Left: Joan's alleged sarcophagus, which can be found in the entryway of St Mary's Church, Beaumaris, Anglesey. Traditionally believed to have been hers since its apparent discovery in the eighteenth century, recent scholarship has called this into question. (*Author's collection*)

Below: The entryway of St Mary's Church, Beaumaris, with both a commemoration and the traditional coat of arms of the house of Gwynedd (Aberffraw) adorning Joan's supposed effigy. (*Courtesy of Llywelyn2000 @ Wikimedia Commons*)

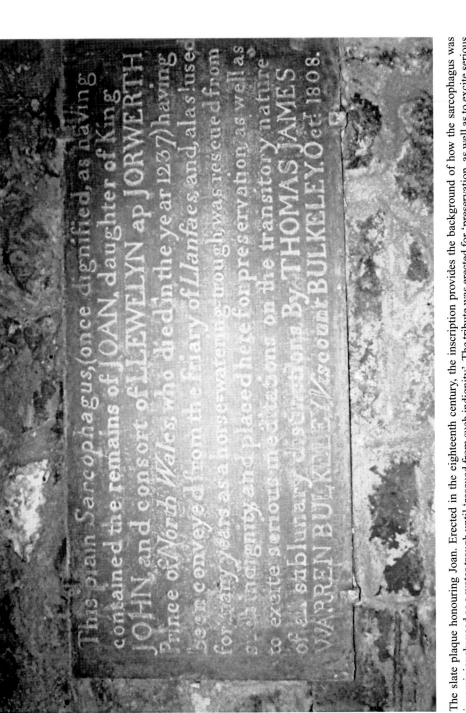

This plain Sarcophagus, (once dignified, as having contained the remains of JOAN, daughter of King JOHN, and consort of LLEWELYN ap JORWERTH Prince of *North Wales*, who died in the year 1237) having been conveyed from the Friary of *Llanfaes*, and, alas! used for many years as a horse-watering-trough was rescued from such indignity, and placed here for preservation as well as to excite serious meditations on the transitory nature of all sublunary distinctions. By THOMAS JAMES WARREN BULKELEY Viscount BULKELEY. O et 1808.

The slate plaque honouring Joan. Erected in the eighteenth century, the inscription provides the background of how the sarcophagus was ignominiously used as a water trough until 'rescued from such indignity'. The tribute was erected for 'preservation', as well as to excite serious meditations on the transitory nature of all sublunary distinctions'. (*Courtesy of Cate228 @ Wikimedia Commons*)

This industrial site sits on the remains of Llanfaes priory, which was founded in honour of Joan by Llywelyn after her death. The *Red Book of Hergest* tells us that in the year 1237: 'Dame Joan, daughter of King John, wife of Llywelyn ab Iorwerth, died in the month of February at the court of Aber; and she was buried in a new graveyard on the shorebank which Bishop Hywel of St Asaph had consecrated. And in her honour Llywelyn ab Iorwerth built there a monastery for the bare-footed friars, which is called Llanfaes in Anglesey.' *Brut y Tywysogion* chronicles that: 'The Lady of Wales, wife of Llywelyn ab Iorwerth and daughter to the king of England, her name was Joan, died in Llywelyn's court at Aber in the month of February and her body was buried in a consecrated enclosure which was on the shore-bank. And there after that Bishop Hywel consecrated a monastery for the Barefooted Friars to the honour of the Blessed Mary. And the prince built it all at his cost for the soul of his lady.' (*Courtesy of RobinLeicester @ Wikimedia Commons*)

Llywelyn ap Iorwerth's supposed sarcophagus housed at St Grwst's Church, Llanrwst, Conwy. (*Courtesy of Llywelyn2000 @ Wikimedia Commons*)

Llanrhychwyn chapel, Llanrhychwyn, Conwy. This late eleventh-century chapel was purportedly a favourite spot of Llywelyn's to worship. Local lore has it that Joan eventually tired of walking the half mile up the steep mountain slope twice a day from their hunting lodge in Trefriw to worship and because of this, Llywelyn had St Mary's church built for her in Trefriw itself. (*Courtesy of Terry Hughes @ Wikimedia Commons*)

St Mary's Church, Trefriw, Conwy. This sixteenth-century church (restored in the nineteenth century) stands on the site of the original church Llywelyn is said to have erected for Joan. (*Courtesy of Llywelyn2000 @ Wikimedia Commons*)

St Mary's Church, Trefriw, Conwy. Stained glass window image of Joan made in the 1930s. (*Courtesy of Llywelyn2000 @ Wikimedia Commons*)

St Mary's Church, Trefriw, Conwy. Stained glass window image of Llywelyn made in the 1930s. (*Courtesy of Llywelyn2000 @ Wikimedia Commons*)

Garth Celyn (Pen-y-Bryn), Abergwyngregyn, Gwynedd. Long-debated as to whether or not this is Joan's and Llywelyn's palace of Aber, support for the notion that it is has gained in popularity, based on recent scholarship. (*Courtesy of John Northall*)

The view from Garth Celyn overlooking the Menai Straits to Anglesey and Llanfaes. (*Courtesy of John Northall*)

The site of the royal *llys* of Rhosyr near Newborough, Anglesey. Considered to have been a royal home, archaeological excavations in the early 1990s revealed a hall, lodgings and barns. (*Courtesy of RobinLeicester @ Wikimedia Commons*)

Llys Llywelyn, St Fagan's Museum National Museum of History, Cardiff. Based on evidence from Llys Rhosyr in Anglesey, other buildings of a similar time frame (c. 1200), and in consultation with historians, archaeologists, architectural and literary experts, Llys Llywelyn is a noteworthy reconstruction of a royal Welsh *llys*; one that Joan would have been more than familiar with and called home. (*Courtesy of Sean Kisby @ Wikimedia Commons*)

Llys Llywelyn, St Fagan's Museum National Museum of History, Cardiff. The courts inhabited by Joan and Llywelyn were much smaller than the royal palaces of England, for instance. Viewing such intimate surroundings, the impression that a Welsh queen such as Joan acted as an integral and visible member of the Welsh court becomes much more apparent. (*Courtesy of Sean Kisby @ Wikimedia Commons*)

The site of Ellesmere manor, Shropshire. This is likely to have been Joan's main English manor, being given to her and Llywelyn on their marriage by King John, and having been held by her aunt Emma of Anjou before her. (*Courtesy of Jeff Buck @ Wikimedia Commons*)

Condover Hall, Shropshire. One of Joan's manors given to her by her brother, Henry III, in recognition of her political diplomacy. Condover is the one manor where clear evidence survives that Joan actively participated in the administration and management of her manorial holdings. This building dates no earlier than the sixteenth century. (*Courtesy of Row17 @ Wikimedia Commons*)

Rothley Manor, Leicestershire. Another manor gifted to Joan by her brother after her successful endeavours as a political diplomat, mediating between Gwynedd and England. Henry eventually confiscated it and gifted it instead to the Knight's Templar. This sixteenth-century building is now Rothley Court Hotel. (*Courtesy of Terry Sheppard @ Wikimedia Commons*)

Llywelyn's death in 1240, Dafydd took measures to secure his occupation of the Venedotian crown, stripped Gruffudd of his lands and locked up both Gruffudd and his eldest son, Owain, in Criccieth castle. From there, they eventually found themselves transferred as prisoners to Henry III and ended up in the Tower of London. The animosity between the half-brothers would result in Gruffudd's tragic and untimely death, in a fall trying to escape his cell in the Tower on 1 March 1244.

It is valuable, and best placed here under the discussion of Gruffudd, to position Joan's role as a political advocate and queen in greater perspective, especially in context to Gruffudd's own wife, Senana ferch Caradog. As will be seen, Joan was not the only royal consort from Gwynedd with a visible and active role in thirteenth-century Anglo-Welsh relations. Her stepdaughter-in-law is also recorded as parlaying with Henry III as the chief representative of her husband's Venedotian authority in 1241, thirty years after Joan first interceded on Llywelyn's behalf in 1211. Senana, in fact, proved to be Gruffudd's staunchest ally in his fight for rights and power against Dafydd and seems to have been a woman of real authority in her own right.[13]

Although the assumed mainstay for a woman who found herself bound in a political marriage was, in theory, to act as a 'merciful' intermediary in the worldly state of affairs largely dominated by men, the evidence surrounding both Joan and Senana suggests that their actions were more than mere gendered, cultural lip-service. The kinds of personal and political connections that warranted their roles as counsellors and envoys, but their influences as 'queens' were far reaching. For these two women in particular, their roles as political diplomats were at the highest echelons of Welsh politics. Their direct involvement in representing and participating in elements of Welsh polity, as advisors, negotiators and ambassadors on a wider political stage leaves us with a tantalising sense of how 'queenship' may have been practiced and, crucially, accepted as an important function within the courts of the Venedotian rulers.

By 1221 Senana ferch Caradog and Gruffudd were probably married. Nothing is known of Senana's early years and frustratingly little is understood about her adulthood. As to when she died, this too remains a mystery. In essence, Senana is a woefully 'forgotten queen'; a woman denied her own rightful claim to power as Gruffudd's consort. Nevertheless, what we do know about her largely stems from a singular event, in which her role, arguably as a contender for the role of queen (against Dayfdd's wife, Isabella de Braose), and certainly as a political diplomat remain unprecedented. Even in comparison to Joan. Senana, in fact, is the most noteworthy example of official 'queenly' authority in practice stemming from native Wales as a whole.

In May 1241, following a failed mission by the bishop of Bangor, who supported Gruffudd's claims to the throne, Senana travelled to the English court at Westminster to appeal directly to Henry III to secure Gruffudd's release from Dafydd's prison. The Curia Regis Rolls record her explaining that her husband's detainment by his half-brother was unjust and that Henry's support in obtaining his release was vital, cleverly arguing that Gruffudd be treated as a tenant of the Crown.[14] To confirm Gruffudd's loyalty to Henry as his overlord, she made promises of hostages on his behalf (similar to Joan in 1211) and also professed his willingness to answer any claims that had been made against him and his case. Furthermore, Senana ensured that pledges of surety from some of the highest ranking Welsh magnates and Marcher lords were offered as a fait accompli. Although Dafydd's own ambassadors also happened to be present in court that day – presumably to hear the case brought by Gruffudd's sister, Gwenllian de Lacy, concerning portions of her dower that had been confiscated from her – and assured the king and Senana that they would take her case to Dafydd and appeal for justice, Joan's son made no attempt to release Gruffudd. Senana again appealed to Henry, subsequently meeting him at Shrewsbury.

On 12 August 1241, after a series of negotiations, Senana and the king reached an agreement, though the terms Senana had to concede to as a means of securing Henry's favour were extreme. A promise to pay an enormously hefty sum, in coins and moveable chattels, was the least harsh of the stipulations. As an assurance that both she and her husband would adhere to the terms of the agreement, Senana was forced to submit to Henry's demand that Gruffudd be transferred to one of his own prisons, along with three of their four sons as additional hostages. The king tempered this punitive requisite with a promise that upon an untimely death of Gruffudd, or their eldest son and heir, Owain, who was already a hostage, the two younger sons would be released and returned to her.

Senana agreed to the terms by swearing upon holy relics. Although it is not entirely unusual that she swore upon holy relics, her undertaking differs from other examples of noblewomen in Wales who observed conditions of agreements through the act. The difference is paramount.

Hers is the only known example of a royal woman giving an oath of her own accord and, crucially, in the highest political capacity possible. This, in itself, is indicative of Senana's recognised 'queenly' status. Such a claim is further bolstered by the fact that she also pledged that Gruffudd would swear to the same, in writing, upon his release and used her own seal and Gruffudd's to finalise the agreement. A number of powerful Welsh magnates and Welsh Marcher lords signed as her sureties.

Similar to all of Joan's mediary roles throughout her life, it is highly conceivable that Senana's very public role as Gruffudd's advocate was a combination of her acting of her own accord, as well as at his behest. Examining her involvement in negotiations is crucial in measuring her own royal authority and how her overall status was viewed by peers. Central to our understanding of the socio-political authority of Welsh royal women, and queen contenders, is the fact that it was Senana, herself, who represented Gruffudd at both Westminster and Shrewsbury in the Summer of 1241, rather than another member of Gruffudd's own court. While Welsh chronicles are silent when it comes to Senana's activities, let alone her involvement the events of 1241, the famed English historian Matthew Paris presents her as the preeminent Welsh magnate (*quod confecit Senena uxor Griffini, et alii terrœ magnates Walensium*) if, indeed, the terminology used refers to her rather than Gruffudd.[15]

As the wife of the publicly and politically rejected illegitimate son of the most powerful ruler in Wales, Senana's success in her political endeavours was crucial. The need to preserve the royal status and authority of her own family was paramount in the midst of a contentious dynastic conflict that had the potential to destabilise not only Gwynedd, but the whole of Wales. Clearly, in a situation in which she was under extreme pressure to protect the physical safety of her husband and children, the terms of the agreement forced upon her a tremendous personal blow.

Politically, her own position and status as queen-contender were precarious and difficult. This she understood having consented to two particular stipulations: one, that her family maintain a 'firm peace' with Dafydd, and two, that they take action against any who rebelled against the English king. By agreeing to these demands, Senana reaffirmed her family's vassalage to the English Crown, using her royal Welsh authority to do so. It was a status that the English King Henry clearly acknowledged. During Gruffudd's imprisonment in the Tower of London, Senana was not only granted permission to visit,[16] she also received payments from the king for maintenance, as well as gifts, between 24 October 1241 and July 1242.[17]

An important mark of her official royal authority is the affixation of the two royal seals – it is a shame that no examples survive concerning actual political negotiations in which Joan was involved. Senana's official use of seals has significant connotations directly linked to assertions of her individual power and authority as a Welsh 'queen'. First, the utilisation of both seals signifies Senana's singular status as a native Welsh royal woman.[18] Of course, there is the possibility that use of Gruffudd's seal indicated that hers alone was not sufficient enough to represent Welsh authority. Yet evidence found in the native laws and acta of the Welsh princes provide evidence otherwise, as do examples stemming from Joan herself, who sent official, diplomatic petitions to the kings of England for the release of hostages. Though they do not survive, references in English chancery enrolments indicate they were probably received in written form, which presumes the use of a seal.

The English chronicler Matthew Paris provides a narrative to the events of 1241 in his *Chronica Majora*, and records that Senana used her own hand to affix Gruffudd's seal matrix.[19] This visible act was a public demonstration of an important role associated with the office of the 'queen' and one that established her royal authority. Senana's signorial status is further underscored when contrasted with extant examples of ordinary freemen in Wales who had to ask their lord to seal charters in their names.[20] As such, Senana's political actions and use of both royal seals seem to be lasting – yet largely overlooked – reminders of the manifestations of women's secular power. They document an extent to which royal wives, like Senana and Joan, were able to employ independent and formal acts of agency in the highest echelons of politics when events called on them to do so. Because both royal seals are attached, along with the king of England's, this agreement remains the only known example of a Welsh 'ruler' and his consort openly collaborating as a force to achieve some elements of native policy.

While it is impossible to identify contemporary attitudes towards Senana's high-level political activities, it seems more than probable that she was encouraged by her husband's supporters. Certainly, the variety of powerful Welsh and Marcher lords named as sureties in the 1241 agreement attest to Gruffudd's own distinguished royal status. Roger of Mold, seneschal of Chester appears. English aristocrats like Ralph Mortimer and Walter Clifford were related to Gruffudd by marriage to his half-sisters, the second husbands of Gwladus Ddu and Marared respectively, and both wielded immense power and influence in English royal circles. Mortimer had extended and consolidated his family lordship and by 1241 had control of vast swathes of lands in mid-Wales, making his the most prominent of Marcher families. As his father was the former high sheriff of England, Walter Clifford had close social links to the English Crown. It is curious that Gruffudd received the support of his half-sisters' husbands. It has been argued that it is unlikely Mortimer, at least, acted as one of Senana's sureties based purely on familial bonds or obligations, and that his claims to Gwerthrynion and Maelienydd alone meant that Mortimer was a key figure in formulating the heavy stipulations in the agreement.[21] Nevertheless, such support may also intimate a sense of familial backing.

The Welsh sureties are perhaps more notable. Maelgwn Fychan was the lord of Ceredigion in west Wales and a strong supporter of Gruffudd. Like Mortimer and Clifford, Maelgwn was also related to Gruffudd through marriage to his sister Angharad. Gruffudd ap Madog of Bromfield, ruler of Powys, was one of the Gruffudd's main supporters, along with his brothers Hywel and Maredudd, who also pledged. Gruffudd ap Gwenwynwyn was himself the ruler of Powys Wenwynwyn in mid-Wales and at the time of the agreement had become a newly recognised baron by the English Crown. He owed no service to the rulers of Gwynedd, having acquired the seisin of his father's estates of Powys Wenwynwyn after paying homage to the king that same year. This made him an extraordinarily powerful Welsh ally.

Crucially, the support from these figureheads attest to Senana's own royal authority in context. This is further reinforced by one particular surety that stands out: the renowned Maredudd ap Rhobert, lord of Cedewain, who was the 'eminent' or 'chief counsellor of Wales'. That Senana either garnered, or in the least maintained the support of these powerful men, and Maredudd ap Rhobert's in particular, is worthy of note. In the least, such support is indicative of the acceptance of her rule as lord in her husband's stead. In numerous circumstances, wives often operated at the helm while their husbands were elsewhere, leaving them directly involved in lordship administration. Senana, as a wife in control of the family lordship during the prolonged absences of her husband, whether in battle or in prison, and on his death, would have had to ensure that previous affiliations were maintained and new ones created. Such connections would have helped her to achieve the results needed to protect her family's interests. At the most, these high-ranking warranties signified a recognition of her status as contender to the Venedotian role of queen.

There is proof that Senana played such an important administrative role and held a position of authority within her own familial lordship on the Llŷn peninsula in 1252. Although a widow by this time, she heads the witness list to an agreement crafted between her youngest son with the monks of Bardsey Island.[22] It is clear that a full eight years after Gruffudd's death, she still maintained an influential status. It is possible that she enjoyed more authority as a widow, though recent research has shown that it was in wifehood that women in native Wales employed the largest levels of agency.[23] Surely, like Joan, Senana's previous political statesmanship secured her position as person of Welsh royal authority and her earlier activities ensured that she maintained a significant amount of influence and authority in widowhood, certainly within her locality, as her appearance as a witness in 1252 seems to imply.

Senana's case says a great deal about the agency connected to a Welsh woman's position as a wife and, more importantly, her status as a potential 'queen'. Like Joan, she acted in an official capacity as the pre-eminent representative of the dynastic authority of her own family. Her achievements lie not in the content of the 1241 agreement itself, which for all intents and purposes was extortionate, but in how she successfully conformed to the political necessities of performing vassalage as a Welsh 'queen'. This agreement is the only surviving piece of evidence from native Wales to showcase the very real level of political agency that a Welsh 'queen' employed at any time during the Middle Ages.

Senana's involvement as the second party in the creation of an agreement with the king of England in 1241 is significant in terms of understanding how Welsh queenship may well have been both practiced and accepted – providing us more insight into Joan's own career, activities, successes and even failures. Senana's participation in 1241 is seminal. First and foremost, that she was a native of Wales presents a singularly Welsh slant to the construction of our understanding of the roles and expectations concerning native queenship. Although evidence survives of 'queenly' economic agency – namely through land transactions that highlight the types power that married royal women could wield within dynastic lordships, such as Joan signing over lands to her daughters on their marriages – there is no Welsh paragon concerning records of practice and a woman's direct involvement in, or influence over, political diplomacy, save for Senana. Further, Senana's documented activities shed light on how female agency was likely exercised with women acting as heads of familial lordships during the absence of their husbands, a stark reality a number of medieval women found themselves in, Joan, herself, included.

The case of Senana contrasts with that of Joan in three clear ways. First, she was a woman of Welsh royalty in her own right, being a descendant of the venerable twelfth-century king, Gruffudd ap Cynan. Second, she was not the reigning 'queen' of Gwynedd while active as a political diplomat, although by Welsh customary rights she should have been. This factor is relational to the third contrast with Joan. Senana can easily be identified as a 'forgotten queen'.

Joan and Senana found themselves in strong positions of formal authority in 1211 and 1241. Such authority was established through their negotiations and settlements of terms with the kings of England: from agreeing to the demands of large (and crippling) financial levies, to the surrender of important and elite hostages, including close members of their own royal families. That they were able to agree to such conditions, let alone participate in such high-end politics, appears to have had much to do with their 'queenly' status and function of the office. In Joan's position as queen, and Senana's as queen-contender, they took different avenues to achieving diplomatic and political goals in ways that neither negated nor lessened the positions of the men they to whom they were intimately connected. Their successes were closely interlinked with their ability to conform to the necessities associated with vassalage and recognising, as Welsh representatives, the distinguished status of the English kings as overlords. For both women, circumstances dictated that they negotiate the interplay between the personal and political, as wives of Venedotian rulers and, importantly, as women of royal stature.

As Joan was a member of the Angevin dynasty it is important to recognise that her natal connections may have provided her special political leverage with kings John and Henry. Further, the more European-wide policies adapted by Llywelyn the Great may have given rise to the publicised role and use of the office of the 'queen' during the thirteenth century. The extent of the 'queen's' own authority may have correlated with Gwynedd's prominence during this time. In many ways, Joan has been viewed as a controversial figure, a perception likely bolstered by all of these factors. Nevertheless, Senana had no such blood relations to the English Crown, yet she is the only known example of a woman of Welsh royalty agreeing to a political treaty, in or out of medieval Wales. As such, it seems that it was precisely within Anglo-Welsh relations that these two Venedotian 'queens' had the greatest scope to exercise official political intervention; activities perhaps supported by real expectations of royal female agency within the Venedotian court.

Chapter Nine

The Legitimate Diplomat

If 1222 was witness to political achievements and familial festivities, the year 1223 was the anthesis. It was a big year that experienced another royal invasion of Wales and Joan's subsequent involvement in quelling overall hostilities. In early 1223 for an unknown reason, Llywelyn antagonised England by carrying out an offensive on the Shropshire border, which included an attack on Kinnersley castle near Knockin and Fulk FitzWarin's caput of Whittington castle.[1] After having been allies for some time in the early thirteenth century, the relationship between Llywelyn and Fulk by this time was contentious, Fulk having abandoned Llywelyn for England after John died.

Fulk tells us that it was Joan who reconciled the two men:

> And from there Fulk and his companions went on their way towards Rhuddlan to have speech with Sir Lewis, the Prince, who had wedded Joan, the daughter of King Henry [*sic*], and sister to King John [*sic*], for the Prince and Sir Fulk and his brothers were nurtured together at the Court of King Henry. And greatly did the Prince rejoice at the coming of Sir Fulk, and he asked of him what accord there was betwixt the King and him. 'None, Sire,' said Fulk, 'for by naught can I be reconciled, and by reason of this, Sire, I am come to you and my good lady, to have your goodwill.' 'Certes,' said the Prince, 'my goodwill do I grant and give unto you, and from me shall you have good welcome. The King of England knows not how to have good understanding with you, or with me, or any other.' And Fulk made answer, 'Much do I give you thanks, Sire, for much trust have I in you and in your great loyalty. And since you have granted me to your goodwill, one thing else will I tell you. Of a truth, Sire, Moris Fitz-Roger is dead, for I have slain him.'

115

> And when the Prince learned that Moris was dead, he was
> much an angered, and he said that if he had not given unto
> him his goodwill, him would have had drawn and hanged, for
> that Moris was his cousin. Then came the good lady [Joan],
> and she made the Prince and Sir Fulk to be reconciled, so
> that they embraced each other, and all anger was put aside.[2]

English reaction to Llywelyn's Shropshire raids was fast. Justiciar Hubert de Burgh on behalf of the king, and Ranulf of Chester, on behalf of Llywelyn, met in Shrewsbury in an attempt to quell the rising conflict. However, efforts were thwarted when, with a large number of knights and foot-soldiers, William Marshal returned to Deheubarth from time in Ireland, and began reclaiming castles and lands in the south. Llywelyn sent Gruffudd to lead the attack on Marshal, but he eventually had to retreat back north due to lack of supplies. As a result, according to Welsh chronicles, Ludlow became the location for a summit that involved Henry, Llywelyn, Marshal, de Burgh and the archbishop of Canterbury.

No resolution was met at Ludlow or afterwards and it seems as if for the first time since 1212, Llywelyn fell out of favour with the Crown. In fact, the English side was remarkably cool in its dealings with Llywelyn afterwards and prepared for war. Soon after Ludlow, Marshal and de Burgh joined forces, which saw the Welsh prince lose much of his authority in south-west Wales. This decline in Venedotian power in the south then saw many local Welsh rulers join the side of the Anglo-Normans. Gruffudd was once again sent south to face Marshal, while Llywelyn himself opted to face his renegade son-in-law, Reginald de Braose, in an attack on Buellt. During the ensuing conflict, even Marared's husband, John de Braose, who was in control of Gower, was under threat of having to choose sides in order to maintain his own hold over his lordship. The loss of Welsh allies and the encroachment of Anglo-Norman power that quickly spread from the south up through mid-Wales was an alarming position for Llywelyn to find himself in and by September, a formal royal campaign against the Welsh assembled at Hereford, putting Llywelyn's Welsh authority in great peril. Consequently, a crucial meeting to discuss peace was called and was held in early October in Montgomery.

There, Llywelyn had to cede his Shropshire conquests, swearing on holy relics to indemnify the king for his English losses on the border and also agreeing to help repair Kinnersley and Whittington castles. It was at Montgomery that Llywelyn received absolution and had the excommunication previously forced on him lifted, which included the lifting of an interdict over Wales generally. It was not just Llywelyn who had to relinquish newly acquired lands. In return, Llywelyn and many other lesser Welsh princes were given back lands taken by Marshal. Nevertheless, Marshal incurred an elevation in his own authority not only being appointed the king's bailiff in the areas of Cardigan and Carmarthen, but also receiving Joan's half-sister, Eleanor, as his wife. The very same formidable Eleanor that would eventually become the wife of Simon de Montfort and the mother of Joan's niece and eventual successor, Eleanor de Montfort. The truce was later made on 4 November 1223 with Llywelyn and his political allies in attendance, along with de Burgh and the Royal Council.

This is another instance in which we do not know of Joan's whereabouts. Conceivably, her presence at Montgomery may have gone unrecorded, perhaps similar to the conjecture that she was at Oxford meeting with John in the summer of 1215. However, there are two justifications on offer as to why she was probably not with Llywelyn in 1223. First, the most observable evidence is that no English manors were bestowed upon Llywelyn at this gathering, or afterwards. This contradicts the discernible consistency in records throughout the early thirteenth century that strongly suggests Joan's career as an envoy was more elaborate than previously understood. As we will see, after 1223 she (and Llywelyn by course of action) were bestowed English manors after Joan's successful participation in political negotiations. Manors gifted before 1223 were largely connected to the Welsh couple's maritagium, implying that Joan may have been rewarded for earlier diplomatic efforts – this is especially pertinent as we know that, in the least, she consented to the alienation of some of these lands to her own children, indicating her rights to them. Second, less than a year later, records tell us that Joan was, in fact, very much involved in organising a peace conference at Shrewsbury as Llywelyn's foremost envoy to help quash the situation once and for all. In fact, records tell us that, on and off for the next six years, Joan was involved in Anglo-Welsh political affairs. It seems, therefore, that had she originally been at Montgomery on official business, in one form or another, her presence is likely to have been noted even if only in the granting of manors that could be tied to her name. Saying that, there is evidence stemming from 1225 (discussed below) which is suggestive of Joan, and indeed one of her daughters, being in Montgomeryshire in 1223.

After Montgomery, a movement was made against the rising power of justiciar Hubert de Burgh, which involved many a powerful Anglo-Norman lord, including Ranulf of Chester, Peter de Roches, the bishop of Winchester, Falkes de Breaute, Engelard of Cigogné and a number of royalists who had remained loyal to John and to the Crown during Henry's minority. Falkes de Breaute himself was one to rival de Burgh's power, though this ended in failure, with him fleeing to Wales for protection in July 1224, where he was hosted by Llywelyn, and Joan.[3] Although Llywelyn essentially chose to remain on the sidelines concerning the ousting of de Burgh, the sanctuary offered to de Breaute in 1224 was a bone of contention for the English Crown who demanded the fugitive be returned. Similarities between de Breaute's refuge at the Welsh court and that sought by the de Braose clan in 1210 may not have been far from the minds of those involved. For Llywelyn, events raised a number of unsolved grievances largely directed at Justiciar de Burgh which, on a larger scale, were connected to how the prince perceived he was being treated by his young brother-in-law and council.

Sometime around July, Llywelyn wrote to Henry claiming it was his right to receive outlaws in his own kingdom; a direct contravention of terms established at Worcester in 1218. In the words of historian J.E. Lloyd, 'His language, though not wanting in dignified courtesy towards a suzerain and near relative, bespeaks the consciousness of power; with a divided England against him, he resumes the tone of confidence and independence.'[4] Llywelyn compared his rights to harbouring the king's fugitives with the same liberties that were enjoyed by the king of Scotland who received 'outlaws from England with impunity'. Llywelyn continued to protest that he was unfairly treated by Crown and council, his rights as a leader continually ignored; so much so that he had no hope in seeing justice (in anything). The Welsh leader commented that he felt he complained so often that it was a source of shame for him to have to even recall his grievances as they were never satisfactorily addressed and the only reason he continued to do so was to follow his own conscience, rather than be condemned by it. Llywelyn ended the letter praying that God would give both the king and the Welsh prince salutary counsel concerning a number of matters; salutary counsel that was much in need.[5]

It is not by happenstance then, that two months later the 'Lady of North Wales' was granted safe passage to meet King Henry and was apparently successful in establishing the preliminaries for another Anglo-Welsh peace conference.[6] In fact, over the next two years Joan was active as a diplomat in similar ways and as this is a period that enjoyed a relatively peaceful interlude in aggressive Anglo-Welsh relations, some credit needs to be given to her for her involvement and apparent achievements. On 19 September 1224 Joan met with Henry at Worcester to lay the groundwork for an upcoming summit due to take place in Shrewsbury five days later.[7] Not only was Joan given safe-conduct to continue on to Shrewsbury, her expenses for travels to Worcester for her initial meeting with Henry were paid for by him, with orders made to the Exchequer and the sheriff of Shrewsbury, totalling £8 7s and 4d.[8] Joan's endeavours in the Autumn of 1224 were successful and five months later, in February 1225, she was greatly rewarded for her political efforts with the manor of Rothley in Leicestershire, valued annually at £25.[9]

The formal grant of Rothley was likely conveyed to Joan and Llywelyn's envoys, Masters Philip and Wrenno, who had travelled to Westminster that month. A show of good faith and relations between Gwynedd and England resided not only in Joan's attainment of Rothley, but that Philip and Wrenno's journey home was paid by the king, a total of 2 marks. More importantly, on their visit to Westminster that month, Philip and Wrenno secured a curious royal writ that may provide evidence of Joan's likely whereabouts in 1223 and also a small, but additional glimpse of her elusive daughter Susanna. The writ was in favour of the widow of a man named Robert ap Madog. Robert was Welshman who had fought on Llywelyn's side in 1223. A tenant of the honour of Montgomery, his wife apparently nursed one of Joan and Llywelyn's daughters.[10]

This daughter must have been the one and only Susanna who appears just once in records by name, dated 1228, and of whom nothing is really known. Though, there is supposition that she was perhaps the unnamed, and therefore unidentified, daughter of Llywelyn who appears in Scottish records in the 1240s who married Malcolm II, the earl of Fife.[11] It is entirely unclear whether being nursed meant that widow Madog took care of Susanna as a young child on a regular basis during visits to the March or that she nursed her through an illness around 1223. If this were the latter, it indicates that Joan would have been most likely in attendance at Montgomery that fall.

In April 1225 a date was proposed for another peace talk, but this ended up being postponed.[12] In fact, four more times over the course of the next year, dates for further peace negotiations were delayed, occurring in July, August and November, and in March 1226. Nevertheless, relations remained on good terms; in the summer of 1225 Joan and Llywelyn gave Henry a number of birds of prey, including goshawks, falcons and sparrow hawks. Fitting gifts, indeed, from the lady and lord who ruled Snowdon, or Eryri, the 'home of the eagle'.[13] However, a much more significant gift was given to Joan in 1226, and by extension her family, in the guise of Henry's support to her achieving legitimate status. It is likely that her prominent diplomatic role and successes between 1224 and 1226, combined with a fraternal bond she may have had with Henry, directly influenced her request to be legitimised at precisely this time.

Evidence shows that Henry and Joan may have enjoyed a rather close relationship as brother and sister, Joan seemingly held in high regard by her younger brother who bestowed many gifts upon her during her lifetime.[14] The way Joan is identified in sources throughout Henry's reign intimates a close familial bond. Although Joan's formal title before 1230 was 'Lady of North Wales', and is used in records in close association with Llywelyn's own designation 'Prince of North Wales' – between 1224 and 1226 in particular – her lifecycle as Henry's sister is used as her primary identifier, before her status and position as Llywelyn's wife. For example, a 1224 record refers to her as *Johanna Domina de Northwallia sorore Regis ac nuper uxor Lewlini Principis Northwall* – 'Johanna, Lady of North Wales, sister of the King and (formerly) wife of Llywelyn, Prince of North Wales'[15] – while in 1226 specifically, she is identified in records as Llywelyn's wife, the king's sister, *uxore ejus sorore Regis; uxorem suam sororem nostrum*. Interestingly enough, during this timeframe, the family bonds between the king of England and his sister's family are were also stressed in documents, Llywelyn being referred to as 'Prince of North Wales, brother of the King' (*Lewlino Principe Northwall' fratre Reg'; dilectum fratrem Lewlinum principem Norwalliae*) and Dafydd as 'the King's nephew' (*filijs suis nepotibus Regis; filium suum nepotem nostrum*).[16] Pointedly, although Joan's royal status was recognised, the employment of her lifecycles in records during this time stress the personal relationships between the English king and the Welsh royals. Joan being at the epicentre of both personal and political relations. It was on the back of this period of closeness between Joan and Henry that, sometime between March and 29 April, she took measures to be legitimised and filed a petition to Pope Honorious in order to receive papal dispensation and recognition of her legitimate status.[17]

For Joan, her newly legitimised status indemnified her rights and equal standing as a Plantagenet, as a daughter and sister of the kings of England. Even though the dispensation oddly does not identify Joan's mother for whatever reason – whether she was low-born and her name truly unknown, or high-born and her identity protected – the fact that legitimisation was given meant that her mother's standing was also legally recognised. Whether she knew her mother or not, religious and royal recognition that her mother was not unimportant in the annals of Joan's own history must have been an emotionally satisfying achievement.

In the context of the function of queenship in Wales, did Joan's legitimisation further transform her queenly status among her Welsh peers and subjects, or further elevate her royal office? This is one of the many questions regarding the life of Joan of England that is fundamental to understanding her life and career, and yet one of the many that have to remain unanswered. Regardless of how momentous the act probably was for her on an intimate level, it is nigh on impossible to determine just how far any changes in perceptions or attitudes towards Joan actually occurred. By nature, however, legitimacy did further enhance her status within her peer-group – arguably, in theory, it may have also enhanced attitudes towards her political career and heightened the clout she carried.

Naturally, the agreement in 1211 that emphasised legitimate succession in Gwynedd by a child from a legal marital union worked to emphasise Joan's overall role and responsibility to become a mother of a legitimate heir. Clearly, her own legitimisation met this new, cultural responsibility of the royal office of the Welsh queen. Who is to say, however, what her role would have been if she had become a widow, or remained heirless, or if Gwynedd had, in fact, escheated to the Crown at some point. Would another woman in her position have retained such an important status had she not been associated by blood to the Angevin dynasty?

The fact that Joan's royal 'authority' was legitimised meant that, in turn, that of her own family was as well. Besides Llywelyn and Dafydd, her daughters and their families, too, would have benefited. In fact, the dispensation states that her 'defect of birth' should not detract from the honour of either her husband or her son.[18] Ultimately, the most driving force behind her petition is that her legitimisation would explicitly shut down any remaining legal – and social – rejoinders concerning Dafydd's patrimony and standing as the rightful heir to the kingdom of Gwynedd. Joan's legitimisation essentially solidified the terms laid out in the treaty that was made between Gwynedd and England fifteen years earlier. It is certainly not unrelated that Llywelyn's own governmental achievements reached yet another climax with the king agreeing that Dafydd should receive fealty from the Welsh princes, or that three years later Dafydd finally and officially paid homage to Henry III at Westminster, accompanied by his mother only, as Llywelyn's chosen successor.

Although Joan's petition for legitimisation was a move that was willingly endorsed by Henry as a symbol of royal friendship, familial bonds and support, we need to ask if it was purely out of brotherly love. As close as sister and brother appear to have been, the political magnitude behind Henry's support of Joan's request for legitimisation had to have been a determining factor. Originally, Joan's illegitimate status was used to by her father to demonstrate his power and benefit his political agenda. By offering Llywelyn a marriage to his bastard daughter, the king of England let the prince of Gwynedd know his 'rightful' place by making it clear Llywelyn's authority was not of an equal standing to his as ruler of England; Joan's illegitimate status was most certainly used surreptitiously to confirm Llywelyn's status as an English vassal. On the surface, through Joan's legitimacy, Dafydd also officially became a member of the English royal family, and in theory, a direct blood-relative would be easier to reign in and create firmer alliances with. This would have been an egregiously erroneous belief on Henry's part as Dafydd as prince of Wales would later prove, but a pragmatic one to begin with.

Most crucial, however, is this. When Joan received her legitimacy, it was specifically without prejudice, or recourse, to the Crown, meaning that neither Joan nor her children could lay claim to the throne of England. It is hardly surprising, therefore, that Henry, who was a year away from coming of age and claiming the full and complete power of his kingly authority, supported Joan's petition. Knowing full well her legitimacy was conditional to this provision offered Henry and his successors security. Regardless of any future conflict with the Venedotian house, threats to England could not include any direct challenge to the English seat of power.

It was at the end of August 1226 when the postponed peace talks finally occurred. Safe-conduct had been given as early as 28 July, but it was not until Thursday, 27 August, when another general safe-conduct was issued, that Joan and her family met Henry, who had been travelling the Welsh border, at Shrewsbury.[19] The Welsh family may have stayed for at least two nights as Henry departed Shrewbury that Saturday, but not before giving Joan yet another manor, that of Condover, five miles south of Shrewsbury.[20] This was another mark of favour and recognition of Joan's political undertakings.

The manor of Condover provides the clearest evidence available that Joan may have directly in charge of the management and administration of the manors that were given to her. Being so close to Shrewsbury perhaps enticed her to travel to Condover to take inventory of her new possession after it was gifted to her. In fact, in August 1226 after receiving rights to assess the state of her manorial holding Joan instructed that corn be sown and livestock and chattels transported. Seven months later, in March, Henry reclaimed both Condover and Rothley as a consequence of hostilities that resumed between Llywelyn and Hubert de Burgh not long after the Shrewsbury conference.[21] As it transpires, Condover and Rothley were confiscated and returned on a number of occasions between 1225 and 1228. Although Joan temporarily lost her ownership over Condover on various occasions, Henry ensured that he honoured her previous administrative orders by sanctioning the removal of her livestock and chattels, warranting the sowing of corn and guaranteeing that these remained in her possession.[22] A year later, in 1227, Joan was excused by her brother from paying tallage tax on Condover and Rothley, with the king even going so far as to make the recommendation to her tenants that they reimburse Joan directly with some form of reasonable aid.[23] No doubt Joan may have had much experience under her belt when it came to running the manors in her custody given she was a woman of standing and it is only right to assume that she may have dealt with her other manors in similar ways. As pertains to the significance of the manors gifted to her by the kings of England, it is perhaps no fluke that the majority of manors in her possession surrounded the important English stronghold of Shrewsbury in the middle of the Welsh March.

Chapter Ten

Hostage and Homage

The relative peace that had heralded the previous three years was soon to draw to a close. In Wales, 1227 was the year that saw Gruffudd finally imprisoned by his father for a six-year duration, leaving Senana alone to manage what was left of their family lordship and raise their children, not least of whom was Llywelyn ap Gruffudd. In England, Henry finally declared himself of age in January 1227 and embraced the full powers of his kingship. The transition of Henry's reign from minority to fully fledged monarchy did little to quell the controversial powers of his justiciar Hubert de Burgh and objectives put into play at this time helped to increase them if nothing else. Both the mounting conflict in 1228 and the subsequent full-scale hostilities in 1231–32 between Llywelyn and de Burgh arguably led to some of Joan's most considerable political contributions.

For an unknown reason, in March 1228, while at Reading, Henry ordered that Rothley and Condover be confiscated by the Crown. The sheriffs of both Leicestershire and Shropshire were commanded to take the manors with all their appurtenances, which had been committed to Joan, into the king's hand and look after them until instructed otherwise by Henry.[1] Doubtless, confiscation of Joan's manors was related to a simmering conflict centred around Llywelyn's dependability as the Crown's political adherent and the increased discord between the prince of Gwynedd and the rising powers of the English justiciar. Exactly a month later, on 27 April, de Burgh received a grant from Henry for the lordship of Montgomery and was allowed to make improvements to the castle. This latter act by the king stoked discontent with Llywelyn who viewed his authority as being challenged. The distrust of the Crown, itself, regarding Llywelyn's own loyalty further complicated matters.

War broke out once again, and records indicate that the conflict during 1228, traditionally known as the Ceri campaign,[2] was indeed Joan's busiest in terms of her political career. Although Llywelyn had not met with the king or de Burgh since 1226, Joan may herself have worked behind the scenes at supressing the escalating situation in the spring of 1228, for it was not three weeks after de Burgh's grant of Montgomery that Henry issued the mandate for her cattle and chattels to be removed from Condover without impediment, even though her ownership of the manor had been rescinded. Was this an act of recognition for her earlier efforts? Most likely, it was. It may have even been decided at this time that another conference would be pursued sooner rather than later in an attempt to keep the situation from reaching boiling point. By the time Henry, while at Hereford, provided the promise of safe-conduct to Joan for her travels to Shrewsbury for further parley in August, the situation was beginning to reach a head.

Henry had been under the impression that Llywelyn, too, might attend and issued a command to dominant Marcher lords like William Marshal, Ralph Mortimer of Wigmore and Walter Clifford of Heredfordshire, that he was not to be molested during his journey.[3] A new Marcher lord, who had inherited his family domains only a month before, was also sent the mandate. In June, Reginald de Braose died leaving William, his first-born son by his first wife, Grecia Briwere – and Gwladus' stepson, although a few years older than her – as his heir. Thrust into the limelight as the head of the de Braose Welsh caput of Buellt, William was hardly allowed any luxury to ease into his new responsibilities and quickly became one of the main players in events between 1228–29. In 1230, it was Joan's connection to de Braose that landed her in prison and ended in his own miserable demise.

Llywelyn, however, deigned not to grace Henry with his presence at Shrewsbury in August, entrusting Joan, instead, to take care of matters on her own. That it was Joan in attendance with her own officials, over other Welsh magnates or court envoys, with the sole purpose of mitigating the situation with the king of England underscores the trust and confidence both sides shared in her consular abilities. Attending as Llywelyn's political diplomat was the role befitting many a medieval queen and one Joan seemingly was efficacious at. As the sole the arbitrator for the Welsh cause, it seems she may have negotiated a successful, albeit short-term, armistice.

Proof of this is the relatively cordial exchange of correspondence undertaken between Henry and Llywelyn in early September after some

125

of Llywelyn's men assaulted merchants taking supplies to the king. The prince of North Wales claimed that he would have sent an envoy to the king regarding the matter of assault if he had thought that the king's counsellors had been with him. Accepting Llywelyn's apology, Henry stated that he did so in spite of wishing that Llywelyn's subsequent actions had been consistent with his overtures of regret. The king denied Llywelyn's claim that he did not have an adequate number of counsellors with him on the occasion mentioned and essentially charged that Llywelyn's excuse of not sending envoys to discuss the matter was entirely unacceptable.

As king, he would have ensured that he honour the truce and the demands made to uphold his side of the bargain. Henry specified that the reason he did not exercise his rights of jurisdiction regarding the matter was down to the truce he had agreed with Joan. Essentially, it seems it was Henry's relationship with Joan that may have kept Llywelyn in royal graces. This the king was not shy to remind his sister's husband of, making it known that if peace and love were breached between them, it would only be down to Llywelyn's own doing; in other words, on the account if further injuries were committed by the prince. The king was very clear in his warning of what would happen if Llywelyn fell out of his brotherly favour.

Llywelyn was to meet with Henry at Shrewsbury on 10 September, a matter of days after he sent his letter of apology to the king. However, in spite of the truce arranged by Joan the previous month, preparations for a royal campaign into Wales, staged from Montgomery, were already under way. The Welsh had attacked the garrison at Montgomery not two weeks after Joan met with Henry in August, and Llywelyn's provocation of the king's merchants was the coup de grâce. Henry made it clear to Llywelyn that negotiation was no longer a viable course of action. Clearly in anger, on 21 September Henry ordered the sheriff of Staffordshire and Shropshire to 'take into the king's hand, without delay, that autumn's harvest at Condover – corn caused to be sown by Joan, wife of Llywelyn, prince of North Wales, who only held Condover by bail of the king for as long as it pleased him.' However, there was some conciliation on Henry's part concerning the impact it would have on Joan as he reminded the sheriff of his command that regardless of the confiscation, it should be remembered that he had also commanded the corn be demised to her 'in peace'.[4]

Four days later on 21 September, war, which lasted only three weeks, started. The campaign was a disaster for the English king. The Welsh terrain and the fervour of the Welsh countrymen and women themselves, proved once again to be formidable adversaries. The size of the English army meant it was difficult to provide sufficient food and other provisions, never mind the reluctance of many to fight a war that seemed to be of only real benefit the justiciar. The biggest, and arguably most humiliating moment of the campaign was the wounding and capture of William de Braose, lord of Abergavenny and Buellt, by the Welsh. William spent months as Llywelyn's prisoner and was only released after a large ransom was met.[5]

Although *Brut y Tywysogion* claims that the Henry's royal advance into Wales in 1228 was 'to subdue the Lord Llywelyn and all the Welsh',[6] analogous with the threat and intention of John's campaigns in 1211 and 1212 according to chroniclers, the royal retreat in October effectively demonstrated that Llywelyn had little to be worried about when it came to facing the English Crown. During the Ceri campaign, the prince of Gwynedd was presented with opportunities to better establish or extend his authority in ways that mirrored those during the baron's rebellions so many years previously. And, they were opportunities that Llywelyn readily seized.

On 24 November, a curious record in the Patent Rolls is found. As faithful servants of the king, Clemence and Nicholas Verdun were ordered to receive, safely and securely, the custody of Susanna, Joan and Llywelyn's daughter. This elusive daughter was likely handed over to the Verduns as a diplomatic hostage of the Crown. When it was agreed that Joan's daughter would be handed over to the Verduns is uncertain. It may have been during Joan's ambassadorial mission in August, but this seems a stiff penalty to agree to at a time when war had yet to break out. By nature of peace and war, it is more likely that it was during negotiations for a truce after the Ceri campaign that it was agreed Susanna would act as an honourable internee to her uncle, in the guise of fosterage. On 8 November, Rothley and Condover were restored to Joan as an overture of peace and perhaps, more notably, as a rejoinder to the conditions agreed to concerning Susanna's essential transference into the king's custody.[7] Simply because details are non-existent does not mean that in October and November 1228 Joan did not parley behind the scenes as she was so wont to do on many occasions. Out of all the important and active

Welsh counsellors to have had the authority to not just agree to such a condition, but to even offer it as a term in the first instance, if indeed the suggestion came from the Welsh side, it would have been Joan.

The Patent Rolls indicate that, indeed, the suggestion to have Susanna 'fostered' (*ad nutriendam*) with the Verduns was one that came from Joan and Llywelyn and it was a grant that Henry agreed to out of good will for his 'faithful vassals', the prince of North Wales and his wife. Susanna was to be kept safely and securely in the Verdun 'possession', without deceit or ill or suspicious intent (*sine omni dampno et occasione suscipiatis*). Reference to potential deceit or ill-intent strongly intimates the political nature behind Susanna's guardianship.

Neither Joan, nor Llywelyn, would have consented to one of their children being a royal hostage, especially not one so young (she was probably under the marriageable age of 12), if explicit guarantees for the child's safety had not been in place. Why the Verduns? The most obvious answer is that Clemence was Susanna's grandmother, Joan's own mother – the most resolute assurance of safety and protection that could be offered. Is it merely a coincidence that Nicholas de Verdun had also been summoned to Montgomery 1228? Was it only to provide the king warfare support? Or were initial talks undertaken in which Susanna's immediate future was discussed? The inclusive importance of family connections in the 1228 Patent Rolls is readily apparent, Joan being referred to as Henry's beloved sister (*dilecta soror nostra*), Susanna his niece (*neptem nostrum*) and even Llywelyn being referred to as the beloved brother (*dilectus frater*). This in itself suggests the overall intimate familial context under which the transfer was agreed to. As a hostage, taking up residence with her grandmother would have been the ultimate guarantee of Susanna's safety. Furthermore, it would have offered assurances that she receive the education expected for a girl of Susanna's status.

Six months later, Dafydd received safe-conduct from the king to travel to Westminster to pay him homage. Dafydd, however, was not to travel alone to England as his older, and recently widowed, sister Gwladus also received safe-conduct for a journey to the king's court.[8] In July the abbot of the Cistercian abbey of Vaundey in Lincolnshire was employed by the king and sent to negotiate the steps that needed to be taken for Dafydd to be formally recognised as Llywelyn's successor.[9] It was probably during this meeting that the details for Susanna's transference to the Verduns for 'safekeeping' were worked out and agreed to as a little less than two months later, on 5 September, Henry once more proffered safe-conduct for Dafydd to journey to England to bend the knee. The grant included safe-conduct for an unnamed sister to accompany him. This unnamed sister must have been Susanna, who was to formally make her way to England as a hostage.[10] Joan chaperoned her two young children to London to meet the king at Westminster and the family likely set off immediately after safe-conduct was received.

It was clear that by Michaelmas 1229 England was concerned about the level of Llywelyn's authority, which had been bolstered by his feats during the Ceri campaign. The Crown appeared eager to continue relations on the most cordial terms possible and this outreach manifested on 13 October when Dafydd appeared before Henry at the great hall of Westminster. The young Welsh prince, the king's nephew, publicly and performed homage to the Crown, 'for all the lands and right that would accrue to him on the death of his father'.[11] In return, Joan's son was formally recognised as Llywelyn's legal successor. He also received an annuity of royal lands in England that valued £40 per annum, with promises of more.[12]

Joan and Dafydd must have stayed in London for a month, time well spent developing the fledgling Welsh prince's understanding of English governance. More to the point, however, their month-long sojourn was likely tied to spending time with Susanna before her resettlement with the Verduns. On 8 November her custody was transferred to Stephen Segrave, who by this time was high sheriff of Bedfordshire, Buckinghamshire, Warwickshire, Leicestershire and Northamptonshire,[13] and who presumably oversaw her safe arrival with the Verduns.

Dafydd's payment of homage in London was a momentous occasion, not least for Joan herself. As a mother, she both witnessed the promised security of her son's future as a leader of Wales and probably spent precious time with her youngest daughter who was soon to begin a life elsewhere. More significantly, however, in political terms, October 1229 marked an unprecedented display of Joan's own status and authority as a reigning queen.

By the close of the 1220s, Joan had become Llywelyn's pre-eminent Welsh envoy and one who seems to have exercised the most influence between the two courts. The fact that she was both predominantly active and effective after two failed royal invasions of Wales in 1223 and 1228 is testament to the level of her own political and royal authority, regardless of her personal connections. Her diplomatic efforts were recognised and rewarded by Henry as king of England, even more so than by her father. The level of respect that Joan commanded is palpable.

Of course her legitimacy in 1226 confirmed her blood-ties to the Plantagenet family, which helped strengthen the status and authority of the Venedotian house, placing it above all others when it came to Welsh connections to the English Crown. However, Joan's attendance in London in October 1229 arguably marks a pinnacle of Welsh queenship in so many ways. It is clear that she attended Dafydd's homage, not simply as a mother, or on behalf of Llywelyn as his wife or because she was the king's sister; because she attended the ceremony on her own, her role as Llywelyn's chief ambassador would have been distinguished, indeed. It can hardly be questioned that in context, it was in her status as a queen that she officially stood as witness to the political tribute that was paid by the heir of the premiere Welsh leader in his absence.

Chapter Eleven

Interlude

'into the good graces of the queen'

Hot on the heels of Joan's attendance at Westminster to witness Dafydd's performance of homage to her brother the king, an additional gift that allowed her to spend time with her daughter Gwladus, who was also there, the spring of 1230 began with great promise and ended in enormous tragedy. The personal, political and public problems Joan and Llywelyn faced in April and May were essentially a power struggle on every front between the Venedotian prince and the most powerful Marcher family, the de Braoses. In 1229/30, marital negotiations concerning the future heiress of the de Braose fortunes, Isabella (r. 1240–1246) and Dafydd as Llywelyn's successor began to take shape. Although by far more significant, the marriage between Dafydd and Isabella was to be the third such alliance between the de Braose clan and Joan and Llywelyn's own children. As an important family that helped define the histories of England and Wales following the Norman Conquest of 1066, and who proffered from their close connection to the Angevins in the late-twelfth and early-thirteenth centuries, it was necessary for the prince of Gwynedd to cultivate a functioning and mutually beneficial relationship that, in theory, he could use to his advantage when needed. Tragically, what started off as a likely celebration of an alliance that had the potential to transform the power structure in Wales for a generation or more, ended in disappointment, detainment and death.

Originating from Briouze in Normandy, the de Braoses were staunch supporters of William the Bastard's (r. 1066–1087) conquest of England in 1066 and, as a result, became one of the first families to settle in the newly taken lands once ruled by the mighty Anglo-Saxons. William de Braose I received rewards for backing the Conquest and gained possession of a number of lands and chattels spread across Britain, from

131

Berkshire, Dorsetshire and Hampshire, to Sussex, Surrey and Wiltshire. Their main lordship-holding was initially based in Sussex, at Bramber Castle. Over the course of the next almost 150 years the family's might and power as significant landholders seemed to grow exponentially. William's son Philip I was the first to infiltrate Wales in the early to mid-twelfth century and gain recognition for the family as prominent Marcher lords, having appropriated the lands of Aberhonddu (Brecon) and Buellt, bordering England and extending into the very heart of mid-Wales. Philip's own son, William III, married Bertha FitzWalter, an heiress in her own right who brought to her marriage the significant Welsh lordships of Brycheiniog and Y Fenni (Abergavenny).

Large expanses of southern Wales and the March became the family's primary annexations, which eventually included the lordship of Gower (Gŵyr) in south-west Wales, granted to the family by King John in 1203. Over a relatively short amount of time, the de Braoses enjoyed such an ascendency that their status was largely unparalleled among their peers. It was a status that reached both its pinnacle and ruin during the early-thirteenth century under the headship of William IV, the son of William III and Bertha FitzWalter.

As the fourth feudal baron of Bramber, William was a considerable court favourite and one of King John's closest allies well before he became king. William was resolute in his support to John's claim to the throne and during his ascendency became lord to numerous Welsh territories – most of mid- and south Wales that bordered England. His landed power was hardly limited to Wales as William was also made lord of Limerick in Ireland.[1] Under William IV's lordship, the de Braose clan became, by far, the most notorious of the Marcher lords as his penchant for vengeful tactics and rule was detested by the Welsh and little embraced by his own Anglo-Norman peers.

William's most infamous and dishonourable act occurred during Christmas in 1175 in what is known as the Abergavenny Massacre when he invited a number prominent southern Welsh chieftains and three princes to his castle of Abergavenny under the pretext of establishing peace. Having the Welsh settled in the great hall and ensuring they were satiated after an impressive Christmas feast, William ordered the doors locked and his guests, who had turned over their arms upon entering in the premise in name of peace, slaughtered. Seisyll ap Dyfnwal, lord of Upper Gwent and brother-in-law to the renowned prince of

Deheubarth, Lord Rhys, was William's greatest adversary and both he and his eldest son, who are believed to have been the primary targets, were among the murdered. But William did not stop there. Leading his men on horseback to Seisyll's stronghold of Castell Arnllt (Castle Arnold), he hunted down the slain prince's youngest son who was only 7 years old and took Seisyll's wife, Gwladus in captivity. The fate she suffered is entirely unknown as she disappears from all records after her kidnapping. The unfortunate lot of the majority of women throughout history.

The presumed pretext to the carnage was that William's uncle, Henry de Hereford (FitzMiles), had been murdered and Seisyll ap Dyfnwal stood as the primary suspect in William's eyes, though proof was slight. Family revenge, however, was far from William's main purpose for directing such a heinous act. It is likely that the underlining intent was to destabilise the vast area of southern Wales, and essentially Welsh leadership, where Anglo-Norman lords, and namely the de Braoses, had not only invested interests, but a strong foothold on the region. Consequences of the aftermath were long-reaching, indeed, as the calamity nourished a festering wound of endless revenge and counter-revenge, discontent, mistrust and hatred between the Welsh and Anglo-Normans for successive generations. Yet even after the genocide of their brethren the Welsh were still unable to unite and cast the foreign invaders out.

Thirty years later, William, the 'Ogre of Abergavenny', and his wife Matilda St Valéry, the famous Lady of Hay, played a large and scandalous role concerning the disappearance of King John's nephew and rival contender for the English throne. To this day, many continue to believe that the king's young nephew, Arthur – the son of John's older and deceased brother Geoffrey, duke of Brittany and his formidable wife Constance, the duchess of Brittany – who mysteriously disappeared in April 1203 met the same fate as the Welsh princes in 1175 while under William's guardianship. It was Matilda's public utterances in 1210, accusing the king of murder at a time when the de Braose were slowly falling out of favour, that led to King John's infamous chase, or rather hunt, of the family across Britain and the subsequent deaths of Matilda, William (in French exile) and their son, William.

Known by the Welsh as Gwilym Ddu, or Black William, Reginald de Braose's heir by his first wife, Grecia de Briwere, was born in the late twelfth, early thirteenth century. Though perhaps seemingly too young in age, William VI may have held a knight's fee in Egerton, Kent, as early as 1210. Certainly, he was of age by August 1218 when his father passed the de Braose family lands in Sussex over to him, including the important stronghold of Bamber. William married Eva Marshal, a daughter of the celebrated William Marshal, earl of Pembroke and Isabel de Clare sometime before 1222. The eldest of their children, Isabella, Joan's future daughter-in-law, was born soon after. Less than ten years later, in 1227, William VI succeeded the de Braose lordships in Wales and on the March. A month after his father died in June 1228, William paid homage to King Henry for his inheritance. Although at least seven years her junior, though probably significantly more, it was this Black William whose acquaintance with Joan ended in betrayal and death.

It was during the Ceri campaign in 1228, in which Llywelyn came head-to-head with Hubert de Burgh, that the new de Braose lord was captured by the leading Welsh prince and subsequently became acquainted with Joan:

> king Henrie came with a great armie to Wales as farre as Ceri, and incamped there, and vpon the other side prince Lhewelyn called him all the power of Wales, and incamped no farre off, and there were diuerse great skirmishes, and chieflie vpon one daie the most part of both armies was in the field, and a great number slaine of the kings men. At which time William de Bruse sonne to Reynald was taken prisoner, who offered for his ransome the countrie of Buelht, and a great summe of monie beside: then there was a peace concluded betweene the king and the Prince, wherevpon the Prince came to the king, and did honor him, but not as his king and lord, and euerie partie returned home.[2]

As Llywelyn's biggest rival in terms of landed power and authority within Wales itself, William's seizure was a pièce d'résistance for the Venedotian leader. His importance as a prisoner was symbolised in the heavy ransom that Llywelyn demanded for his release – an astonishing sum of £2,000, which in today's money is close to £1.5 million. It was a sum that would have had the purchasing power of over 2,500 horses, 5,500 cows, 15,000 stones-worth of wool, 12,500 quarters of wheat and

200,000 days' worth of wages for skilled tradesmen.[3] It was an amount that was particularly useful to Llywelyn as it allowed him to continue his war against Hubert de Burgh and his ongoing role as a powerful combatant to the English Crown. Indeed, £2,000 was the exact sum Llywelyn had agreed to pay Henry in October in return for the Crown's acquiescence to destroy de Burgh's half-built castle at Ceri.

As monetarily debilitating as the exchange for William's freedom was, it was not the definitive crushing blow that diminished the Marcher lord's power. Llywelyn demanded that he agree never to take up arms against the Welsh leader again and made it clear that William would only be released once he agreed to a proposed marital alliance between Dafydd and Isabella. It was hardly the alliance that was so enervating to William, whose feudal status to Llywelyn was to be made clear upon the marriage. It was the fact that the prince of Gwynedd demanded the principal lordship and castle of Buellt as Isabella's marriage portion. Essentially located in the centre of Wales, the *cantref* of Buellt promised Llywelyn solid control over huge swathes of Wales, including areas that were strongly divided between the more Anglo-Norman controlled south and the native-run north. Losing control over Buellt meant a demotion in authority for William and a significant decrease in the de Braose legacy. Surprisingly, or perhaps not as the case may be, the prince was successful in his negotiations and after garnering de Braose's assent to the marriage, let the Marcher lord go on 12 February 1229.

One wonders why William would have acquiesced to Llywelyn's demanding terms, especially to the loss of Buellt. Could part of the reason perhaps be that Joan and William had become close – too close – during his confinement, and that the lord of Bramber was, rightly, concerned about the consequences if the truth were revealed? In many ways, William's own notoriety equals that of his grandfather's, the 'Ogre of Abergavenny', though for entirely different reasons. The sixteenth-century historian David Powell relates that William was brought to Llywelyn and Joan's court and there enjoyed 'an honourable confinement'. Honour soon disappeared as he 'had not continued there very long, when he began to be suspected of being too familiar with the princess, King Henry's sister'.[4] The nineteenth-century antiquarian T.J. Llewelyn Prichard, and anti-Joan crusader, goes further:

> The Welsh prince treated him less like a captive than as an
> honoured guest. He ate at his table in company with the

> sovereign and his queen, and passed his hours pleasantly, in social intercourse, without the least appearance of restraint ... but the baseness of this man soon became hideously apparent by the unworthy returns which he made for this generous confidence and princely treatment. However, his ingratitude was not of a darker dye than might have been expected, had the character of the perfidious prisoner been sooner known ... it follows that this captive was the grandson of the infamous man-slaughterer of Abergavenny castle ... and quite worthy of the line from which he descended ... this Baron, though less celebrated for blood-shedding propensities, was, like his grandsire, one of the most unprincipled of men.[5]

William had remained in captivity for months and there may have been much speculation that it was during this time that he and Joan became better acquainted.

According to tradition, the supposedly amorous couple sought solitude together 'in a deep glen, adjoining the grounds, belonging to the palace of Aber', at some point during William's captivity. While in apparent throes of passion – or in the longwinded and pedantic words of Pritchard while they were 'under circumstances too decisive to admit of the least incertitude respecting their guilt' – they were observed by a court officer. The officer's apparent determination to keep the secret, his steadfast silence on the matter, seems to have been driven by what can only be perceived as devotion to both Joan and Llywelyn as he was reluctant to slander 'the character of the queen'. Rumours seem to have swirled around the *llys* about the clandestine liaison and upon William's release from prison, Llywelyn was apparently informed of the intrigue between his wife and former prisoner, information that covered 'all the particulars of his dishonour'.

The provocateur is named as none other than Hubert de Burgh, who ostensibly heard of the affair first-hand from William. Obviously, de Burgh had incentive to sow incredible discord and distrust between the Welsh prince and Marcher lord and Llywelyn surely would have had cause for serious doubt about the veracity of such alarming claims, especially if they came from the justiciar. Nevertheless, if Llywelyn's suspicions were raised, they were quickly confirmed when the officer who witnessed Joan and William in the glen was finally exposed 'as the original master of the secret' and Llywelyn approached him, asking for his testimony. The officer's response was to 'relate all he knew when authoritatively so required':

> It appears that during the light of pleasant captivity of William de Breos, according to the heartless profligacy of his character, forgetting all ties of honour, gratitude or friendship towards his confiding host, as Llewelyn may truly be considered, rather than the rigid master of his fate, he insinuated himself into the good graces of the queen; and ultimately was admitted into criminal familiarities with her.

Llywelyn's reaction was that of a greatly aggrieved husband who was,

> Exasperated to frenzy on fully ascertaining the infidelity of his wife, whom he had so fondly loved and tenderly indulged for the twenty-seven years that she had been his queen, to the very summit of her expressed desires, he determined to be most signally revenged on her atrocious gallant.[6]

As such, the prince devised a plan to punish his uxorious adversary by inviting William to return to Aber to partake in Easter festivities in 1230. Once the lord was fed and satiated (a lure into false comfort and security comparable to the 4th Lord of Bramber's own exploits that fateful Christmas at Abergavenny in 1175) Llywelyn pounced. Accusing him of the crime of adultery and excoriating de Braose in the great hall in front of the prince's own adherents, Llywelyn commanded that the Marcher lord 'be ignonimosously [*sic*] dragged out of his presence, and hanged upon a tree of conspicuous appearance, situate on a rising ground within the immediate precincts of the palace.'

Further according to folklore, William was mightily aware of the dark energy hanging over the court like a toxic miasma during what should have been a joyous occasion. Joan's apparent absence as hostess from the table she was so accustomed to gracing 'doubtless surprised' the amorous visitor and the ominous silence during the meal itself was one 'befitting a feast of vengeance, the prolonged continuance of which was calculated both to astonish and alarm the guilty guest.' It was a situation William would not, and could not, have escaped from, even if his survival instincts had kicked in as the prince's orders for death were,

> readily obeyed; for there was no friend at hand to intercede for a mitigation of his punishment: and vengeance on the villainous foreigner who had dishonoured their prince and nation and abused the sacred attributes of friendship and hospitality, was the general feeling of that assemblage of Welshmen. Foredoomed as he was, the business of his execution was brief enough and soon over; when a wild, savage shout from the surrounding guests, vassals, and intimates of Aber, rent the air nd [*sic*] announced that the enemy of their sovereign, the high and haughty William de Braose was no more to be numbered among existing mortals.

Such quixotic accounts written hundreds of years after the actual events are certainly entertaining. Though undoubtedly embellished upon, they should not be written off entirely as regards their legitimacy. Indeed local, oral tradition has a way of preserving threads of history otherwise lost. The Welsh Triads, for instance, are a perfect medieval example in and of themselves; preserving traditions and some historical truths. Contemporary sources are hardly as informative, or dramatically engaging, but collectively they do insinuate that the subsequent and unforeseen events that took place during the Easter festivities which ushered in the spring of 1230 stunned Wales and the March. This scandal was tragedy of epic proportions, one that escalated from the personal to political with potentially dire consequences.

Whether Llywelyn knew of an affair between Joan and William before April 1230 is unknown, but it seems incongruous to what we know of his character to destroy de Braose with such an odious plot of entrapment.[7] It is more probable that William returned to Aber to finalise the marriage arrangements for Isabella and Dafydd and perhaps contend with other issues of grievance between the two families, as Gwladus Ddu had brought a suit against William in March concerning her manorial rights in Surrey as Reginald's widow. At any rate, it was sometime during his visit that his relationship with Joan was publicly exposed. The monks of Ystrad Fflur (Strata Florida in Cardiganshire) recorded the event in simple, yet ominous terms in *Brut y Tywysogion*:

> In this year, William de Breos the Younger, lord of
> Brycheiniog, was hanged by the Lord Llywelyn in Gwynedd,
> after he had been caught in Llywelyn's chamber with the
> king of England's daughter, Llywelyn's wife.[8]

This is the only full and complete record we have from contemporary Welsh chronicles. A number of English annals are modest in their approach to the incident, mostly stating that Llywelyn captured and killed, or hanged, William. Still, the fact that the incident is recorded at all highlights how momentous the occasion was.

The only known detailed account is provided by Nicholas, abbot of Vaundey who wrote to Ralph Neville, the bishop of Chichester who also happened to be England's lord chancellor, some two weeks after the event:

> On 2nd of May, at a certain manor called 'Crokein', he
> [William] was made 'Crogyn', i.e. hanged on a tree, and this
> not privily or in the night time, but openly and in the broad
> daylight, in the presence of more than 800 men assembled
> to behold the piteous and melancholy spectacle.[9]

Llywelyn's seemingly impulsive reaction to the supposed affair that sealed de Braose's fate was, in many ways, inevitably influenced by his personal feelings and pride. As a husband of twenty-five years and the father of at least five children by Joan, the prince's confidence must have been rocked, as was his faith in her as his wife – her loyalty and her love – never mind his faith in her as his principal political partner.[10]

Certainly, at the outset, it seems to have been the ultimate act of vengeance by an aggrieved husband, yet they were actions that were a far cry from the prince's general level-headed approach to governance. The hanging of a nobleman, not in private or in the dark of night, but in broad daylight in the company of so many noble witnesses was a shocking thing to do. In particular, the hanging of the powerful William de Braose was an astonishing act of defiance by Llywelyn and one that made him potentially vulnerable to extreme retribution by the English Crown, regardless of his personal relationship to the king. A possible and vital form of retribution would have been the loss of Buellt for certain. Never mind some version of retaliation in how Joan was dealt with that may have been displeasing to her brother.

However, Henry's reaction was remarkably detached. When the king first heard of William's imprisonment after being caught with Joan, he went to great pains to ensure provisions were made to safeguard the crucially important de Braose territories to English advantage by transferring the custody of all lands and castles to Peter FitzHerbert, John Monmouth and William Marshal, the new earl of Pembroke who was also the brother of Eva de Braose, William's wife, and soon to be widow.[11] At the time of William's execution, Henry was preoccupied with gathering his military for his long-anticipated expedition to Poitou and, as a result, it was Robert de Neville, his chancellor, and Stephen of Seagrave, his new justiciar, who dealt with the political repercussions of Llywelyn's surprising actions.[12]

Ultimately, the Crown's response was also surprising. Instead of reacting to the threat of Llywelyn's open display of what was essentially defiance by killing a potent vassal of the English king, Llywelyn's brother-in-law sent a letter three whole months after William's execution, stating that the issue at hand was domestic and was, therefore, not a concern to the English Crown. This is an interesting response considering Wales promised to be a greater threat to England than previously if Llywelyn took all the de Braose lands under his full control – and would have received much support from his adherents in doing so.

William's daytime death was not just an act that glorified the humiliating demise of one of Llywelyn's greatest adversaries, a traitor that caused him public 'disgrace and injury', and real personal anguish, it was also an act of significant political meaning. The abbot of Vaundey, himself, understood William's death to be retribution for the general reign of terror that largely defined de Braose legacy in Wales; his execution by the leading Welsh prince was likely backed by the majority of Welsh who deeply, and rightly, mistrusted and detested the Marcher family.[13] This is the perception also alluded to by the annals of Margan, which record that Llywelyn's hatred for William, the 4th lord of Bramber who caused the deaths of so many Welsh natives, was, in part, motivation for William's execution.

William's public hanging was an act that was weighted with particular meaning. First and foremost, punishment by hanging was for the lesser gentry, the criminal, the common thief, not for a patrician. It was a remarkably dishonourable way to die; if carried out correctly, the neck breaks and death comes quickly, but decapitation is also a very real possibility if the neck breaks. Further symbolism more apropos to this situation, death by hanging can produce what is referred to as a 'death erection', an effect that the pressure of the noose places on the cerebellum. The quicker a man dies by hanging, the more likely it is for this to be the case. Thus, the public performance surrounding William's death was one enacted to visibly showcase the shame, humiliation, disgrace and degradation of his character and, if he died quickly enough, a grotesque reminder, though far from needed, of the debased act that led to his public demise. If Joan was made to watch the spectacle, all would have been witness to the chastening mockery surrounding William's last erection for her.

Attempts to pinpoint the location of where the Easter court was held, the infamous affair discovered, and exactly where William was executed are very convoluted by nature. The preferred, and long-established contender for all of the above, is the royal Welsh *llys* of Aber, traditionally held to be the main Venedotian court in Gwynedd. It may be that 'Aber' is actually Abergwyngregyn on the north coast overlooking the Menai Straits, roughly seven miles from the cathedral town of Bangor. Tradition says that the princes of Gwynedd had a castle in the parish of Abergwyngregyn on a hill by the church, where remnants of medieval buildings are still to be found.[14] Pen-y-Bryn, also referred to as Garth Celyn, is an Elizabethan manor house in Abergwyngregyn, with much older medieval origins, which is believed to have been the historical palace of the princes of Gwynedd. Although previously having been much debated by historians and archaeologists about the veracity of the claims, strong evidence has emerged that has greatly increased support for this theory.[15]

Certainly, the fact that after Joan died at the *llys* of Aber, her body was transported across the Menai Straits to Llanfaes in Anglesey for internment helps strengthen the argument surrounding Abergwyngregyn – Llanfaes lies directly across the straits from Aber. Further, association of this particular location with Joan and William's affair is intimated in local lore contending that the lord of Abergavenny was hanged in Garth Celyn over the *llys* cesspit, still referred to as 'Hanging Marsh'. In addition, antiquarians such as Thomas Pennant and A.B. Williams who toured Wales in the early-nineteenth century record convention that:

Less than five miles away from Aber, in a sheltered cave in the majestic Snowdon mountains flanking the Irish seaboard, is

> a place identified by tradition as *Cae Gwilym Ddu*, or Black
> William's Field. It is here that local lore insists William's
> body was interred after his public demise on suspicion of
> too great familiarity with [Llywelyn's] royal consort.[16]

Another contender for the location of William's hanging is an area in Gwynedd Is Conwy called Crogen, near Bala. There have been arguments that taking Crogen as the actual place for William's death, as mentioned in the abbot of Vaundey's letter, at face value is etymologically problematic. In the Welsh language, *crogen* refers to 'hang-dog', which could easily hint more at a description of what happened to William, or *of* William, rather than the actual place where he died.[17] Nevertheless, there was a princely manor there and one day before William was hanged, Llywelyn undertook administrative duties while at Ystrad, another princely manor just seventeen miles from Crogen. Additionally, Crogen is roughly ten miles from Ellesmere and it is here that Joan was perhaps imprisoned – or more to the point, kept under house arrest. Abbot Nicholas' letter mentions a meeting with Llywelyn at Ellesmere not long after William's death. Again, if Joan was detained here, the significance of the location would not have been lost on either wife or husband, Ellesmere being the first manor given to them as a marital gift. Importantly, it may have been at Ystrad where William's death sentence was delivered by Llywelyn's magnates and perhaps the decision made for Joan's punishment. Also present with the prince at Ystrad in the midst of this extremely fraught situation was Joan and Llywelyn's teenage son, Dafydd – a jarring reminder of the deeply personal trauma that Joan's entire family experienced in the aftermath of her supposed adultery.

The de Braose family suffered too, but Eva, William's widow, did not accept the fait accompli submissively, nor is it likely that she viewed Llywelyn's actions in the same light as many of her peers. While Henry was on campaign in France, Stephen Segrave was appointed joint regent of England (along with chancellor Ralph Neville, and William de Warenne, earl of Surrey) and it was to Stephen that Llywelyn wrote to complain about Eva's reaction to her husband's death, and her retaliation. Unsurprisingly infuriated by William's execution, in anger and openly supported by her brother William, the earl of Pembroke, Eva repeatedly had her own chaplain excommunicate Llywelyn as a reprisal for her husband's execution. It was an act that apparently so aggrieved

Llywelyn that he made it clear to Segrave that if excommunication – or threats thereof – continued, open war would be his only alternative form of retribution. Further insult to injury was Eva's repeated attempts to secure the release of hostages previously taken in exchange for the return of her fosterling, the son of Einion Fychan, one of Llywelyn's top ministers.[18] Fosterage was an important cultural practice in Wales and Eva's actions showed disregard for the honour with which she, and her family, had been endowed. Her actions challenged not only etiquette, but Llywelyn's own authority.[19]

Eventually, Eva received a letter from her husband's executioner, beseeching her to enlighten him as to whether or not the marriage between Dafydd and Isabella was going to go ahead, in spite of what happened. With a notable air of humility, the prince told Eva that if she chose to end all discussions, it was a decision he would honour, but one that would never fully rest with him. In fact, Llywelyn relinquished notions of accountability by stressing that it was his governing council that insisted William be hanged.[20] Sidestepping the audacity of making such an enquiry or even taking ownership for his actions, Llywelyn insisted that the outcome of events could not have been prevented as final judgement lay at the feet of his magnates who sought to rectify the great dishonour and insult done to Llywelyn's own person; that William's blood, so to speak, was not on his hands.[21] The fact that English and Welsh sources both record Llywelyn's response to the situation without condemnation and the fact that Llywelyn did not have to endure any political ramifications for his actions suggests that his judgement was widely supported because de Braose abused his hospitality.[22]

Whether true or not, we will never know, but Llywelyn certainly consented to the decision and it is expected that he took part in, if not led, the actual discussions and probably proposed the sentence, being a shrewd adjudicator himself. The division of the de Braose lands among William's daughters was politically advantageous, which probably also swayed sentencing to a large extent. The conciliatory, nigh on remorseful, tone of his letter to Eva carries a certain level of surprising intimacy as, in the same breath in which he uses her title of lady (*domine*) as acknowledgement of her social status and power in southern Wales, he also refers to her as his beloved friend (*dilecte amice sue*). Such a reverent combination certainly suggests that the alliance was not simply one between powerful lordships, but also one between families.

In fact, a few days after Llywelyn wrote his entreating letter to Eva, he also wrote to her brother, William Marshal, earl of Pembroke, who became the custodian of Buellt, immediately after William's execution. Similar to his letter to Eva, Llywelyn was active in seeking some sort of confirmation that the marriage between Dafydd and Isabella would still go ahead. To William, the prince also expressed concern that their affable alliance remain intact, claiming that the last thing he had wanted was for their friendship to end because of what happened or because 'of anything else in the world'.[23]

In spite of what appears to be genuine declarations of friendship, the letter Eva received from Joan's husband was also slightly intimidating, Llywelyn telling her that she needed to inform him whether or not she had decided to continue marital negotiations as the proposed alliance affected the rights of her daughter. Rather more menacingly, Llywelyn stressed his need to know one way or the other 'so that nothing worse can result from the misfortune'. Whether this is a veiled threat being made directly by the prince of Aberffraw, lord of Snowdon, as Llywelyn styles himself, to a lesser subject, or a more genuine concern for the fate of a widow and her daughter, cannot be known. However, it is easy to dismiss Llywelyn's protestations as 'a cynical effort to excuse an act of private vengeance and protect a politically advantageous marriage'.[24]

Certainly, attempts to discern how Llywelyn really felt by reading these letters are non-sequiturs. It is clear that his own political requirements were in the forefront of his public persona. The diplomatic advantages that would, and did, result from William's death superseded the shame of a cuckolded husband and likely swayed sentencing. Upon William's death, the de Braose lands were divided among his living daughters and heiresses, including Isabella. In any case, threat or no threat, it appears that Eva did not exactly resign herself to the situation that she found herself in.

The possibility that Eva, herself, may have been more involved in the initial marital negotiations and knew Joan should be kept in mind. Based on evidence in other studies, and the fact that she was Anglo-Norman and brought up in circles where women often did partake in marriage negotiations, it is not an improbable proposition. Moreover, in his letter to her, Llywelyn refers the alliance (*confederationem*) between Isabella and Dafydd, whereas in his letter to William Marshal, he refers to it as a friendship that was made (*amicitiam factam*). This was a very political episode in which Eva was thrust to centre stage in dealing with the aftermath and the consequences of events. She found herself acting as a key player, not only as a widowed wife and a mother, but also as a powerful female 'lord' in her own right. A situation that, though little documented in terms of women's movements and actions, was hardly unique. Wales was a warrior society after all and many women had to act as heads of households 'on the home front' while their husbands were away on campaigns or securing the family lands. In this way, both William's wife and assumed lover were similar.

Chapter Twelve

Reckoning

'the Woman'

What *was* Joan's role in all this? What was her reaction? Did she plead innocence? Did she admit to betraying her husband of twenty-five years? Did she witness William's death? Where was she incarcerated? How did all of this affect her relationship with Llywelyn and their family dynamics overall? Shockingly, it is the 1821 telling by the Rev. A.B. Williams in which Joan first appears as a primary character in any source; a full 600 years after the event.[1] The tenets of Williams' version are highly embellished up on in an 1845 rendition written by Louisa Stewart Costello in which Joan is portrayed as a lovelorn, almost feckless woman. It is worth providing her narrative on Joan in detail:

> There are many stories told of the princess Joan, or Joanna, somewhat contradictory, but generally received; she was, of course, not popular with the Welsh, and the court bard, in singing the praise of the prince, even goes so far as to speak of a female favourite of Llywelyn's, instead of naming his wife: perhaps he wrote his ode at the time when she was in disgrace, in consequence of misconduct attributed to her. It is related that Llywelyn, at the battle of Montgomery, took prisoner William de Breos, one of the knights of the English court, and while he remained his captive treated him well, and rather as a friend than enemy. This kindness was repaid by De Breos with treachery, for he ventured to form an attachment to the Princess Joan, perhaps to renew one already begun before her marriage with the Welsh prince. He was liberated and returned to his own country;

but scarcely was he gone than evil whispers were breathed into the ear of Llywelyn, and vengeance entirely possessed his mind: he however dissembled his feelings, and, still feigning the same friendship, he invited De Breos to come to his palace at Aber as a guest. The lover of the Princess Joan readily accepted the invitation, hoping once more to behold his mistress; but he knew not the fate which hung over him, or he would not have entered the portal of the man he had injured so gaily as he did.

The next morning the Princess Joan walked forth early, in a musing mood: she was young, beautiful, she had been admired and caressed in her father's court, was the theme of minstrels and the lady of many a tournament – to what avail? her hand without her heart had been bestowed on a brave but uneducated prince, whom she could regard as little less than savage, who had no ideas in common with hers, to whom all the refinements of the Norman court were unknown, and whose uncouth people, and warlike habits, and rugged pomp, were all distasteful to her. Perhaps she sighed as she thought of the days when the handsome young De Breos broke a lance in her honour, and she rejoiced, yet regretted, that the dangerous knight, the admired and gallant William, was again beneath her husband's roof. In this state of mind she was met by the Bard, an artful retainer of Llywelyn, who hated all of English blood, and whose lays were never awakened but in honour of his chief, but who contrived to deceive her into a belief that he both pitied and was attached to her. Observing her pensive air, and guessing at its cause, he entered into conversation with her, and having beguiled her of her tears by his melody, he at length ventured on these dangerous words:

'Diccyn, doccyn, gwraig Llywelyn,
Beth a roit tiam weled Gwilym'

'Tell me, wife of Llywelyn, what would you give for a sight of your William?'

147

The princess, thrown off her guard, and confiding in the harper's faith, imprudently exclaimed:

'Cymru, Lloeger, Llywelyn,
Y rown igyd am weled Gwilym!'

'Wales, and England, and Llywelyn – all would I give to behold my William!'

The harper smiled bitterly, and, taking her arm, pointed slowly with his finger in the direction of a neighbouring hill, where, at a place called Wern Grogedig, grew a lofty tree, from the branches of which a form was hanging, which she too well recognised as that of the unfortunate William de Breos. In a dismal cave beneath that spot was buried 'the young, the beautiful, the brave'; and the princess Joan dared not shed a tear to his memory. Tradition points out the place, which is called, Cae Gwilym Dhu.

Notwithstanding this tragical episode, the princess and her husband managed to live well together afterwards; whether she convinced him of his error, and he repented his hasty vengeance, or whether he thought it better policy to appear satisfied; at all events, Joan frequently interfered between her husband and father to prevent bloodshed, and sometimes succeeded.[2]

Other, shorter, antiquarian versions exist, all largely taken from Williams and Thomas Pennant. Although they obviously preserve local tradition to an extent, the story itself ostensibly morphed into legend. Moreover, such retellings also adhere to the gendered stereotypes that so dominate history and literature. Joan's infidelity was much like Queen Gwenhwyfar's of Arthurian lore, and was met with retribution and ritual humiliation for crossing culturally accepted gendered boundaries, however nebulous they may have been; retribution that involved some form of public shaming.[3] For both women, the public shaming continued in the form of denigration of their characters in the medium of the written word during the late eighteenth and early nineteenth centuries; writings that perpetuate the sexual woman as the calumniated wife. For Joan in particular, some commentaries are especially dreadful:

As this lady ultimately attained the utmost height of the vilest species of notoriety that can distinguish a bad woman, that of the faithless wife and paramour of the profligate, we hold ourselves justified in pausing at this period of her history, to scrutinize the motives which would actuate her in the assumption of a characteristic in reality so foreign to her as piety: especially as certain authors, more Quixotic than judicious, have embraced the *honour* of becoming her vindicators, her knight-errants forsooth! to do battle for her with the perverted pen of pseudo history, by aspersing the character of her heroic and too indulgent husband and sovereign ...

In Wynn's history of Wales, Joan is emphatically styled 'a sly woman;' and doubtless she is open to more than suspicion, as an intriguante, both in political and amatory matters: and it is not to be imagined that a woman of her character was without her devoted and favoured admirers before she left her father's court, or that she afterwards failed to divulge those political occurrences of her time, to favour the land of her birth at expense of the country which had adopted her as its daughter when she became its queen.[4]

The motif of the calumniated wife is found widespread across medieval European literature (and fundamentally figures in a number of Arthurian stories, including the original Welsh tale 'Culwch and Olwen') and is associated with the notion that women, royal ladies especially, were subject to seemingly strict socially and culturally controlled rules regarding behaviour.[5] Obviously the stressed importance of uxorial chastity was founded in rules and practices of medieval inheritance where the legitimacy of an heir and the longevity of a family fortune depended on the chaste behaviour of a wife and her fidelity. Largely, women were faced with the juxtaposed expectations of being both fertile and chaste (read faithful). The sexual disloyalty of both Joan and Gwenhwyfar remain the root cause to political upheaval in native Wales: Gwenhwyfar's led to the Battle of Camlan and Arthur's death. Joan may have escaped such calamitous ignominy, but her sexual infidelity too 'shamed a better man than any (of the others)'.[6]

Queens were hardly immune from medieval criticism and the double-standards faced by women, especially those in the upper echelons.

In fact, as the public models of wifehood, they were subjected to even further scrutiny. Even though a queen's agency was often promoted and accepted because of her intimate proximity to her husband as the king, it was precisely because of this visible position that many royal women were exposed to public ridicule and judgement simply because they were more closely observed. English queens like Joan's grandmother, Eleanor of Aquitaine and Isabella, the 'She-Wolf' of France (r. 1308– 1327) were no strangers to the widespread condemnation expressed by their peers for their perceived defiance of cultural and social gender norms. Because the fears and expectations associated with the female sex were further enhanced in the persona of the queen, who was in a public position, the same fears and expectations also worked to shape the role of the queen herself. It is for these reasons alone, if nothing else, that the silence of contemporary sources concerning Joan's character is so utterly intriguing.

Of course, medieval history is a both fascinating and frustrating subject of research, and the situation Joan found herself in in 1230 is a noteworthy example of both. Sources elude to an intrigue that is comparable to today's tabloid news stories and gossip columns, which not only held the attention of many for weeks and months after the fact, but for centuries. Through the ages it has been wildly contended that Joan and Llywelyn had a strong, and even loving, marriage. That it was certainly one in which a mutual respect for royal status and duties abounded, there is no doubt. Unquestionably, up to this point, their twenty-five year marriage was one of success and stability. Thus, endless questions of how and why the affair could have happened, coupled with widespread gossip, must have been in abundance. How could a woman of her stature, the daughter and sister of English kings no less (!) be so wanton, or at least foolish enough to be caught? Were Joan and William in love? Was it a matter of lust? Were they in cohorts to bring Llywelyn down? And though unrecorded, surely Joan's 'misstep' must have called into question her overall loyalty as Llywelyn's wife, especially as a foreigner, and legitimacy of their progeny. Was Dafydd even Llywelyn's? Where did this leave the succession of Gwynedd? Would Gruffudd, rightly, take the gauntlet as Llywelyn's successor? With the facts being few and far between, speculation seems endless.

Modern historical silences on Joan as a subject in her own right are also remarkable. Although, in essence, she was truly at the heart of the episode, and certainly the more important participant in relation to Llywelyn than William himself was, by and large, discussions of events and the sheer significance of her involvement, or even about her as a person, have been completely been marginalised. Fundamental questions have never been explored: How far did the temporary loss of his most ardent diplomat shape political spheres and Llywelyn's agendas during the rest of 1230 and 1231? Did they at all? Was her incarceration short-lived due to a wariness of how the king would react if his own sister continued to remain detained indefinitely? More to the point, was Joan even incarcerated?

In the most critical of terms, why have questions like these never been asked by historians? It seems to be a glaring oversight to understanding not only the events of 1230, but to Llywelyn's reign as a whole. Given what we do know, it seems unlikely that Joan was a meek and silence woman, hidden away in her chambers, with her ladies-in-waiting, spending her days embroidering while sat in a window seat. The agency she wielded up to 1230 increased in importance year after year; agency as a queen and as Llywelyn's visible, trusted and successful political cohort. It is here that the context of the situation is addressed for the first time, with Joan's role, status and position as queen-consort at the epicentre of historical investigation.

To begin on a more cursory level, as with Eva, it is likely that Joan, too, was integral to working out marital arrangements with William. Again, this is a role that many royal and aristocratic women played and there is evidence that Joan had certainly been involved in 1222 with the marriage of her daughter Elen to John the Scot. Regardless of how, when, and if a relationship began during William's imprisonment, once he returned to the Venedotian court to finalise details of the marital alliance, Joan would have had at least first-hand knowledge of negotiations. Llywelyn's later letter to Eva is even suggestive of the fact that Isabella was already at the Venedotian court at the time of her father's death. Perhaps William's visit at Easter 1230 was to accompany his daughter to her new home. Joan's assumed presence during talks leads to the much deeper examination of her actual political role she would have been privy to discussions involving the creation of an alliance that had the potential to shift the axis of Welsh power in Llywelyn's favour – especially if she had forged a relationship with William during his earlier detainment, romantic in nature or not.

William would have easily been welcomed at the royal *llys* and bestowed the honours of gifts, foods and festivities that the Welsh were so renowned for. Accommodating guests and gift-giving were integral and expected customs to be undertaken by the royal couple in tandem. It was anticipated that the husband *and* wife would entertain important guests and dignitaries in the royal *llys*. Easter, in particular, was one of the main court festivals and Joan would have been present as the symbolic female face of royal authority and honour during such an important occasion. Aside from antiquarian accounts in which William would have been surprised at the absence of Joan at the high table simply because she was his supposed lover, her absence from the court as Llywelyn's queen would have been more questionable during such an occasion, especially at their main residence, and highly unlikely. Moreover, the reasons for William's attendance would have made the occasion doubly important for her to make an appearance. Public honour would have been bestowed upon him as a royal guest, through the offering of wine and mead as a means of showing the alliance was graciously supported, regardless of personal feelings toward him one way or the other.

In fact, there is no doubt that Joan was expected to attend court for those Easter celebrations. The Laws of the Court (particularly the Iorwerth redaction) tell us that the ritual of feasts concerning Christmas, Easter and Whitsun, especially, were of great importance and suggest that the queen played a publicly important role during these festivals, particularly in the form of giving gifts and acting as a hostess. In fact, her role as a hostess was fundamental to aligning political friendships within the court. Comparable to elsewhere in Europe, even in Wales, ideals of 'monarchy' often assumed that there was a supposed partnership between husband and wife, king and queen, that helped strengthen and define rulership overall. As such, it was the Welsh queen's role to be visibly present in the royal hall during such occasions as a means of further manifesting the ideals of kingship associated with Welsh custom and ritual.

So many examples are found in the tales of the *Mabinogion*, where royal wives are gift-givers, and in Welsh poetry across the breadth of the Middle Ages where they are lauded for their roles as hosts, that this must have been an important aspect of practice. It was a tradition strongly associated with the widespread imagery of the lady with the 'mead cup' discussed earlier, one that was reminiscent of the more ancient depiction of the Goddess of Sovereignty offering a drink of libation to a chosen king who was to symbolically marry the land. In Wales in particular, the offering of drinks by both the king and queen in native Welsh society was an act that symbolised honour and the creation of alliances; it was a public act associated with the recognition of friendship. During the Easter feast in 1230 there was much to celebrate and expectations must have been high, with Joan surely playing host and the lady with the mead cup in the truest of senses.

To tackle the real crux of the matter, there are a number of issues that need to be addressed which highlight the complexity of the situation at hand; complexities which may or may not explain why so little information was recorded by contemporaries. The first issue involves rape. If it were a case of rape, it could be that at the court of Ystrad on 1 May when sentencing (for both?) was likely decided, William did not have oaths of the fifty men he legally needed as character witnesses to let him walk free: 'If it happens that a woman says of a man that he raped her and the man denies it, let him give the oath of fifty men without aliens and without designated men.'[7] Indeed, the antiquarian account mentioned above claims that 'there was no friend at hand to intercede for a mitigation of his punishment.' Though unlikely, given Joan's subsequent imprisonment, the notion that rape was involved cannot be dismissed entirely. Indeed sources may have been silenced, not by the idea of Joan's traumatic physical defilement, if this had been the case, but by the public defilement of Llywelyn's honour.

Nevertheless, although it cannot be determined how far the written laws were put into practice, it does seem extremely unlikely that Joan, and Llywelyn to be sure, would have been subjected to the more demeaning demonstrations of proof legally required when accusations of rape were involved. If it happened that a woman made a legal charge of rape the laws declare that she must,

> take the man's member in her left hand, with her right hand on the relic, and let her swear by relic that that member had connexion with her by force and that blemish and *sarhaed* were done to her and her kin and to her lord. Some of the justices do not allow denial against that.[8]

In reality, it is hard to believe that Joan, as queen, would have been forced to be centre-stage in a court, surrounded by her husband, likely her own son, and other men of the realm under the expectation that she would publicly grab William's penis and swear such an oath.

153

Moreover, if William had raped Joan, it would have afforded Llywelyn and his adherents ample ammunition to implement a full-scale retribution and take the de Braose lands by force, ending up in the chronicles. Writers of the sources would have also been able to use the state of affairs in a propagandistic way to help garner further support for such an attack. Nevertheless, a good indicator that this was not an occasion in which sexual assault occurred is, again, related to the silence in the records. As such, one would assume the native chronicles, in the least, would have been more excoriating towards William and his character, even while maintaining silence on Joan or even the act of rape itself, if it had actually happened.

The themes of honour and shame are so widespread throughout native Welsh sources that it is clear they were important cultural characteristics unique to Wales. By definition, honour was associated with one being able to exact respect by living up to social and cultural expectations, and Welsh laws identified the importance of someone being accused of an offence being able to have the chance to 'save face' in order to maintain social harmony.[9] In many ways, the strong cultural influences concerning honour and shame ensured that women and men stayed within their culturally defined gendered boundaries. For example, shame for men was aimed at dereliction of primarily public (and political) duty. For women, shame was directly associated with female sexual transgression. The Welsh laws are explicit in their codification of punishments for women who dishonoured themselves, and their families, through contravention of accepted sexual roles and duties.[10]

Under this pretext also falls the quality of uxorial chastity. Even the Welsh Triads make distinctions between three chaste and three unchaste wives. These triads appear in great contrast to, and in fact may have been written in imitation of, the list of the three faithful and unfaithful war-bands from Britain, which unquestionably highlight pervasive attitudes concerning masculine attributes associated with honour, the physical stamina of the warrior and loyalty. The term *diweir* used in association with chastity and honour was often applied differently to women and men. For women most connotations denote 'unbending', 'constant, faithful and loyal' in specific relation to sexual chastity. In contrast, also denoting 'faithful', 'loyal', 'reliable', 'honest' and 'true', in the masculine context *diweir* mainly relates to political allegiances. Although for both sexes chastity appears as an attribute, it does seem to be strictly defined by notions of gender.

For a woman, and especially a legal wife whose perceived failures (and disobedience) as a dutiful wife were exposed, public and communal shame was the normal reprisal – often as seen in themes associated with the calumniated wife mentioned above. In spite of the fact that concubinage was a common and legal Welsh practice, the *gwraig briod* was expected to be honourable by remaining sexually loyal to her husband. The Iorwerth redaction is emphatic in making it clear that if a man wants to marry a woman, he was to be promised surety from her parents that 'she will not cause him shame by her body'.[11] The Blegywryd redaction of the laws state that the wife has to pay her husband's *sarhaed*, or shame fine, if she commits adultery, allowing the husband to leave her and freely repudiate her.[12] Nevertheless, it should be noted that maintaining honour in the face of marital infidelity was not simply a one-sided gendered expectation. Interestingly enough, the Iorwerth redaction allows the wife to receive compensation for her shame if she finds her husband with another woman. If she was (un)lucky enough to find that he had transgressed up to three times, she was free to leave him without losing anything that rightfully belonged to her.[13]

We could speculate that for women like Joan, their status as the wives of the imminent Welsh rulers overshadowed such cultural transgressions. For Joan, certainly, silences in native sources regarding her uxorial 'dishonour' strongly suggest that, first and foremost, her status as Llywelyn's wife offered a layer of protection; that his overall status in Wales ensured a modicum of silence when nothing polite could be said.

Interestingly, in Joan's case, it appears that one particular member of their ministerial elite, his *distain* Gruffudd ab Ednyfed, son of their greatly valued and highly trusted Ednyfed Vychan, fled to Ireland after publicly slandering Joan, presumably in light of the events of 1230.[14] Ultimately, it is likely that Joan's status as a queen, and position as Llywelyn's wife, overshadowed unconcealed criticisms relating to her cultural and sexual transgressions. In the end, it seems as if Llywelyn's dependence on Joan's ability to mediate and play her important part as a diplomat outweighed any crime at hand. Are the silences in the sources further proof of recognition by contemporaries that her status and political position were deemed too inherently valuable to jeopardise with public reproach, offering her yet another layer of protection?

It is remarkable that a woman of her calibre, and one as well-known as she, is not referred to in the sources for 1230 by name, especially in the context of such a calamitous event. The neutral tone of the sources regarding Joan's 'misbehaviour' suggests an earnestness to ensure that Llywelyn's status as a leader, and a strong one at that, remain intact. Unquestionably, regardless of her actions, as Llywelyn's wife Joan remained a public and viable symbol of his overall power and authority and even reminded the Welsh of Llywelyn's greatness due to his intimate connection with the Plantagenet rulers. Again, we refer back to the ideals of honour and shame and how these shaped perceptions and attitudes. A wife's sexual violation of her husband's trust, and specifically in such a public way as Joan's assumed perfidy, had a direct impact on perceptions of masculine power, descriptions of which are deeply underscored in the political contexts of the entries found in chronicles of 1230.

Silences notwithstanding, there is also a curious impartiality on the part of sources that record events regarding Joan's assumed actions as an adulterous wife. This is especially noteworthy given the majority of the sources were written by religious establishments who considered adultery to be principally a female offence and one that incurred harsh penalties for women who were deemed to be unfaithful wives.[15] Although religious writers often used hyperbole to discuss the polarity between the positive and negative attributes assigned to each sex, the accomplishments and failings of women were often particularly popular and pointed. Wales' own famous cleric Gerald of Wales found plenty of space in his writings to pontificate about the assumed 'natural' rights of husband over wife, and how the overtly sexually active nature of the married woman was parallel to her being a usurper of social order and masculine authority.[16] Yet in religious sources, Joan is hardly blamed for the affair and her fate met with abject silence.

The Chester annals are the only known source to comment on Joan's fate of imprisonment, and in context, the scribes simply refer to her as 'the woman' (*mulier*). Welsh chronicles are silent on her incarceration and mention her in context using lifecycle labels, as wife of a prince and daughter of a king. Both examples seem to be indicative of judgement, even if they are subversive ways of condemning the king of England's sister.[17] In relation to Joan's participation in the affair, the lack of finger pointing for her role as a seductress is also interesting. It has been suggested that the political ramifications were too widespread and shocking in their own rights for the religious authors to have to manipulate gender to embellish the narratives. This is undoubtedly in stark contrast to many other women who suffered worse fates of slander, like Isabella of Angoulême, Joan's own stepmother.

Only the Welsh laws, namely those found in the Iorwerth redaction written in Gwynedd during Joan and Llywelyn's reign, provide hints of judgement actually aimed at the reigning queen of North Wales. First of all, there is a curious passage found in the tractate on adultery that seems to emulate antiquarian versions about Joan and William being seen committing adultery outside: 'If it happens that a woman is seen coming from one side of a grove and man on the other, or coming from an empty house, or under one mantle, if they deny it, the oath of fifty women for the woman, and as many men for the man.'[18] This passage is intriguingly reminiscent of the one discussed above that seems related to William not having enough, or any, character witnesses to help save him from his fate.

Secondly, multiple versions of the Welsh laws discuss the idea of marital separation, known as *ysgar*, and indeed, some may be quite noteworthy when it comes to attitudes towards Joan. Divorce was not an unusual practice in Wales and legal writings concerning the practice of it have been roughly dated to the second-quarter of the thirteenth century, meaning that discussions concerning *ysgar* are contemporaneous to the events that took place in 1230.[19] This certainly is an indication that they may, indeed, reflect political and social commentary regarding Llywelyn's adulterous, foreign wife. The laws declare that the infidelity of a wife was the greatest disgrace that a Welsh ruler could face and provide what is essentially a homily concerning problems and inequity caused by divorce. Perhaps very real attitudes towards Joan's actions permeate legal content.[20]

For a man renowned for his statesmanship and political acumen, Llywelyn's reaction to the affair was extreme, even for a cuckold. Nevertheless, the utmost form of shame, or *gwarthrudd*, in native Welsh society was that of the adulterous wife. It was not just the shame incurred on the woman herself for being involved with a man other than her husband, it was the insult afforded to both the woman's husband and his kin. A scandal such as this, referred to as *enllib*, could openly be refuted by the suspected wife with the backing of compurgators (*rhaith*) who were asked to provide oaths to clear the woman's name. Always a double-edged sword with most rules and expectations regarding the behaviour of women in the Middle Ages, the need for an accused wife to provide character witnesses and/or compurgators was also deemed an affirmation of her guilt, or in the least, proved a further disgrace.

Being found guilty of adultery was no easy walk in the park for a married woman. A man who lain with another man's wife was not necessarily bound to pay anything towards an insult price if the woman was an active participant. Nevertheless, if the deed became known, it was the woman who paid *sarhaed* in the hopes that her husband would not repudiate her as he was free do.[21] Personal and public shame and humiliation aside, being found guilty of the offence (*cyflafan ddybryd*) ultimately meant that a woman's husband was allowed to formally reject her, in which the loss of all her rights as a married woman followed.[22] That adultery was one of the mainstays for ending a marriage is also found in the legal Welsh Triads. The Triads discuss the *sarhaed* specifically belonging to the king of Aberffraw and the very first of three and most important insults suffered by the Venedotian ruler was shame relating to his wife.[23] Is this particular triad a direct attack on Joan specifically; a contemporary political commentary on the scandal of the age? It seems a very likely possibility.

The mild nature of Joan's own sentence is decisive in our understanding of the delicate political and personal nuances that underlined 1230. First, it is important to note that if Llywelyn had repudiated Joan, which he certainly had the right to do – especially once the affair became public knowledge – it would have freed him to seek another marriage. Nevertheless, pragmatically speaking, the odds of him finding a more lucrative union than that with a daughter and sister of the kings of England were little to none. Certainly, Llywelyn's alliance with Philip Augustus seventeen years earlier was not going to provide the Welsh prince with a marital alternative, Princess Marie of France (already in her second marriage) having died in 1224. Second, and more importantly, divorce from Joan could have jeopardised Dafydd's successorship to Gwynedd. It would have provided the English Crown ample ammunition to refute his legitimacy, and therefore ammunition to refute his claim to the Venedotian throne if Joan were no longer the prince's legitimate wife. Third, and most important, all evidence points to the fact that Joan's role as Llywelyn's queen, essentially her role as political emissary, was far more important to him and to the hegemony of Gwynedd, if not Wales itself, than the consequences of personal anguish and angst that must surface with any sexual infidelity. This is likely why she was only incarcerated for one year, which we are made aware of by only one source, and an English source at that. At the end of 1231, the Chester annals note that Joan – identified only as Llywelyn's wife (*uxorem suam*) and King John's daughter (*filiam Johannis Regis*) – had been released from custody.[24] By 1232, she had once again taken the gauntlet as Llywelyn's emissary, pleading his interests, publicly, with the English Crown.

Joan and Llywelyn had at least five children together during that time and it seems they enjoyed being a strong family unit – grants of lands made to their children and records of travel seem to indicate this. Ultimately, it may be that the punishment of having to watch William die, if indeed Joan was witness to his hanging, or in the least knowing that relationship ended in her assumed paramour's death, was deemed her real punishment. Not only was it literally a public affair, where she would have been shamed on some personal, if not public level to which we are no longer privy, the shame of betraying her husband, never mind her children by extension, all made this a tragedy that surely changed Joan forever, in ways we will never know or can ever fully understand.

It is very unlikely that Joan was 'banished' for a year as a means to hide a pregnancy that resulted in her affair with William. In 1230 Joan would have been at least 40 years old, probably older. Not an age entirely beyond the capabilities of childbearing, as our modern society increasingly shows, but the sustenance needed in the mid-thirteenth century, even for a royal woman, to carry out a successful pregnancy, one in which both the mother and child survived, would have been difficult to maintain.

Furthermore, a royal pregnancy, especially one that was the result of dishonour and shame according to custom, would have been difficult to hide altogether. It is in human nature to gossip and the only way to keep a pregnancy hidden would have meant that Joan remained under strict house arrest – perhaps similar in kind to that her grandmother Eleanor of Aquitaine endured at the beginning of her sixteen-year long incarceration in 1173, in which she was limited to her one trusted lady-in-waiting and was not allowed to receive visitors. Certainly not beyond the realms of possibility, but the odds of probability assume otherwise. Besides, the idea that Llywelyn would have forced Joan to give up William's child and have her or him raised in a religious house or adopted by another family seems unlikely, especially as he openly embraced his own illegitimate children. It is not hard to argue that, given what (little) we know of Llywelyn's personality, he comes across as a man of great magnanimity, and one who may have really loved his wife. The child would probably have been raised as his own, or at least in his household.[25] How far he would have been eager, or even able, to place Joan's illegitimate child as a fosterling to another Welsh aristocratic family and keep it secret is another matter.

Surely, Joan and William had been well-acquainted, probably from as early as Gwladus' marriage to Reginald in 1215. It is more than likely that their paths crossed again in 1219 with the marriage of Marared to John de Braose. And the fact that William was Gwladus' own stepson, never mind at least seven years Joan's junior, further muddies any sense of clarity on the situation. Factors like these make the situation even more intriguing and it is important here to put forth the argument that Joan and William had no affair at all. In fact, it is from this standpoint that a more political reasoning behind events holds suggestive sway; with innuendos of a 'set-up' underlying the 'anecdote' as a whole.

Kate Norgate, the author of the first entry written about Joan in the *Oxford Dictionary of National Biography* penned in the 1920s, proposed that William's death was the result of a secret and cunning plan hatched by Llywelyn, and agreed to by Joan, to eliminate the prince of Gwynedd's most ardent adversary.[26] Further to this, the de Braoses were patrons of Margam Abbey, whose chronicles of the events intimate that an affair between Joan and William was only suspected by Llywelyn, rather than discovered by him as is recorded in the Welsh chronicles. This leads one to ask numerous questions: Would Joan have had any reason to bribe William with sex? For information? For lands? For power? Did Llywelyn have reason to get rid of him beforehand, making the Easter drama a simple ruse? Why are there no records? And why was Joan not really punished?

The phrase 'being caught in the prince's chamber' needs to be analysed here as there perhaps lays a deeper importance behind the terminology and description used in Welsh sources as to where the affair was discovered. In other words, why were Joan and William found in *Llywelyn's* chamber and not Joan's? It is unquestionable that the stakes for being caught in the prince's chamber, and the likelihood of it happening, were much higher than if the two were squirreled away in Joan's separate quarters, wherever those may have been located. Importantly, Welsh sources highlight that there was a very indistinct nature concerning the function of and differences in 'chamber' and 'court', of which the queen seems to have been allowed, or enjoyed, more freedom of movement.

This is very important in context with how 1230 is recorded and in terms of Joan's subsequent, and lenient, punishment.

Native Welsh courts were not nearly as grand in structure and size as many of those from other European countries. The royal Welsh *llys* was a much more intimate setting all round and interestingly there is a revealing ambiguity in the nature of definitions concerning 'private' and 'public' spheres within the Welsh court, as well as an ambiguity concerning the expected setting of the queen herself within the *llys*. There is no doubt that both earlier and later redactions of the Welsh laws, such as Cyfnerth and Iorwerth, seem to emphasise the queen's general quarters as her own 'chamber', seemingly situated on the periphery of the court. The laws even endow her with her own 'officers of the chamber' or *swydogyon yr ystauell*.[27] The male officers are set apart from the queen's quarters at night and the attendance of female servants within the queen's own chamber hint that she was to live in the more traditionally acceptable realms of female domesticity, or within a private sphere, to use a pejorative term. This image is concomitant with numerous medieval sources in Western Europe especially where the queen was portrayed as isolated and disconnected from the public and thus political activities of her husband's court. In stark contrast, the Welsh king's household as laid out in the laws is more masculine in nature, and combined, these descriptions presuppose that the king would visit the queen in her space and vice versa, but not inhabit those spaces together.

The notion of the Welsh queen being separated in a 'private' sphere, and more specifically the bedchamber and kitchen is illustrated in sources other than the Welsh laws. As always, examples can be found in the *Mabinogi*, specifically the First, Second and Fourth Branches – from the wives of Arawn, Teyrnon and Math fab Mathonwy to the famous Branwen – as well as in other tales of the *Mabinogion*, such as 'The Lady of Well', where the female protagonist being confined to her chamber is the dominant theme throughout. Unsurprisingly, queens found in the Lives of Welsh Saints are more often than not sequestered in their bedchambers, usually in juxtaposition as women giving birth or playing out the role of seductress.[28] Further illustrations of the queen being portrayed in private chambers are also found in the Welsh chronicles beyond Joan, from the abduction of the princess Nest of Deheubarth in the early twelfth century, to the simultaneous birth of the princess Gwenllian and the death of her mother, Eleanor de Montfort, at the end of the thirteenth century.[29] Such examples of the queen's own chambers being prevalent to her expected location within the court are in curious contrast to the chronicles claiming that Joan was found committing adultery in Llywelyn's court. Or are they really?

The ubiquitous links between the queen and the chamber by no means indicate that such a space was solely her remit. In fact, recent studies on medieval queenship have shown, and continue to show, that royal chambers were not simply domestic. For Wales in particular, earlier editions of the laws, such as the twelfth-century Cyfnerth, highlight the ambiguities in trying to make a distinction between the chamber (*ystafell/camera*) and the hall (*llys/curia*) and suggest that the *ystafell* was a space that was shared by the queen and king and not simply as a privatised domestic environment.[30] Certainly in earlier times, the king's chamber itself seems to have been more largely defined by the administrative and public duties that took place there, rather than as simply a personal space. The boundaries overlapped between what we consider to be 'public' and 'private'. If the *ystafell* was purely the private space of the king, one has to ask why the laws ensured that the court justice was provided lodgings there?[31]

Furthermore, archaeological evidence also adds weight to the argument that the chambered spaces that the queen and king circulated within the court were shared by many, again highlighting these areas as the hub of governance. The queen's own chamber may not even have been separated from the king's and was most likely connected[32] as her own chamberlain who was wont to conduct his errands 'between the chamber and the hall', and who was in charge of her coffers, apparently had his own lodgings situated 'with his bed in the garderobe, so as to be ready to serve the needs of the King and Queen', naturally implying that the royal chambers were connected.[33] Such activities and setups indicate that the queen was neither segregated, nor on the periphery of royal administration and political action.

Even the later Iorwerth redaction has sections that imply a presumption that the queen and king were together within the royal household, regardless of the more defined division of the private chamber. In fact, taken together, the Welsh laws seem to presume overall that in the space of the royal household, and even attendance in court, was expected to be shared by the king and queen and that they be together. Thus, although images of royal women are often visibly structured within the privacy of the bedchamber, this does not preclude their presence or involvement in the politics or governmental administration that took place in the king's own chamber. Joan being found in Llywelyn's chamber is important. As the prince's chamber may have been the hub of administrative activity, Joan's place within the court, and her status as Llywelyn's advisor and counsellor assumes she would have been there.

Indeed, it is clear from other sources that the queen's presence within the public areas of the *llys*, the king's *ystafell* included, was both accepted and expected. This is in spite of various statements in the Welsh laws, such as Cyfnerth and Latin B, that situate the queen, during feast times, within the chamber.[34] It has been assumed that this meant the queen was secluded from hubbub of great hall – a belief further championed by the Iorwerth redaction itself where various sections emphasise the queen's location in her chamber. The Laws of the Court, for instance, describe that the queen should be 'quietly' sung to by the household bard (*bardd teulu*) 'so the hall is not disturbed by him',[35] which has been interpreted to mean that the queen was situated in the in the *ystafell*. However, this is largely circumspect and other evidentiary material from native Wales indicates the opposite was true. It is much more likely that the queen was *not* supposed to be secluded in the *ystafell*, but was expected to be among the court patrons. The fact that the bard was to sing quietly as to not disturb the rest of the hall certainly suggests that the queen was there.[36]

Even though the queen is not given a placement at the high table in any of the legal treatises, which again has led many to assume her insignificance, her presence and power within the royal court is evidenced in a number of other native Welsh sources. In the Blegywryd redaction of the laws, the queen's presence seems to have been expected in the court, with her power on display – her own steward casting royal protection, that of both the queen and king, over guests gathered in the hall.[37] Other sources, like the Welsh Lives of Saints, provide numerous examples of royal women being seated and visible in the public realms. For instance, the future and virginal Queen Gwladus, in the Life of St Cadog, is placed in the narrative sitting outside her chamber door with her sisters.[38] In the Welsh Triads, Queen Gwenhwyfar receives the ultimate insult by being physically struck from her own royal chair situated in Arthur's great hall.[39] In the *Mabinogion* a plethora of royal woman partake in gathering and feastings in the royal halls of ruling kings, many often seated at the high table.

Based on evidence, it seems erroneous to assume that even if the queen were placed in the *ystafell* during feast times, this meant she remained wholly separate from events. In reality, the *ystafell* likely functioned as a host to, or an extension of, the more private political undertakings and activities of the great hall. Indeed, Joan entertaining William in the beating heart of the ministerial body that would have been Llywelyn's chamber (sexual innuendos precluded), may have hardly been circumspect. It may have been a very commonplace location and occurrence in which queens fulfilled their political and social duties. It cannot be stressed enough that the very symbolic purpose of any medieval queen's status was adjunct to the king's as she, too, acted as the public face of masculine authority.

This contextual background provides much hitherto overlooked evidence regarding the culturally political and social role of the queen within the Welsh *llys*. Because the masked commentaries found in the chronicles do not feature any sort of remarks regarding a profound distrust in Joan, either by Llywelyn or, perhaps more importantly his adherents – which certainly would have been the case given she was a foreigner, related to the Angevin empire no less – the urge to jump to the unquestioned conclusion that this simply was an affair of lust, or the heart, should be tempered by both the knowns and unknowns – why they are there, why they are not there, and collectively, the deeper significance of what both statements and silences possibly imply.

Specifically, in terms of the possibility that Joan and William were found in Llywelyn's chamber, sources certainly intimate that the politically functionary purpose of the king's chamber was an accepted placement for the queen. It was here where she was in the hotbed of the political sphere (pun intended). Accordingly, such an impression is persuasive in suggesting that there might indeed be a stronger political emphasis underlining the whole affair than has ever seriously been considered. Ultimately, this political undertow may, in part, explain: one, the silence and lack of condemnation towards Joan and her role in the part of the story that was made public, and two, the moderate nature of her 'punishment'. In fact, in many ways, scribes specifically recording that it was in the prince's chamber that the couple were found seems to be a very overt way of highlighting the magnitude of the queen's actual position and role within the Welsh court overall.

Though the younger William was not known for the levels of intense cruelty exercised by his grandfather, his disrepute is parallel in its infamy.

Not only did his butting of heads with the most powerful prince in Wales end in his own execution, his death also meant the death knell for the de Braose legacy, with the Welsh lands being distributed among his four daughters. Isabella aside, all the de Braose women intermarried with other prominent Marcher families such as the Bohuns and Cantilupes. William's titles were carried down the junior branch of the family, with the only surviving male heir being Marared's husband, who had already inherited the titles of Gower and Bramber from his far-sighted uncle Reginald de Braose. But with his death in 1232, the de Braose clan was essentially no more.

As told through history, Joan has always been painted as a secondary character, the main event occurring between the two men in her life. Seemingly stuck between two apparent lovers, on the surface, her role portrayed throughout history all too easily falls into the trappings of the traditional trope of the woman as seductress, the traitorous wife, or the lovelorn anti-heroine. This event is tragic, but not all together telling. In fact, placing the remaining pieces of the puzzle together leaves more questions than answers and the melding between the personal and the political in such a public way should give cause for serious debate as to why and how the events actually occurred. Thinking about the expectations and roles of the queen in the Welsh court itself does, however, shed more light on the shadowy figure that is Joan, as Llywelyn's consort and what was expected of her in this esteemed role. It is because of this status alone that the astonishing silence of the Welsh sources concerning her person, her role, her reaction, her imprisonment, or in the least, the castigation of her character is noteworthy.

It seems no coincidence that as tensions further flared between Llywelyn and Hubert de Burgh soon after April 1230, that by 1231, Joan was released. During her time under arrest, England's notorious justiciar had extended his authority in southern Wales to the point of becoming unprecedented breach of trust. Political negotiations and parlays for peace were unsuccessful and when meetings involving even the king failed to procure any solution to the crisis, war broke out. Llywelyn and the king both needed an experienced, trusted and efficacious political envoy to broker a much needed deal. By 1232 it was clear that there was no better candidate than Llywelyn's hitherto indomitable adherent, his wife, Joan, now Lady of Wales.

Chapter Thirteen

On Bended Knee and Shedding of Tears

'Llewelin, prince of Wales, took back his wife, the daughter of King John, whom he had formerly imprisoned.'[1]

While Joan remained confined from the public eye throughout 1230, life and events within both her family and Wales carried on without her. She missed out on important family occasions as not one, but two crucially important political marriages concerning her children took place. Although a specific date is not known for either set of nuptials, Gwladus Ddu married her second husband Ralph Mortimer in 1230[2] and Dafydd and Isabella de Braose were probably married in August, because on the 10th, Dafydd was granted de Braose lands by the Crown.[3]

As lord of the house of Wigmore in Herefordshire, Ralph Mortimer had succeeded his older brother Hugh following Hugh's death in 1227. During the twelfth and thirteenth centuries, as Marcher lords, the Mortimers were a considerable thorn in the Welsh side concerning the middle March, particularly in the region known as Rhwng Gwy a Hafren,[4] and specifically the *cantref* of Maelienydd. After conquering the territory, it was the Mortimers who became the lords of Maelienydd in 1200, though it remained an issue of significant contention while Llywelyn was leader, he himself eventually backing the dynastic rights of the descendants of the Welsh prince Cadwallon ap Madog (d. 1179) to claim the lordship of Maelienydd over the Mortimer family. Given the upheaval in the middle March with the hanging of William and the division of the de Braose lands among his daughters as heirs, Gwladus' marriage to Ralph Mortimer was another perceptive political move by Llywelyn in attempts to both reign in growing dissident to his own dynasty's hold over the area in the vacuum that resulted in the collapse

166

of the de Braose lordship, and harness power through a potentially supportive alliance.

The continued support that Llywelyn needed from Joan grew readily more apparent during her imprisonment. Although the death of William de Braose is not believed to be the reason per se that led to a clear outbreak of aggression between Llywelyn and Hubert de Burgh at this time, it may have played a part in its own matter of ways, not least of which could have been Llywelyn's umbrage at de Burgh's supposed involvement in publicising Joan's supposed affair with William. More likely, the power struggle between the two was related to the de Braose lands. On William's death, oversight of the de Braose lordship was initially given to William Marshal, which was a disturbing turn of events for Llywelyn who wanted control of Buellt – and essentially had it in the guise of Dafydd's marriage to Isabella. In April 1231, luck – if it can be called that – seemed to shine on Llywelyn when Marshal died. The prince made a move to attack Radnor and take control. It was a crucial effort on the Welsh leader's part with Henry's senior minister de Burgh having been entrusted with the de Braose lands after the death of the earl of Pembroke.[5]

With de Burgh in charge, local princes and tenants revolted and broke peace with the English. They were joined by Llywelyn who, during that time, enjoyed a number of successes in strategic areas in the south of Wales and southern March, including at Montgomery, Radnor, Hay, Brecon and other places like Neath, Carmarthen, Cardigan. Between May and August, King Henry sought to negotiate a truce before hostilities intensified to the point of yet another war. On 27 May Llywelyn had envoys meet the king at Worcester, under safe-conduct, to discuss the renewal of tensions between himself and the English justiciar. The purpose was to lay the groundwork for a forthcoming conference scheduled to be held at Shrewsbury seven days later on 3 June. However, the subsequent summit at Shrewsbury was a failure, delegates falling far short of reaching any kind of resolution. A stalemate occurred and it was not long after the discouraged king returned to London that the Welsh began a campaign in south Wales, which ultimately led to Llywelyn's excommunication and yet another royal expedition being organised.

From May and throughout the summer of 1231, Llywelyn led his forces through the de Braose lands and those of other prominent

March lords, sparing nothing in his wake and compromising the safety of the innocent, including, according to Roger of Wendover, women and girls.[6] In retaliation, a number of Welsh fighters were captured by the English and, thereafter, grossly decapitated. Even though Henry excommunicated his brother-in-law (for burning churches and not guaranteeing the safety of church officials), Llywelyn continued with his agenda, ravaging the south and by the summer had a considerable amount of lands, extending from Montgomery, to Radnor, Hay, Brecon, Cydweli, Neath and Caerleon – itself the traditional location of the Welsh Camelot. According to the Chester annals, Ranulf of Chester, likely acting on Llywelyn's behalf, met with the king that summer at Painscastle. The king and powerful magnate apparently quarrelled and Ranulf returned to his own lands without any success.[7] Eventually, in November, a truce was agreed upon; Llywelyn wrote to his brother-in-law, requesting that respite be extended another year.

Once again, records for this time offer a curiosity that, upon further reflection, may intimate another occurrence in which Joan participated in political discussions behind the scenes, without either public acknowledgement or even knowledge. Twenty-four days after the failure of the Shrewsbury conference, rights to the Welsh couple's manors of Condover, Rothley and Ellesmere were revoked. By order of the king's hand while he was at Windsor, the sheriffs of Shropshire and Leicestershire were tasked with taking the manors back and keeping them safe until the king ordered otherwise. The sheriff of Shropshire, in particular, was ordered to take with him the whole of the king's posse of the county of Shropshire to reclaim Ellesmere.[8] Less than ten days later, between 6-7 July, Henry gifted Rothley in Leicestershire to the Knights Templar. The mandate specifically states that the Knights' rights to the manor were not to be hindered in any way by either Joan or Llywelyn.[9]

As we have seen, Rothley and Condover in particular were manors Joan distinctly had possession of in her own rights, and managed, while Ellesmere, too, was probably a manor in which she had some oversight seeing how it was a portion of her dowry and was also linked to her aunt and predecessor Emma of Anjou, suggesting some form of traditional female proprietorship. The question remains as to why rights to these manors specifically were revoked after the failure at Shrewsbury to reach any suitable mediation. It is the gifting and revocation of manors related to Joan that happens over and over again during times of political turbulence and subsequent peace which provides a more distinct indication of her possible activities and influences than are formally recorded. June 1231 seems to be no different from the other examples.

The Chester annals are the only source to tell us both that Joan was imprisoned in the first place and released a year later stating that 'Llewelin, prince of Wales, took back his wife, the daughter of King John, whom he had formerly imprisoned.'[10] To meet his agenda and to safe-guard his political gains under the threat of the increased power of England's justiciar, Llywelyn needed his most stalwart and successful diplomat to work with the English Crown. Thus, it seems no coincidence that Joan was released from prison and took up her position once more, both as Llywelyn's reigning consort and political legate, apparently reappearing by the summer of 1231, having been reinstated as Llywelyn's political diplomat. However, it may even have been that while incarcerated, Joan was not entirely bereft of her former duties. Parlaying for peace with England was an activity she may have undertaken nearer the end of her incarceration rather than simply after it.

The growing hostilities between de Burgh and Llywelyn after William's death may be an important indicator that Joan was perhaps needed to mediate between Gwynedd and England in 1230–31. Although it is difficult to date, two possibilities being available,[11] the one and only surviving letter from Joan herself indicates she took quill to parchment in a political context during this time. In fact, the letter addressed the king of England can easily have been one she wrote while still in prison. It is a source which greatly illuminates her own awareness of the importance of her queenly role in both an official and personal capacity:

> To her most excellent lord and dearest brother, Henry, by the grace of God, King of England, Lord of Ireland, Duke of Normandy and Aquitaine and Count of Anjou, the Lady of Wales sends her own greetings.
>
> Know, lord, that I am grieved beyond measure, that I can by no means express, that our enemies have succeeded in sowing discord between my husband and you. I grieve no less on account of you than on account of my husband, especially since I know what genuine fondness my husband used to have, and still has, for you, and how useless and dangerous it is for us, with due respect, to lose true friends and have

enemies instead. Thus on bended knee and shedding of tears, I beg your highness to alter your decision, as you may easily do, and do not fail to be reconciled to those who are joined to you by an unbreakable bond and learn both to love friends and oppress enemies. With regard to this, lord, you may know how some have wrongly suggested to you that you should not trust Instructus, your clerk and my lord's, in whom I do not believe you could have a more faithful clerk in England, may God help me. For this reason, he is no less faithful to you if he is faithfully carrying out the business of his lord, because he behaves in the same way carrying out your affairs in the presence of his master; neither you nor anyone would rely on him if he handles the business of his master in a half-hearted or careless manner. Therefore if you wish to have confidence in me for anything else, put your faith in me for this. Farewell.[12]

There is much to unpack in this crucial and lasting testimony we have of Joan as a person through the expression of her own voice. The 'personal as political' elements that dominated her life, her position and her status are readily evident and highlight the considerable weight she carried throughout her career.

For the standard diplomatic practices of her age, Joan demonstrates that she was adept at understanding, acknowledging and playing on the different levels of relationships she was involved in, and the expectations encompassing her position as a family member to both royal houses and status as queen. The political dimensions stand out, as does the fact that she wrote this in an official and formal capacity, for she promptly addresses Henry as her lord (*domino*), before referring to him as her brother. This establishes the acknowledgement that her relationship with Henry was first and foremost a feudal one. As the king of England, Henry had status over her (and her husband) as overlord; using the king's complete title was both a mark of respect and a further appreciation of his sovereign power. Such formalities are instantly contrasted with Joan's reference to Henry as her brother (*fratri suo*). Such a juxtaposition in letters was commonplace in medieval diplomacy where the personal and political were often interwoven. But for Joan, this provides especially important insight given that her letter skips the more formulaic protocol of the common supersalutatio, the additional phrases used to wish success upon the addressee and confirm a friendship further, found in medieval correspondence. Indeed, instead of outlining the particulars of her petition first and foremost as was customary, Joan skips such precedents and jumps to the heart of the matter.

Being 'grieved beyond measure' that discord had been sowed between the king and her husband, Joan humbly submitted to begging 'on bended knee' with the 'shedding tears' to entreat her brother, the king, to reconciliation. Remarkably, rather than presenting any preferred outcome, or, indeed, defining any potential (political) consequences if Henry chose to ignore her petition, she elected instead to beseech the king (pointedly *not* her brother) to trust her authority above all else. The magnitude of this is highlighted by the fact that Joan simply ends her letter, so that her plea, and the import of it, are not lost in the final and more formal valediction, or formal subsalutatio.

In her letter, Joan adopted the position of the medieval queen's accepted role as the subservient intercessor founded in biblical ideology. Yet, in spite of her modest overtones, which are unmistakably gendered based on the social and cultural expectations and standards concerning the political movements and activities of women to act as humble petitioners for the 'defenceless', Joan makes both her political point, and own official role, clear. It was her belief that Henry as a ruler had made the mistake of listening to the misgivings of his own advisors. Such an undertaking was patently detrimental to the already precarious political relationship between Gwynedd and England and Joan's position as both Llywelyn's wife and Henry's sister gave her the right to say so accordingly. Moreover, it is implied that her status as queen and her role as a political diplomatic in her own right, and one with broad experience, meant that her advice was to carry even more weight.

Her letter adeptly recognises the crux of the duality of the relationship between the Venedotian and Plantagenet houses. It was one that existed between vassals (herself and Llywelyn as a Welsh royal couple) and overlord (King Henry). But it also existed on a personal level, between beloved sister and beloved brother. In this guise, Joan skilfully adhered to the widespread gender expectations that allowed women a place in politics and polity by being involved in the personal. Her appeal to her brother as king was emotive and one that played on the importance of familial ties, but always highlighting political associations. This is no better demonstrated than in her employment of a new and previously unused title – Lady of Wales, which was conventional epistolary practice to be sure, but its use further substantiates the diplomatic aim of her letter, and thus her official capacity as the wife of the leader of Wales, never mind queen. Perhaps Joan's use of the royal 'we' and 'our' in her letter is indicative of her own perception of her status and authority.

Up to 1230, Joan had obviously been a significant figure in maintaining a diplomatic relationship between Gwynedd and England. Interestingly, her imprisonment had little effect on either her reputation or her activities after this time. In fact, just the opposite rings true as a controversy did not truly exist concerning Joan's assumed relationship with William and the consequent punishments, neither Llywelyn's nor Joan's power or reputation were tarnished. In fact, it may have even been the result of events in 1230 that Llywelyn found the means to express the true extent of his authority as the leading Welsh ruler, with Joan herself arguably becoming the most resourceful and most dominant channel through which it was achieved.

Before 1230, English chancery records use the title of 'Lady of North Wales' in relation to Joan's status as a Welsh queen-consort. However, during 1230 or shortly after, Llywelyn decided to change his own title to underscore the advancement of his authority within Wales, meaning that Joan's own designation changed to follow suit. Previously, Llywelyn went by the designation of 'Prince of North Wales', but officially changed it to 'Prince of Aberffraw and Lord of Snowdon'. The change in Joan's title corresponded with Llywelyn's, but did not exactly mirror it. In point of fact, as Llywelyn's consort, the change in Joan's title to 'Lady of Wales' (*domina Walliae*) was more overtly allied with the change in elevated status of the rulership of Gwynedd. With his consort being identified as such, Llywelyn's claims to overlordship and his status as prince, or king, of Wales were unambiguously reinforced.

Yet, how far was the use of *domina*, like *dominus*, considered merely a title of courtesy when paired with a woman's name, status or position? There was, after all, a commonality in the term *domina*, or 'lady', used to address women of status in the Middle Ages. Records show that for Joan, *domina* was a complementary use of Llywelyn's own *dominus* on occasion, such as in a grant and confirmation made to Basingwerk Abbey in July 1240 by Dafydd for salvation of his soul and those of his mother and father.[13] In such an instance, the style of Lady Joan is less about queenly status and authority than it is about her lifecycle position as mother (and

172

wife) and is used as a general mark of respect. Similar occurrences can be found in both the annals and chronicles of Wales, *Annales Cambriae* and *Cronica de Wallia*, which jointly identify her as 'Lady Joan, daughter of the king of England and wife of Llywelyn prince of Wales' (*Domina Johanna, filia regis Anglie et uxor Lewilini principis Wallie*).[14] Nevertheless, against the setting that such entries are found, Joan's official and political status as Llywelyn's consort is hardly underestimated.

The *Brutiau* (different versions of *Brut y Tywysogion*) in contrast, do emphasise Joan's official status and role as queen, referring to her by her official post-1230 title, 'Lady of Wales'.[15] Such usage specifically in her obituary signifies a status that was rightfully understood and accepted to be her own; this is in an interesting juxtaposition to the fact that in the entry, Llywelyn is proffered no title whatsoever and is only identified as her husband. Joan's official title is also used in her obits found in the Tewkesbury and Chester annals. These examples and those found in the Chancery records where Joan is clearly identified as 'Lady of Wales' are indicative of a regnal status that was acknowledged by her peers.

In comparison, *domina* is certainly how many well-known Anglo-Saxon queens appear in contemporary sources. Furthermore, the use of the title *domina Walliae* for Joan, as lady of the land, was reminiscent of that used by her own great-grandmother, the Empress Matilda of England, who in the mid-twelfth century employed the label as a means of emphasising her position and status as the declared heir to the English throne, 'lady of England', or 'lady of the English'. The *Mabinogion*, once again, is a vital source in assessing contemporary perceptions of queenship and here, too, royal women are often referred to as 'lady' in a number of tales, not just out of a gendered mark of respect, but from perspectives that relay female agency and responsibilities.[16] In terms of Gwynedd specifically, *domina* was a term that became intimately associated with the queen-consorts of Gwynedd during the twelfth century, often in a context associated with the agency of foreign wives.

The term *domina,* as it is associated with Emma of Anjou, likely reflected her own standing as a member of the English royal family, as it did with Joan of England. And like Joan, the narratives in which Emma appears, she too is styled as *domina* in a more gendered mark of respect, often in association with her lifecycles. For example, Gerald of Wales refers to her as 'the sister of King Henry II' (*sororem regis Henricis secundi*), thereby signifying the importance of her association with the

Angevin dynasty and the authority that Dafydd acquired through his marriage to her.[17] The *Brutiau* also refer to Emma as 'the king's sister' (*chwaer yr brenhin*), yet in reference to her marriage to Dafydd, she is emphatically addressed as *'Dam' Emma'* who married king Dafydd (*Brenhin Dauyd*), use of which is indicative of both her gendered position and her newly acquired Welsh royal status.[18] This latter point is made in the acta issued by Emma and her family during their reign. *Domina* was employed to mark her status, authority and royal responsibilities as the wife of a ruling Welsh prince. This is especially noteworthy as it is a title which was dropped in the charters that Emma issued or consented to after Dafydd's fall from grace in the 1190s.[19]

It must be also noted that Joan's title of Lady of Wales is different from that taken up by her own niece and eventual successor, Eleanor de Montfort, who, upon her marriage to Llywelyn ap Gruffudd in 1278, acquired and used the title 'Princess of Wales, Lady of Snowdon' (*principissa Wallie, domina Snaudon*).[20] The paralleled titles between Eleanor and her husband is remarkedly different than between Joan and Llywelyn. In context, this further reminds us that the status Joan and Llywelyn enjoyed as rulers of Wales was incomparable, and that in 1230 the change in royal style for Joan was one that helped reinforce Llywelyn's claims and status as prince of Wales.[21] With her change of title to Lady of Wales, Siwan became the paragon and embodiment of full and complete Welsh power.

Although Llywelyn's determination to change his style marked his need to find a title befitting his increased hegemony, it was also a move that helped to revive his own reputation after the fateful events of 1230. His specific choice to adopt a designation that candidly referred to the authority of the house of Aberffraw above all others, indeed, may have helped him to further justify his hanging of William as his inalienable right to judge without explanation.[22] In many ways, the change in titles for the ruling couple helped them redefine themselves, their power and their authority. Such a consequence of which just may have been a greater elevation of status for both overall. For Joan, her formal transformation to the Lady of Wales might also reflect an elevation of her own, very real, political status and responsibilities after 1230, perhaps even beginning before her release from prison if her letter stems from this time.

It may be that *domina Wallie* used her own position as a member of, and status within, the Angevin dynasty as a means of being able to represent 'her husband's aspirations to Welsh authority rather than employing any real constitutional or politically significance her new title may have implied.'[23] While this may be true, it is important to place Joan's letter in further context in terms of political diplomacy and the expected roles and responsibilities of not only the medieval queen, but a Welsh one at that.

Joan refers to the clerk Instructus, who was shared jointly as messenger between the two royals courts. In terms of Gwynedd, traditionally rulers were inclined to prefer to use members of their own ministerial elite as clerks and political envoys. Llywelyn's grandfather, Owain Gwynedd demonstrated this in letters he sent to the king of France between 1163–66, in his desire to establish a political alliance between the Venedotian house and the house of Capet.[24] During Llywelyn's reign, his *distain*, Ednyfed Fychan, was his most respected emissary after Joan. Ednyfed, like Joan, also received gifts from the English king as rewards for his diplomacy. It is clear from Joan's letter, and from corresponding records from the English chancery, that Instructus was also a trusted royal messenger, employed by Llywelyn and used by both courts.[25] Joan, herself, may have used Instructus on occasion, as well, which is most telling.[26] If Joan and Llywelyn shared a royal messenger, this implies a level of duties directly associated with the office of the Welsh queen in the court of Gwynedd. Most vividly, it provides a vibrant and well-defined image of the king and queen working together in various political capacities.

Thus, as yet another crisis brewed between 1230–31, Joan's place, both in Llywelyn's home and within his court, were neither forgotten nor ignored. In August 1231, the English crossed the Welsh border when it became obvious that the preponderance of Welsh princes supported Llywelyn's actions against the Crown in south Wales; it was they who helped the Venedotian ruler take back Welsh territories occupied by the Anglo-Norman leadership. Although all-out war did not break out and both sides enjoyed moments of victory and suffered losses, Llywelyn was perhaps the winner in the political gamut, if there were one. Uninterested in wrangling with ineffectual arbitration, he made his point to both his allies and his enemies that his authority as the Welsh overlord was one not to be contended with. Llywelyn's overall successes either laid the groundwork for Joan's release from house arrest sometime in 1231, or were, in fact – and more likely – a result of her release earlier in the year. In any event, in 1232 the Lady of Wales once again traversed the Welsh-English border on more than one diplomatic mission to establish peace.

Chapter Fourteen

Lady of Wales

The year 1232 witnessed an attempt by both Gwynedd and England to make amends and negotiate for peace after such an unforgiving and bitter clash the year before. Royal plans to use the sea, and the Irish, as weapons against the Welsh had come to no avail and Hubert de Burgh was eventually ousted from power and replaced by Stephen Segrave as justiciar. For Henry's part, by the spring of 1232 turmoil was developing among his own aristocracy and Wales, in the form of the agitated stand-off with his brother-in-law, was not a situation he had either the time or the inclination to continue, not when his attention was desperately sought elsewhere in his own lands. Llywelyn, for the most part, had successfully ensured that his point – that he was the premiere Welsh leader not to be challenged – had, once again, been made; with the demise of de Burgh, immediate threats to his power assuaged to a large extent. It was in this light that Joan fully employed her status as Llywelyn's primary representative and met with Henry on more than one occasion to negotiate peace. 1232 is also the last year of any recorded activity of her as a travelling diplomat.

Through February and March, the Venedotian clerks Masters Instructus and Philip were granted safe-conduct to Westminster to begin talks of amity. However, in March it seems that Philip's visit was a general failure as any outcome is inconclusive. Nevertheless, he must have met with some success assuming it was because of his visit that the manors of Bidford and Suckley, which had previously been confiscated, were returned to Elen and her husband of ten years, John, the earl of Huntington.[1] However, it should be considered that it may have been after these failed attempts at negotiation by Instructus and Philip, and before her visit in person with the king in May, that Joan sent her letter pleading for peace to her brother. More accurately, Joan could have written her letter and sent it around 12 March 1232, perhaps following the failed diplomatic visit, after which correspondence between the two courts refers to breaches in truce. Indeed, Henry's distrust of Instructus to which Joan alludes may have been sown at this time. It may have also been Joan's intercession via her letter around this time that compelled Henry to return manors to his niece and her husband, which had been confiscated on account of his war with Llywelyn. Doing so would have easily followed the traditional trend of rewarding Joan for her diplomatic contributions with the gifting or re-gifting of manors, and although Suckley and Bidford had been passed to Elen and John on their marriage, they were still, in essence, associated largely with Joan.

A mere two months later, on 19 May 1232, the body of King John was reinterred at Worcester cathedral. The late king's body was covered in silk and a newly carved lifelike effigy solemnly placed over him. The tomb itself was crowned with a silk canopy to hang over it. Candles paid for by the royal government were placed around the tomb and lit in prayer for his soul.[2] It was an official and sober ceremony attended by Henry, and possibly by Joan, who may have been eager to attend to bid honour to her beloved father and her memories of him.

A trip to Worcester and Joan's attendance at John's reinterment could have also been a precursor to her meeting scheduled days later with the king at Shrewsbury. In fact, it was while at Wenlock in Shropshire that her brother issued her safe-conduct on 24 May to meet him on the 27th in their familiar stomping grounds in Shrewsbury. As such, Joan and her brother may have had 'behind-the-scenes' discussions at Worcester before formal parlay took place at Shrewsbury. Joan seems to have been the lead negotiator as part of the larger delegation, which also included Venedotian envoys Ednyfed Fychan and Einion Fychan. It seems Llywelyn was supposed to travel separately as he received safe-conduct which was issued on 28 May, when the king was already at Shrewsbury.[3] However, it seems that he did not attend any of the scheduled meetings with Henry over the next six months, leaving Joan to parlay for him in his stead. The meeting in May seems to have come to nothing, as does her meeting with the king at Shrewsbury that took place in early August.[4]

Personal tragedy struck Joan and her family in 1232. Marared's husband, John de Braose, died suddenly at the age of about 34, after a fall from his horse while in his estate at Bramber in Sussex. Regardless of how Marared felt towards John personally, it must have been a devastating blow to be widowed in her mid-twenties with young, vulnerable children at her side, and especially during a time of instability in Anglo-Welsh relations, which meant a troubling sense of insecurity in regards to maintaining her hold over the family lordship. Marared's son and John's heir, William, was still at a young age when he became his father's successor and took up the title Lord of Bramber, having only been born in early to mid-1220s. If she had been worried, the king proved Marared right to be so as he took Gower and Swansea and passed them to Peter des Riveaux, who in essence became the 'new' Hubert de Burgh after the latter's downfall. Nevertheless, by the following summer her uncle had promised Marared that she would not be married against her will, perhaps the king felt some sense of familial obligation and protection of Marared as his niece, regardless of whether the agreement was concessionary to formal peace talks with Welsh envoys.

Soon after, Marared moved closer to home when she married her second husband, Walter de Clifford, a Marcher lord in Herefordshire – a man her mother's age. Although Walter initially rebelled against King Henry in baronial discontent faced by the English Crown in 1233, much like her sister Gwladus' first husband, Reginald de Braose, Walter soon switched sides and found himself fighting against his new father-in-law. Marared's marriage with Walter may have not been an easy one for a handful of reasons, not least because of his struggles with her father. Walter's temperament may have also proven difficult to contend with. It is reputed that during a dispute he had with King Henry, Walter forced the royal envoy, who brought Walter a king's writ that displeased him, to eat the writ, wax seal and all.

Another blow occurred in October 1232 with the death of friend, family member, advocate and chief ally Ranulf, earl of Chester. Although the eastern frontier of Gwynedd remained secured as the earldom of Chester was passed to Elen's husband, John the Scot, in November, the enormity of losing such a stalwart and political behemoth must have weighed heavily with Llywelyn and Joan herself. Naturally, if her mother were Ranulf's wife, there was further need for condolences and emotional support to be offered during the changing of the guard.

In early December, less than two months after Ranulf's death, the king of England issued safe-conduct to Joan and Dafydd, with a promise of safe travels that also extended to those whom they should bring with them, to attend Shrewsbury to pick up the peace negotiations that had floundered over the summer. This venture was much more successful as it resulted in an agreement that was acceptable to both parties. To the king, it was likely Joan who promised that Llywelyn would pay all excesses made against him, and importantly, restore all the lands that the Welsh leader had seized the year before. Also on behalf of Llywelyn, Joan probably complied to the assignation of William de Braose's lands to Dafydd and his wife, Isabella. This latter concession was no hardship for Llywelyn. In fact, it fell right in line with his long-term goal of establishing Dafydd as his heir. Once Dafydd succeeded the Venedotian throne, he would already be the established overlord of those lands in the middle March long coveted by Llywelyn, and over which his control was a strong determinant in a successful rule throughout Wales. How awkward it must have been for Joan to negotiate terms regarding the vast lands once held by her supposed former and deceased paramour. To have to confer over them in front of her son, in particular, must have been uncomfortable for her, but the political substance at the heart of the assignation would have been more important to focus on.

That Dafydd, who was of age by this time, attended with Joan on this mission and agreed to terms is important, especially in light of the fact that this is the last official record we have of Joan on a formal diplomatic mission. It only makes sense that Dafydd, who was to be heir as the essential ruler of Wales, supersede his mother's diplomatic status. Attending diplomatic missions and partaking in conferences of negotiation with Joan would have been valuable, educative measures taken by the Welsh royal family to train Dafydd for future missions when he would meet the king, ruler to ruler. With his mother's insight, experience and presence at the forefront of mediation, Dafydd was probably provided safe opportunities to quietly assess how the king reacted to situations, learn to read his mannerisms, and even between the lines of what was said or not said. Diplomatic ventures with Joan would have helped foster in Dafydd an understanding of how personal relationships could be manipulated or managed in order to effect political gain. From Joan, Dafydd probably learned a most important lesson in how best to negotiate familial ties with political needs and aspirations. It is no coincidence that the Lady of Wales stops appearing in chancery records as an official envoy after December 1232. The years 1233 and 1234 were turbulent for the English Crown, but advantageous to Venedotian rule and to the continued training of Llywelyn's chosen *edling*.

The growing dissention in the English court reached an apex in south Wales in the summer of 1233 when Richard Marshal, who succeeded his brother William as earl of Pembroke, challenged the royal government. Marshal led a baronial campaign specifically against the influences of the king's new favourites Peter de Roches, the bishop of Winchester, and his nephew Peter de Riveaux. According to Roger of Wendover, the fast-track to power enjoyed by these men after the fall of Hubert de Burgh the previous year flouted justice and threatened the rights of the English race. For Marshal and his adherents, 'the oppression of the Poitevins' (referencing the increased and unpopular power of the queen of England's family members) was of utmost importance.

Llywelyn used the disturbance and the distraction of English power to his own advantage to further mark his influence and authority within Wales and along the border. Through significant areas of the March, the Welsh ruler sieged and destroyed towns such as Oswestry and Clun and castles like Brecon. In spite of such destruction the relationship between Gwynedd and England was not one that was irrevocably broken by any means. In fact, on 14 October Dafydd was granted Purleigh manor in Essex. A new truce was not initiated as this gift to the king's nephew may suggest. The grant, however, may have been an extra show of good faith in the renewal of truce first established in 1231.

Llywelyn eventually joined the baronial opposition in October, making 'a solemn pact' with Marshal and continued his side of the offensive by attacking much of south and western Wales, from Cardiff to Abergavenny and Carmarthen. The conflict, a burgeoning civil war reminiscent of John's reign, raged on until it finally became clear to the king that the only real solution to ending the struggle would be to instigate the reform sought by the rebels and clean up his government. Providence, however, seemed to be on the side of the Crown because in early 1234 Marshal was killed in Ireland, where he had been led by the rebellion. In March, Llywelyn agreed to a truce with the English at Brocton in Shropshire, which was later ratified in June.

Safe-conduct lasting for three weeks was granted to Ednyfed Fychan, 'and to those he brings with him', to treat with the king at Worcester for peace between the Crown and Llywelyn. Under the same safe-conduct the king had given to Dafydd, as Llywelyn's son, 'and those he brings with him', if he, too, would come to Worcester with the said Ednyfed.[5] Though unrecorded, it is very probable that Joan was one of the unnamed travellers to Worcester under safe-conduct; this time in the capacity as the king's sister, Dafydd's mother and Llywelyn's wife. What later became known as the Pact of Myddle, a truce was sealed in June 1234 and subsequently became known as a significant watershed moment in Llywelyn's reign.[6] One would like to think that after all of her endeavours, Joan, too, would have been there to witness proceedings.

Although in the summer of June 1234 it was unknown to be the case, the Pact of Myddle essentially established a permanent peace between Gwynedd and England, and more significantly, Llywelyn's supremacy as the leading Welsh ruler. The truce was renewed time and time again, lasting for the remainder of both his and Joan's lives. Surely having been such a crucial adherent and formative political diplomat in Anglo-Welsh relations for the previous twenty-three years, and most recently as 1232, she knew the terms to be offered by the Welsh side, and also what they would agree to. Given her experiences in the field, there could have been some inkling of the potential for long-lasting peace on the face of it. Although it is only on reflection that in so many ways the Pact of Myddle was a culmination of her many political endeavours, whether or not she was one of the behind-the-scenes arbitrators chosen by Llywelyn to outline the details of the treaty itself, the result must have been a richly rewarding one for her on a personal front in the end. The effects of loyalties being torn between her natal and marital families for a quarter of a century surely had an impact on who she was as a person. How she operated. How she thought. How she felt. There are likely no words to be able to describe her experiences in wondering just how far after that summer day in 1234 that such a deeply personal struggle may have finally reached its end.

Epilogue

After 1232, Joan disappears from official records. The only indication that we have that she remained active on any diplomatic front resides in her very last petition made to Henry in November 1235, asking for the pardon of one Robert, son of Reginald, who had been accused of the death of a man named William, a son of a man referred to as Ralph of Credenhill.[1] In this apparently final act Joan proved she was still a skilled petitioner as her request was granted.

From the summer of 1234 until her death in February 1237, Joan experienced a peace that had largely evaded her for the majority of her life. Save for the very first years of their marriage, the last three years of her life may have been on particularly special period in which she and Llywelyn may have spent time together in their own lands, in their own courts and in their own homes, on a consistent basis. Thus, in her twilight years, the Lady of Wales was probably able to retire to a quieter way of life so unbeknownst to her for close to twenty years.

On 2 February 1237, between the ages of 47–50, Joan of England closed her eyes for the final time and died at her home in Aber. It would be nice to think she was surrounded by her loved ones – in the least, the man she called her husband, the father of her children and her king for thirty years. The founding of the friary of Llanfaes in her honour seems to have done little to temper Llywelyn's profound sense of loss that was both deeply personal and which held great political significance across his realm. Having lost his wife and confidant, the mother of his children, and his queen of more than thirty years, the grief that Llywelyn likely experienced was palpable. In April he made a grant to the prior and canons of Ynys Lannog, an Augustinian priory opposite to that of Penmon which sits on the mainland of Anglesey, not far from Llanfaes.[2] It was a grant he made at his royal *llys* in Rhosyr, where he and Joan surely sent many an occasion. It may be time spent at Aber, at least so soon after Joan's death, was too painful an experience for him and he made a conscious decision to grieve in another location that brought him happier memories un-associated with the trauma of 1230 and Joan's recent passing.[3]

The obituaries found for Joan across all the Welsh chronicles are befitting such a woman of royal stature and though they say little in words, they say a great deal in symbolism. In comparison to any of the other obituaries found for women in these sources, Joan's are by far the longest and most honourable of their kind. Such rectitude is indicative of her status as a queen, but may also intimate how she was actually viewed among her adopted people and how she was recognised as an individual in her own right – as a women who wielded successful agency and who, certainly on occasion, worked tirelessly for the Welsh cause. The fact that her titles are used to define her first and foremost, such as *domina/dam/ arglwyddes*, indeed, Lady of Wales, accentuates her symbolic stature as the wife to the leading Welsh ruler, if not the symbolic importance of her own status as queen in and of itself.[4]

Joan's death seems to have had a great impact on the aging ruler, who was by then himself in his late sixties, and in that same year, Llywelyn, the prince of Aberffraw, lord of Snowdon, suffered a devastating stroke that left him paralytic and apparently unable to rule, effectively putting an end to his reign. In 1238, at the abbey of Strata Florida, the princes of Wales swore fealty to Dafydd as their leader. Short of receiving homage, which had been Llywelyn's original intent, but denied by the king, this event remained the crowning glory for all the intents and purposes towards which Llywelyn and Joan had worked their whole lives. In 1238, Dafydd became the true heir and on Llywelyn's own death in April 1240, he became the first and true prince of Wales.

Conclusion

The rule of Llywelyn the Great dominates much of the discussion about political life during the Age of Princes. Seen as one of the greatest rulers of an independent Wales, his ambition to create a single principality was novel, if not ambitious and maybe even a little naïve. The changes he made to Venedotian polity, the flourishing of the arts and his generosity to the church during his reign were but a few of his achievements. It is largely agreed that his triumphs and rise to power were not just down to his astute political acumen, but personality. This is especially relevant in the knowledge that all he achieved in his lifetime dissipated soon after his death.

His biographer, Roger Turvey, has rightly pointed out that what we know of Llywelyn, and how we are able to assess elements of his character, are 'by means of what he did and how he did it'.[1] There is no starker contrast than how historians are able to approach the life of the first Lady of Wales. In some cases we know what she did, but in only one case do we know how she actually did it. The hows, whys, and importantly, her reaction to events, the problems she faced and the burdens she carried, can only remain matters of contexualisation. Her person, her actions, her relationships and her life overall have remained a mystery for 800 years and will continue to remain so forever more.

One of the fundamental purposes behind this study of Joan of England is to help supply the woefully anorexic historiography concerning women and medieval Wales with some constructive food for thought. It has not been about simply discussing Joan's life and the events that happened. That would have been an impractical task when there were so many cultural and social dynamics at play that had bearing on her movements and participation in political life. In fact, rummaging through Joan's personal history we can see that there were a number of factors that defined both her personal life and her career – factors that tied into the hows and whys – she was intimately involved in the Anglo-Welsh political forum on a number of important occasions; factors that contributed to her political responsibilities.

Yet, by placing Joan within the principal narrative of Anglo-Welsh relations in the early thirteenth century we achieve a greater sense of who she may have been – certainly, our understanding of her role as Lady of Wales, on both the personal and political level, becomes slightly sharper. Perhaps the biggest changes that occurred in Llywelyn's own kingdom was the move towards the more centralised bureaucracy of his own government, and more specifically, a more ordered structure to the organisation of a prince's council to which, it seems, Joan played an integral part. Her role as Llywelyn's closest advisor and emissary was based on a number of factors, including her position as his wife, her position in and intimate connection to the English Crown and court and her position as Dafydd's mother.

Wide networks of family connections such as these, and diplomatic necessities, allowed women movement in the wider political realms of the Middle Ages. Yet, more often than not, movement was dictated by personal and individual circumstances and not all women can be presumed to have undertaken such an essential role as Joan did. For Joan, however, her anticipated career as a political diplomat was firmly established in 1201 when Llywelyn reinforced his newly formed relationship with the king of England by agreeing to marry her.

Throughout this book the intention has been to get readers to think more about the possibilities of Joan's political role – activities that have been left unrecorded. It is important to consider how far a role she may have actually played acting in Llywelyn's place during his long absences from Gwynedd, possibly as 'regent' or even 'justiciar'. Joan may have been a controversial figure, as suggested largely by the law of Gwynedd and her obvious support for her son's succession over his older half-brother's, which may, indeed, have made it more difficult for her to act as Llywelyn's representative than if she were by his side. Nevertheless, it is important to consider the wider range of activities, duties and responsibilities which she may have had, and the real nature of her position as a royal wife and queen. As Llywelyn's closest advisor and emissary, Joan's role was dictated by expectations of her status as a royal woman in her own right, as the reigning consort of the leading Welsh ruler of the time. Even if only a figurehead, Joan's eminence above her peers was unmistakable. But she was not just a figurehead. She was active and successful on important occasions. The queen in Welsh culture, certainly in Gwynedd, had expectations of office; expectations that seemed to advance during Joan's reign.

When Llywelyn adopted the regal designation Prince of Aberffraw, Lord of Snowdon, as a means of reflecting the nature of current political circumstances, and to echo his ancient rights to overlordship, in Wales, Joan's own change of title echoed this Wales-wide authority in a more explicit way: Lady of Wales. All of her titles, but overtly that of Lady of Wales, implies that her position and status were proportionate to those of a traditional medieval queen. The fact that her title changed later on in life seems to reflect not only the increase in her status, concomitant to Llywelyn's own, but the increase in her activities. In many ways, the two seem relational.

The political marriages of Europe's ruling elite in the Middle Ages were intrinsically tied to ideals and expectations of rulership, and medieval Wales was no exception to this rule. Marriage was a tool to form alliances early on among the Welsh-Welsh, and by Llywelyn's reign, a tool that was increasingly used to form important Anglo-Welsh alliances, as a means of procuring peace. The marriages of Joan and Llywelyn's own children to Marcher families are testaments to the wide-ranging importance of such a policy. If marriage was a political instrument based on opportunity and ambition, then it is vitally important to reflect on how Welsh rulership was both conducted and perceived as a whole and not in isolation, where only the man, the husband, the king, was the sole public figure, or the only half the royal couple who had power, authority or status above peers.

Examining Joan's life and her activities especially expose the need to have more balanced, critical discussions concerning traditional forms of Welsh rulership, and in particular, traditional forms of royal female power. In other words, how both kingship and queenship operated as a united front. Sources suggest a lingering expectation spilled over from much more archaic times, that wife and husband, queen and king, acted together both as a unit and individually, but always as expressions of masculine power. Overt expressions of masculine power dominate the original sources which, by extension, has meant that historical discussions have also been dominated by a painfully male-centred perspective.

By and large, Welsh history has been very contracted and chiefly, the position of women has hardly been discussed outside the terms of law, literature, marriage and a genealogical milieu. Even within these individual strands, the popular approach remains the use of a masculine lens. Joan's experiences and activities illustrate just how problematic, and detrimental, this is to our knowledge and understanding of native Wales as a whole. Both women and men were defined by gender expectations and ideals, both of which were large determinants to how women and men interacted and how their positions and roles in life were defined. It is only through the interpolation of the experiences of both women and men that we are able to reach a more egalitarian understanding of 'reality' as it was. The study of history is left wanting if it does not incorporate the way that the activities, roles and expectations of both sexes have been socially constructed *across* gender. This means rethinking and offering new interpretations of source material. It means questioning traditional 'givens'. Joan was not alone in the roles she undertook as the queen consort to the reigning Venedotian leader. But arguably, she is the important bridge between her predecessors and her successors – Siwan was the model of Welsh queenship in its many guises.

The authority and esteem of the queen in Gwynedd is found in the more arcane Welsh sources, steeped in the much older and highly revered oral tradition. For instance, the *Mabinogion* and Welsh Triads tell us of the wife of the Roman Emperor Maxen Wledig. Elen was not just Maxen's wife or the Empress of Rome. She was Elen of the Hosts from Caernarfon, a royal woman of authority in her own right, renowned for creating the infrastructure that united all four corners of the island of Britain in sovereignty, summoning a great host to aid her husband to siege Rome, and his advisor in matters of polity.

The Welsh Triads, themselves, declare that the kingdom of Gwynedd was 'held by the distaff' no less than three times.[2] Crucially, this reference is linked to *The Descent of the Men of the North* (*Bonedd Gwŷr y Gogledd*), a pedigree of the sixth-century rulers of northern Britain. It is more than noteworthy that the Venedotian dynasty, founded by the legendary Welsh hero Cunedda Wledig, is explicitly descended through the female line. Moreover, is it only a fluke that early Welsh poets refer to Gwynedd as the land of Esyllt, the mother of Rhodri Mawr, the ninth-century 'King of Wales'? Sure, these examples could simply indicate claims to male rulership through the maternal line, but this in itself showcases, in the very least, a semblance of reverence for the status, power, authority and reputation of royal women. It is not difficult to argue that these references may also collectively also refer to times when the north of Wales could have actually ruled by women.

We know that by the twelfth century the Venedotian queen was one of esteemed status, who beheld duties and expectations that mirrored those of her husband. The biography of Gruffudd ap Cynan tells us that Queen Angharad was noteworthy for being generous to the poor and mild-tempered, compared to the occasional ferocity of her husband. She was honoured for being wise and prudent, but above all, a woman of good counsel – a counsel-woman, an advisor. She also held and managed a significant portion of lands in widowhood, including the crucial harbour and *commote* of Porthaethwy on Anglesey.[3] The fact that it is recorded that Gruffudd left her half of all his possessions on his death is testament to the potential power she wielded as consort. Perhaps it was even Angharad herself who commissioned the biography in honour of her husband's memory and was concerned with the dual portrayal of her person as one who prescribed to Welsh socio-cultural gender expectations and stereotypes (literally being the opposite of Gruffudd in every characteristic), but also honouring her own independent influence and authority as a queen in the twelfth century.

The queenly agency of Angharad's immediate successors are no less significant, even if references to them are meagre. Regardless of how she is portrayed in the small handful sources to be found, it is clear that Angharad's niece, Cristin, the wife of Owain Gwynedd, also exercised independent political authority and influence. After all, she is accredited with orchestrating the political rise to power of her own sons by Owain, who wound up governing Gwynedd, regardless of the difficulties that followed. Similar to cases found elsewhere in Europe, say in Anglo-Saxon England or thirteenth-century France under the regency of Blanche of Castile (r. 1223–1234, 1248–1252), it may be that Cristin's status as queen dowager, and the mother of Gwynedd's potential rulers, was significant enough to allow her to craft her own political identity and agenda by exerting her influence and power through the advancement of her sons' claims to succession. Surely, as young rulers, her sons may have been subject to her will, or even that of their maternal kin. Cristin's role and her power to influence was crucial to the establishment of her sons' increased hegemony.

Joan's own aunt and immediate predecessor, Emma of Anjou, issued charters jointly with her husband Dafydd, but also independently, using her own royal seal. This is especially important when noting that she did so while her husband was under exile in England when some were enacted. The very purpose of her marriage to Dafydd ab Owain in 1175 was to instil peace and carve out a mutually supportive relationship between Gwynedd and England. Sources like Gerald of Wales and the chronicles make it clear that it was Emma who was the crucial link, implying that it was expected that she play the role of advisor and emissary between Dafydd and Henry II, her half-brother, when required.

Although previously 'unified' by cultural practices, norms and perceptions, largely through laws, literature, legends and lore, Llywelyn's peripatetic rise to power meant that Wales witnessed a form of unification that it had never really experienced before – Llywelyn's feats and achievements earning him the eponymous epithet 'the Great'. At the beginning of the thirteenth century, Wales embarked on an era that can be considered one of great change – change arguably instigated by Llywelyn, and even Joan, themselves as important cultural vicissitudes in social practices occurred during their reign, not least the removal of successorship for illegitimate sons and the practice of concubinage as an accepted form of marriage. The impact of this transformation alone affected and elevated the status of the royal woman who was the ruler's chosen *gwraig briodas*, as Joan was. As such, women who found themselves in the more inferior marital relationships that defined concubinage, were in possession of fewer rights and less legal protections than legitimate wives.

Of course, on the flip side, it can be argued that the rise in the practice of primogeniture in Wales meant that status of *gwraig briodas* declined, because in essence the status of the son would eventually overshadow that of his mother, in effect, demoting her to something no more than a procreatrix. Thinking about the wording of the 1211 agreement which stresses the need for Llywelyn to ensure he had a son by Joan specifically, or else his kingdom would escheat to England on his death, certainly gives an impression that Joan's main duty was as a procreatrix. Yet the elevation of Gwynedd's status over that of any other Welsh kingdom through the adoption of primogeniture also suggests that the queen's status, Joan's status, in fact, may have increased in tandem. Adhering to more established European practices like primogeniture that secured and advanced rights to rule, meant that both Joan and Llywelyn were, in effect, on par with their European counterparts – their own dynasty was secure and established. If nothing else, a royal woman's role as mother of a potential heir afforded her power simply by association. We know, of course, that Joan's authority was much more than being perfunctory. Understanding the exact terms used to define a woman in a Welsh court as queen highlights the fact that there was a culturally constructed concept of queenship itself.

Such transformations helped elevate Llywelyn's authority, eventually solidifying his right to reign as the nominal prince of Wales. His marriage to Joan, daughter to one of the most powerful, albeit largely flawed, rulers of thirteenth-century Europe further propelled the movement of Wales – and if not Wales as whole, certainly Gwynedd – to further embrace the systems and cultural routines of wider western European societies, bringing it into the fold rather than allowing Wales to remain on the periphery of medieval Europe. Although Llywelyn had much to do with these developments and has been given mostly sole credit, Joan likely had a hand in this Welsh renaissance of sorts.

Laws, arts and religion also flourished during Joan and Llywelyn's reign – another symbol of their success – and some of the older oral sources, especially those that have references to strong queens, like Elen of the Hosts, were codified at this time. The Iorwerth text, the updated Venedotian version of the native Welsh laws of Hywel Dda written during the married couple's rule, is witness to the rise in status and increase in numbers of officers of the court, including the queen's. The queen in the Iorwerth certainly has a more elevated standing than compared to other redactions and the expansion in the number of her officers is a good indication of the elevation of her own status within the royal court – even in light of the contradictory suggestion by Ior that the queen remain in a more private sphere. Examples of the queen having her own scribe and her own coffers, and more importantly, her own seal in Iorwerth hints at the very real duties and responsibilities the Welsh queen was to undertake and, in fact, did.

As such, two pertinent questions need to be asked: does the emphasised status of the queen reflect Joan's own authority and agency? And, how far, if at all, did Joan act as a patron, of the arts or the church, or how much influence did she have over how the laws of her realm represent the queen? The laws stemming from Gwynedd in particular are noteworthy as arguably, they may reflect how Joan and Llywelyn, and the Venedotian court of Gwynedd as a whole, viewed and expected queenship to operate, and thus reflect much of Joan's actual duties. That there is French vocabulary within the text itself, not found in other versions of the laws, indicates her own cultural influences and the impact Joan had within the Welsh court overall.

However, we cannot take the status of the queen in these laws strictly at face value and categorically declare that she (i.e. Joan) was at the vanguard of political activity or that she regularly carried out municipal duties. Iorwerth has a particularly moralising tone uncommon in the other, earlier law redactions stemming from other areas of Wales. On the surface, the seemingly greater emphasis on the queen's placement in the royal chamber in this text, in particular, seems to suggest that the relevance of the queen, and Joan specifically, was simply as a figurehead only; that the ruler's wife was to enjoy the opulence of her royal status, but to take no part in the day-to-day functions of monarchical governance. Indeed, subversive as they may be, the exhortations that the public role of the queen are believed to be aimed specifically at Joan and the supposed isolation of the queen in the chamber, or 'private' realm, was a real and contemporaneous reproach aimed at the woman who played a very real role in Anglo-Welsh relations.[4] Yet we know from other versions of the laws, and other contemporary sources like the *Mabinogion*, for instance, that the chamber was the traditionally the hub of royal governance and diplomatic activity. That the laws suggest the queen's and king's chambers were interlinked, physically connected to each other, is indicative that there was an expectation of the queen to be involved in various levels of governance, even if as a host to political dignitaries.

It is important to consider that the conservatism of the lawyers and the moralising tone of the thirteenth-century Venedotain text may not actually be aimed at Joan as an individual, but at the office of the queen itself; one that was public, visible and active in very real ways. Iorwerth was written during the time of change in Wales and one that especially observed an increase in bureaucracy. Llywelyn's exploitation of the flexibility of Welsh laws to adapt to changing circumstances meant that within his own kingdom there was much assimilation of Welsh courtly culture to match the more obvious conventions used on the Continent. This is particularly noticeable in Llywelyn's efforts to establish a more centralised form of governance.

These aspects are crucially important to understanding the events in Joan's life because her story in this context of great change has additional significance. During eras of great change it is generally believed that women were increasingly denied opportunities to profit from the changes that took place. The rise of monarchical and governmental institutionalism during the twelfth-century Renaissance across Europe, for instance, seemingly pushed the power and authority previously enjoyed by royal and aristocratic women to the background. Before the twelfth century, the aristocratic household stood at the centre of power. Yet with the rise of feudalism and the changes associated with it, the domestic sphere became increasingly 'private' and increasingly viewed as the woman's domain.

A new order of society always entails a revamping of gender norms, and often hones the limits of social acceptability concerning 'femalesness'/'maleness' and 'femininity'/'masculinity'. A royal couple was not exempt from adhering to these rules. Indeed, as models of femaleness and maleness, and as wives and husbands, they were intrinsically bound to them. But did such institutional changes really affect attitudes towards gender so drastically that women were suddenly inherently denied any form of agency? The simplest answer is, no. Just because women were largely excluded from government and the creation of public policies on the outside does not mean that they took no part in the decisions of any kind, especially decisions and polity that intimately affected them.

The adoption of European conventions by the foremost reigning Welsh dynasty must have also included an adoption of ideals and values, including gendered stereotypes and expectations, concerning kingship and queenship. This acculturation could have involved a shift in the official agency of the queen and her visibility; her authority, indeed, may have shifted to a more domesticised and unofficial ambit. However, it is imperative to understand that the distinguished position of the queen depicted in the Iorwerth redaction is believed to be contemporary commentary that specifically relates to Joan and her special standing as queen in Llywelyn's court. The blatant irony of laws stemming from Llywelyn and Joan's court that somewhat portray the queen as a domesticised figurehead when the real queen herself was visible, mobile and a prominent dignitary during some of the most tumultuous times in Venedotian rule is not lost on any reader. Similar to a number of male writers throughout the Middle Ages, the conservative lawyers of Gwynedd played with common hyperbole concerning the activities, and perhaps even personality of Joan as an individual woman, in furtive attempts to outline the limitations and expectations of the role of the office she held, as queen and as the king's wife.

For Joan, the importance of the counsel she provided Llywelyn throughout their thirty-year plus marriage, and which he relied on, certainly provides a strong argument that the queen in the Welsh court, and expectations of her office, were more active, influential and politically significant than has ever really been previously considered. Throwing into the mix our understanding of the activities of Joan's predecessors and successors, there seems to have been a sense of long-term continuity in expectations of their roles and how they may have practiced queenship. Perchance Joan's successes were informed by the roles undertaken by her predecessors, which also informed the activities and roles played by her contemporaries and own successors.

Was the role that Senana ferch Caradog played in meeting with Henry III in 1241 to (unsuccessfully) secure the release of Gruffudd from English custody based, in some part, on Joan's political conducts? She initially appeared in person at Westminster on Gruffudd's behalf rather than any other member of their royal *llys* – a particularly notable event given that one of the sureties on the subsequent peace treaty that was to follow after their convention in Shrewsbury was Maredudd ap Rhobert, lord of Cedewain, the 'eminent' or 'chief counsellor of Wales'.

In fact, her conduct in many ways bears all the hallmarks of queenly intervention – whether at the instigation of Gruffudd himself or not. She pledged an oath on Gruffudd's behalf on holy relics, indicative of the acceptance of her rule as lord in her husband's stead. The use of her own seal on the document was a clear representation of her own agency and independent identity, symbolic of all associated with one authoritative enough to carry a seal: rights to and ownership of lands, wealth, status and power. Further, Matthew Paris, who records that it was 'by the hand of Senana' that Gruffudd's seal was affixed to the treaty also intriguingly seems to reference Senana's status specifically as a Welsh magnate. During Gruffudd's imprisonment, she was given special privileges to the English Crown to visit him and her eldest son in the Tower. She was also looked after by the king from whom she received 10 marks of gift on one occasion while Gruffudd was in captivity. After his death, the king still looked after her providing her with 100 shillings for maintenance and a robe worth 2 marks. These were annual gifts from the king. She also received an additional one-off payment of another 100 shillings for her continued maintenance.

Senana is the first and only recorded royal Welsh women (for all intents and purposes, we could argue a Welsh queen without a throne) to actually sign a peace treaty with a king of England. In fact, the settlement that Senana negotiated is the only surviving document of its kind, relating to the power and authority of Welsh royal women. In order to obtain her husband's freedom, Senana agreed to a number of extraordinarily crippling terms, including the promise of handing over her remaining sons as additional hostages if required, and had a handful of the most important men of the time who acted as her sureties, including Gwladus' second husband, Roger Mortimer. Like the other royal women before and after her, the Welsh chronicles remain silent on Senana's involvement in 1240–41, which, indeed, may have been a pointed commentary in itself.

Eleanor de Montfort, the wife of Llywelyn ap Gruffudd, daughter of Simon and Eleanor de Montfort, cousin to King Edward I and Joan's own niece, was herself successful in political mediation during the waning years of Welsh independence. Though a shockingly short reign, having died in childbirth six months before the death of her husband in 1282, as small as it is, her own surviving acta is authoritative enough to indicate that in the six years she was married, and the four she lived and ruled in Gwynedd as a lady of Wales, she was proving herself to be an astute representative of her Welsh home, never mind one to stand up for her own personal demands. Records certainly indicate that Joan's own political conduct and diplomacy were exemplary models of how to conduct the role of queen with success. In an undated letter sent by Eleanor to Edward I, with whom she was extremely close, she castigates the English king for his actions towards her husband, and with uncanny similarity to Joan's own letter to Henry thirty years earlier, Eleanor also pleaded for mercy on bended knee and with the shedding of tears. Indeed, it is clear that Eleanor was shaping into a formidable political opponent, and one whom the king of England himself initially admitted to being fearful of having enough support and power to potentially raise a rebellion similar to her father's.

The last reigning royal wife of Wales was Elizabeth de Ferrers (d. after 1283), wife Dafydd ap Gruffudd (d. 3 October 1283), son of Senana, brother to Llywelyn ap Gruffudd and the last prince of independent

Wales. Like Joan, Senana and Eleanor, Elizabeth is documented as travelling to England to parlay with the king of England. Even before Elizabeth de Ferrers, the last official female royal of Gwynedd, disappeared without a trace after the death of her husband, she is recorded as pleading to the English king for clemency and for her husband's release from the king's prison. For the last reigning queen, it was a final, yet unsuccessful, attempt to plead for mercy during the final vestiges of native Welsh rule. It is not hard to imagine that Elizabeth conducted herself in a manner that mimicked her previous queenly exemplars.

The extraordinary exception to the list of active royal wives is Isabella de Braose, Dafydd's wife. Unfortunately, her life is so terribly obscure, evidence verges on the point of non-existence. This is not to say she did not undertake duties similar to these other women once Dafydd became ruler in 1240. In fact, she may have been educated in the particulars and expectations of Welsh queenship by Joan herself, regardless of a relationship that must have been inherently difficult for the both of them given William's death in 1230. Royal protocol always outweighs personal considerations. Senana, too, knew Joan of course. How much or how little is unknown and perhaps even unimportant, but it would be surprising if Senana did not look to Joan's own accomplishments – whether through Joan herself or by word of mouth – and how she conducted herself in political forums as a means of helping her outline her own path to achieving her goals.

Against a century's worth of circumstances in which a long succession Venedotian queens participated in various political undertakings with the English Crown, Joan's own standing and activities seem less particular to her personal circumstances and more particular to her office as queen. Yet as specific circumstances largely dictated female involvement in the predominantly masculine realm of politics, what does it tell us that Joan is, in fact, the only queen to appear in Welsh sources in a political context? Although it has long been assumed that it was her positions as Llywelyn's wife, as King John's daughter and as Henry III's half-sister that afforded her the opportunities to partake in serious political matters, the successful results of her intervention suggests a woman of aptitude for negotiation and diplomacy. Her efforts were rewarded with the receipt of manors and, most importantly, her legitimisation, which was backed by Henry and the pope.

The familial-political context of her involvement in Anglo-Welsh relations may have been defined by the accepted boundaries wherein a Welsh queen was expected to operate as a diplomat and counsellor. That the documented activities of other reigning Venedotian consorts are similar to her own suggests an overall expectation of native Welsh queenship that was, in a number of ways, akin to more prevalent European standards wherein queenly intervention was largely accepted when the fate of either the royal family itself or the greater family lordship were at stake. Joan's own activities highlight some of the parameters of governance in which a royal woman in Wales could manoeuvre, and in fact did – as is also illustrated by the examples above. Joan, of course, stands apart from the rest because the power and status that Llywelyn, and her as his reigning consort, wielded in the early thirteenth century was not only unparalleled during their lifetime, but has remained so throughout Welsh history.

Welsh customs aside, it is likely that Joan herself brought some ideas of 'queenship' and the career of the royal woman as a political diplomat with her on her marriage to Llywelyn and that some of her own understanding of Norman-French customs were subsumed in some aspects of Welsh culture. It is vital to remember that Joan not only stemmed from royalty herself, but that she also ran in the same circles as the biggest of names in early to mid-thirteenth-century Europe. She may have spent time with Isabella of Angoulême on various occasions when meeting with her father – never mind the possibility that perhaps she spent time in the queen's household in Normandy before she sailed to Britain in 1203. Joan also must of have spent some time with Eleanor of Provence (r. 1236–1272), Henry III's wife on occasion. Recent scholarship that is emerging on Eleanor shows that she was an astute political diplomat in her own right. Did Anglo-Welsh discussions take place between these two women on their own; discussions that could have also altered the views of their husbands as rulers? By no means should this notion be ruled out.

Joan's much younger half-sister was the famous Eleanor de Montfort, countess of Pembroke and later Leicester. It seems unlikely that she would not have at least met the young Eleanor at some point, especially as her brother-in-law was one of Llywelyn's adherents in the 1220s and she was a young widow at the time. As for her other half-sister, Joan Makepeace, queen of Scotland, it is hard discern if they connected in any way, but again, hardly beyond the realms of possibility. Siwan may have also met the formidable and politically active queen of Scotland,

Ermengarde de Beaumont (r. 1186–1214) on at least one occasion, not least perhaps when her husband, William the Lion, paid homage to John in 1212, if Joan attended the event. Perhaps some of William's knowledge of the organised coup to take down John that year reached his ears by the way of his wife, who may have been in contact with Joan. It is important to remain circumspect with these types of suggestions, but equally important to simply consider such possibilities all the same.

In fact, the family of women that Joan was fundamentally connected to were all active and powerful queens in their own rights. Another of Joan's sisters was Isabella of England, who herself became Holy Roman Empress (r. 1235–1241).[10] Her aunts included Eleanor, Queen of Castile, Joan, Queen of Sicily, and Matilda, duchess of Saxony and Bavaria, who was the mother of the Holy Roman Emperor, Otto IV (r. 1209–1215). Blanche of Castile, the queen of France was Joan's cousin and her sister, Urraca of Castile, Joan's other cousin, was queen of Portugal (r. 1212–1220). As a collective whole, traditional definitions of medieval queenship, and the roles and duties of the office of the medieval queen, are arguably the influential and lasting legacy of these Angevin women spread far and wide across Europe and beyond. Joan certainly had knowledge of these women and knew they were her immediate relations.

Regardless of who her mother was, bastard or no, Joan was of royal and esteemed stock and as such, she could have had communications with any of these women in her family. She knew her paternal background and the celebrated and powerful extent of her extended family. It cannot be stressed enough that being made legitimate by the pope in 1226 placed her on the exact same standing as them in European eyes. Nor can it be stressed enough that sheer knowledge of these female relatives and their own roles as queens must have informed Joan's own perceptions and attitudes towards queenship. Never mind that her paternal grandmother was Eleanor of Aquitaine. And just as importantly, her great-grandmother was the Empress Matilda.

Perhaps later descendants and claimants to the English Crown in the fourteenth and fifteenth centuries who used their direct blood ties to Joan to showcase their rights and prerogatives had more to do than simply with heritage. Conceivably, the weight and solemnity of her position as a queen and successful diplomat were better remembered, understood and revered 200 years after her death than the 780 plus years that separates us now. Indeed, Joan's royal lineage was revered by her descendants. Future generations celebrated her status and the importance of position as a member of the Angevin dynasty to enhance their own political ambitions. During the Wars of the Roses both the houses of York and Lancaster asserted their rights as claimants to the throne through two of her daughters by Llywelyn.

It is no wonder that as a choice of wife for an aspiring Welsh prince who had set lofty ambitions for himself, Llywelyn the Great could not have been made a better offer than that of Joan's hand in marriage. But what about Joan? Would there have been a better offer in place for her somewhere down the line if the agreement between Llywelyn and John had been dropped? Although royal illegitimate daughters in particular had been used previously as 'peace offerings' and some married into other royal European houses – such as Sybilla (r. 1107–1122), Henry I's bastard daughter who became queen of Scotland when she married Alexander I (r. 1107–1124) – by the thirteenth century, a bastard woman's prospective for a higher marriage than to a lord were at a low. Llywelyn was a 'catch', so to speak, in many ways. He was still a royal and one from an ancient and dignified lineage that harkened itself back to Arthurian lore – legends and stories of which were at their height by the early-thirteenth century. Llywelyn was ambitious, even in his early days, and that ambition promised great rewards in the long-term. Further, the Welsh had no issues with illegitimacy whatsoever, or Joan's 'questionable' parentage. The bonus of being married to a Welsh prince meant that, even though she was far away from where she grew up and seems to have never returned to France that we know of, she was much closer to her father and kin than she may have been if married to an Irish lord or a Castilian duke.

Of course there were many failings in her life, as there are in all of ours. Her first sojourn as a diplomat in 1211 was due to catastrophic circumstances; her stepson and son battled to the bitter end for supremacy over one another; she purportedly had an affair and was imprisoned – probably the most horrific set of personal circumstances that a woman of her status could imagine because there was no way such particulars could possibly remain private. Not when the queen was involved. And yet Joan is not castigated by contemporaries for being a traitor and a foreigner. And yet, she regained her freedom and her political stature.

This is surprising as many royal wives were foreigners and seen as such. They were exposed to xenophobic attitudes, largely made up of suspicions that foreign queens were in pursuit of their own inimical interests and agendas. As such, foreign queens often received unwanted and negative attention and many found themselves to be popular scapegoats during the turbulent times when their husbands (or sons) found themselves floundering. It is surprising, given Joan's situation, that her loyalties seem not to have been vigorously questioned by her adopted country women and men, especially after her supposed infidelity with Llywelyn's biggest adversary. Maybe condemnation is to be found in the silences of the sources. Court poets do not even address Joan or mention her in their poems about Llywelyn.

For a women such as Joan, wifehood and queenship were intrinsically linked. When she entered the wilds of North Wales as a new bride in 1205, she was abruptly confronted with the seemingly arcane customs and practices of her new home, which sometimes greatly differed from what she had been used to. Joan's background and the story of her life are interwoven within thirteenth-century Anglo-Welsh politics and themes associated with her identities as wife, daughter, mother, sister, bastard, foreigner and queen – who she was, literally and figuratively. It is impossible to make any definitive statement as to who Joan really was, which identity she felt perhaps defined her the most, or exactly how she was perceived by her contemporaries. However, it is clear to us, as observers of history, that all these identities defined her life, her relationships, her career, her movements and her history. In spite of the hardships she and her family, on both sides, faced, and in spite of her own failings, there is absolutely no doubt that the bastard child whose true origins are shrouded in mystery, but who rose to the prominence of queen, played a crucial and central role during her thirty-year reign. That she was 'of great service in a diplomatic capacity' there is simply no doubt.

In spite of Welsh antiquarian musings about Joan's life and their dislike of her as an English foreigner who betrayed their glorious prince, through her 'savviness' and 'wiley' and 'cunning' ways, it seems that Joan was, indeed, accepted by her Welsh subjects to a large extent. The fact that she was involved so heavily in parlaying for peace and did much to protect Wales from a seemingly inevitable English onslaught, must have abetted much wariness toward her. Her supposed affair with

William de Braose did little to taint or tarnish her status or reputation among the Welsh. That in itself speaks volumes as to the acceptance of her place in 'their' world. Perhaps the lenient Welsh culture regarding the different levels of marriage and practice of concubinage, attitudes towards divorce and separation, and some of the identifiable parity in the laws regarding women and men meant that, if she did actually embark on a romantic journey with de Braose, moral judgement was less likely to mimic the types of outrage that would have been – and was – expressed in other parts of Europe when it came to a queen's perceived misstep outside gender expectations, roles and duties. For all intents and purposes, Joan fought on the side of the Welsh, and for this loyalty, it seems that she may have received the loyalty of the Welsh in return.

Siwan's importance in early to mid-thirteenth-century Wales, and Anglo-Welsh relations, should no longer be downplayed or ignored. Nor should her importance be unnecessarily hyped. It is a fine line to walk in attempting to find the balance between emphasising the true import of her role as a wife, as a daughter, as a sister, as a mother and her functions as duties as a political diplomat, and most significantly, as a queen. But indubitably, a queen she was, and it was a role she fulfilled that met all the standards of its day.

Abbreviations

ABT	*Achau Brenhinoedd a Thywysogion Cymru*, in P.C. Bartrum, *Early Welsh Genealogical Tracts* (Cardiff, 1966), pp. 95-110.
AnnCestr	*Annales Cestrienses*, ed. R.C. Christie, *Record Society of Lancashire and Cheshire*, 14 (London, 1887).
AM	*Annales Monastici*, ed. H.R. Luard, 5 vols (Rolls Series, London, 1864–9).
AWR	*The Acts of Welsh Rulers 1120–1283,* ed. H. Pryce (Cardiff, 2005).
BS	*Brenhinedd y Saesson, or The Kings of the Saxons: BM Cotton Ms. Cleopatra Bv and The Black Book of Basingwerk NLW Ms. 7006*, ed. T. Jones (Cardiff, 1971).
BT, Pen20	*Brut y Tywysogyon Peniarth MS. 20*, ed. T. Jones (Cardiff, 1941).
BT, Pen20Tr	*Brut y Tywysogyon, or The Chronicle of the Princes Peniarth 20 Ms. Version,* trans. T. Jones (Cardiff, 1952).
BT, RBH	*Brut y Tywysogyon, or The Chronicle of the Princes Red Book of Hergest Version*, ed. and trans. T. Jones (Cardiff, 1955).
CCR	*Calendar of the Close Rolls preserved in the Public Record Office* (London, 1900–).
CFR	*Calendar of the Fine Rolls, 1–57 Henry III*, Henry III Fine Rolls Project, *https://finerollshenry3.org.uk/content/calendar/calendar.html*.
CPL	*Calendar of Entries in the Papal Registers Relating to Great Britain and Ireland: Papal Letters*, i. *A.D. 1198–1304*, ed. W.H. Bliss (London, 1893).
CPR	*Calendar of the Patent Rolls preserved in the Public Record Office* (London, 1891–).

Gir. Camb., Op.	*Giraldi Cambrensis Opera*, (eds) J.S. Brewer, J.F. Dimock and G.F. Warner, 8 vols (Rolls Series, 1861–91).
HGK	*Historia Gruffud vab Kenan*, (ed.) D.S. Evans (Cardiff, 1978).
HW	J.E. Lloyd, *A History of Wales: From the Earliest Times to the Edwardian Conquest*, 2 vols (London, 2nd edn., 1912), ii.
LTMW	*The Law of Hywel Dda: Law Texts from Medieval Wales*, ed. and trans. D. Jenkins (Llandysul, 1986).
Rot. Claus.	*Rotuli Litteratum Clausarum in Turri Londinensi Asservati A.D. 1204–A.D. 1227*, ed. T.D. Hardy, 2 vols (Record Commission, London, 1832–44).
Rot. Pat.	*Rotuli Litterarum Patentium in Turri Londinensi Asservati*, I. i., *A.D. 1201–A.D. 1216*, ed. T.D. Hardy (Record Commission, 1835).
TYP	*Trioedd Ynys Prydein: The Triads of the Island of Britain*, ed. and trans. R. Bromwich (Cardiff, 3rd ed., 2006).
Vita Griffini	*Vita Griffini Filii Conani, The Medieval Latin Life of Gruffudd ap Cynan,* (ed.) and trans. P. Russell (Cardiff, 2005).
WKHC	*Welsh King and His Court*, (eds) T.M. Charles-Edwards, M.E. Owen and P. Russell (eds), *The Welsh King and His Court* (Cardiff, 2000).

Endnotes

Introduction

1. Mnemonic learning devices for lawyers and storytellers.
2. See D.R. Messer, 'The Uxorial Lifecyle and Female Agency in Wales in the Twelfth and Thirteenth Centuries', PhD Thesis (Bangor University, 2014).
3. Although based on later medieval England, for additional context and comparison see B.J. Harris, *English Aristocratic Women, 1450–1550: Marriage and Family, Property and Careers* (2002).
4. J.E. Lloyd, *A History of Wales: From the Earliest Times to the Edwardian Conquest*, 2 vols (2nd edn., 1912), ii, p. 685.

Chapter One – Roots and All

1. *Regesta Honorii Papae III*, ed. P. Pressutti, 2 vols (1885–98), ii, pp. 417-18; *Calendar of Entries in the Papal Registers Relating to Great Britain and Ireland: Papal Letters, A.D. 1198–1304*, ed. W.H. Bliss, 5 vols (1893), i, p. 109. For the discussion on the implications of Joan's illegitimate status and the reasons for her request for legitimisation see Chapter Nine.
2. It is most unfortunate that the papal decree does not name Joan's mother. Her identity remains hotly debated, especially among medieval genealogists.
3. As a grown man and reigning king, Henry was known to throw himself on the floor and roll around in full toddler-tantrum mode.
4. '*Annales Monasterii de Waverleia*', in *Annales Monastici*, ed. H.R. Luard, 5 vols (1864–9), ii, p. 282.
5. W.L. Warren, *King John* (1997), p. 259.

6. See S. Church, *King John: England, Magna Carta and the Making of a Tyrant* (2015) and M. Morris, *King John: Treachery, Tyranny and the Road to Magna Carta* (2015).

7. Giraldus Cambrensis, *Opera,* (eds) J.S. Brewer, J.F. Dimock and G.F. Warner, 8 vols (1861–91), viii, p. 316.

8. *The History of Fulk Fitz-Warin*, trans. by Alice Kemp-Welch (1904), pp. 68-69.

9. *Rotuli de Oblatis et Finibus temp. Regis Johannis*, ed. T.D. Hardy (1835), p. 275; Warren, *King John*, p. 190; S. Painter, *The Reign of King John* (1949), pp. 231-32.

10. Richard of Devizes, *Chronicon de rebus gestis Ricardi I regis Angliæ*, ed. J. Stevenson (1838), p. 10.

11. James Brundage is the most prominent historian to discuss medieval concubinage, canon law and marriage. See, in particular, 'Concubinage and Marriage in Medieval Canon Law', *Journal of Medieval History*, 1 (1975):1-17; *Law, Sex and Christian Society in Medieval Europe* (1987) and *Sex, Law and Marriage in the Middle Ages* (1993).

12. In Iceland and Ireland, for example, women involved in extramarital relations often went on to marry. In fact, in both these places concubinage and polygamy were mutually practiced and openly accepted. It is not clear if polygamy was openly practiced in Wales at this time, though the very definitions of the archaic nine legal couplings found in the thirteenth-century version of the Welsh laws stemming from Gwynedd (the Iorwerth redaction) suggests that it was to some extent.

13. T.M. Charles-Edwards, 'Nau Kynywedi Teithiauc', in D. Jenkins and M.E. Owen (eds), *The Welsh Law of Women* (1980), pp. 23-39.

14. Ibid., p. 27. It appears that these unions are listed in order of declining legal and honourable status.

15. *Vita Griffini Filii Conani: The Medieval Latin Life of Gruffudd ap Cynan,* ed. and trans. P. Russell (2005), pp. 76-79; *Historia Gruffud vab Kenan*, ed. D.S. Evans (1977), p. 22; *Trioedd Ynys Prydein: The Triads of the Island of Britain*, ed. and trans. R. Bromwich (3rd ed., 2006), triads 56 and 57, pp. 161-64; *Achau Brenhinoedd a Thywysogion Cymru*, in P. C. Bartrum, *Early Welsh Genealogical Tracts* (1966), pp. 95-103.

16. *Llyfr Iorwerth: A Critical Text of the Venedotian Code of Medieval Welsh Law Mainly from BM. Cotton MS Titus Dii*, ed. A.R. Wiliam

(1960), p. 26; *The Law of Hywel Dda: Law Texts from Medieval Wales*, ed. and trans. D. Jenkins (1986), p. 49.

17. National Library Wales, Penrice and Margam, 289 (60) roll.
18. Warren, *King John*, p. 182.
19. D. Powel, *The Historie of Cambria, now Called Wales: A Part of the Most Famous Yland of Brytaine, Written in the Brytish Language aboue Two Hundreth Yeares Past* (1811), p. 103. For the year 1203.
20. See S.M. Johns, *Noblewomen, Aristocracy and Power in the Twelfth-Century Anglo-Norman Realm* (2003), pp. 67-69.
21. Rachel Swallow, 'Gateways to Power: The Castles of Ranulf III of Chester and Llewellyn the Great of Gwynedd', *Archaeological Journal*, 171 (2014): 299-300.
22. The historical novelist Sharon Penman seems to have been the first to explore this idea. See S. Penman, 'The Mother of Joanna of Wales, wife of Llywelyn ab Iorwerth' (2009), accessed 30 December 2018, http://sharonkaypenman.com/blog/?p=88.
23. April 1203 was also the date that Llywelyn received dispensation to marry the princess of Man.
24. Llywelyn's first-born, illegitimate son Gruffudd became King John's most important hostage after events that took place in 1211–12.
25. See M. Hagger, 'The De Verdun Family in England, Ireland and Wales, 1066–1316: A Study', PhD thesis (University of St Andrews, 1998), p. 10.
26. Joan, Geoffrey, Oliver, Richard and Osbert. See C. Given-Wilson and A. Curteis, *The Royal Bastards of Medieval England* (1984), pp. 126-31.
27. Although this was incest, none of the parties seemed to have been castigated for the relationship. If Joan, however, had been a product of incest (i.e. Agatha de Ferrers), there would have likely been more implications for her, being a reigning queen and mother of Llywelyn's chosen heir – and as a woman.
28. Painter, *The Reign of King John*, p. 233.

Chapter Two – Gwynedd and the Rise of Llywelyn Ap Iorwerth

1. Gerald of Wales, *The Journey Through Wales and The Description of Wales*, trans. L. Thorpe (1978; repr. 1988), p. 187.
2. The medieval *cantref* was an administrative division of land, similar in kind to the English hundred.

3. R. Turvey, *Llywelyn the Great* (2007), p. 7.
4. For the use of styles found in Welsh charters and what charter production reveals about the power of the native Welsh princes see C. Insley, 'From *Rex Wallie* to *Princeps Wallie*: Charters and State Formation in Thirteenth-century Wales', in J.R. Maddicott and D.M. Palliser (eds), *The Medieval State: Essays Presented to James Campell* (2000), pp. 179-96
5. *Vita Griffini,* pp. 88-91; *HGK*, p. 32.
6. This distinction also appears in the genealogies of the princes of Wales where the order of women named associated with a leader starts with the wife of the highest status. *ABT*, pp. 95-110.
7. This is in stark contrast to her obituary found the Welsh chronicles where she is simply referred to as Gruffudd's wife. Nevertheless, Angharad was a widow for almost thirty years, and one who seemed to have wielded much power (bestowed upon her at Gruffudd's death), so the simplicity of the entry in the chronicles may also have much to do with a sense of familiarity and retainment of her royal rank during her widowhood. *Brenhinedd y Saesson, or The Kings of the Saxons: BM Cotton Ms. Cleopatra Bv and The Black Book of Basingwerk NLW Ms. 7006*, ed. T. Jones (1971), pp. 162-63; *Brut y Tywysogyon Peniarth MS. 20*, ed. T. Jones (1941), p. 108; *Brut y Tywysogyon or The Chronicle of the Princes Peniarth 20 Ms. Version,* trans. T. Jones (1952), p. 62; *Brut y Tywysogyon or The Chronicle of the Princes Red Book of Hergest Version*, ed. and trans. T. Jones (1955), pp. 142-43.
8. The chapter is entitled, '*Literae reginae Norwalliae Giraldo directae*'. Gir. Camb., *Op.*, i, p. 13.
9. W. Davies, *Wales in the Early Middle Ages* (1996), pp. 63-64.
10. Originally seven degrees of separation, this dropped to four in 1215.
11. John of Salisbury, *The Letters of John of Salisbury (1153–1161): Volume One, The Early Letters (1153–1161)*, eds. and trans W.J. Millor and H.E. Butler, revised by C.N.L. Brooke (1955), pp. 135-36.
12. *The Acts of Welsh Rulers 1120–1283*, ed. H. Pryce (2005), pp. 74-75; Id., 'Owain Gwynedd and Louis VII: The Franco-Welsh Diplomacy of the First Prince of Wales', *Welsh History Review*, 19 (1998–9), pp. 20-21, 23.

13. *The Correspondence of Thomas Becket, archbishop of Canterbury, 1162–1170*, ed. and trans. A.J. Duggan, 2 vols (1999), ii, pp. 842-43, 875-77.

14. The 1175 entry of events found the Red Book of *Brut y Tywysogyon* describes Dafydd's rise to power, not as Cristin's son, but as the uterine brother of Rhodri, whom he turned on and imprisoned in his grasp for power. *BT, RBH*, pp. 164-65.

15. *Welsh Court Poetry*, ed. R.M. Andrews (2007), pp. 26, 114. For a crucial discussion on kinship bonds in Wales see Charles-Edwards, *Early Irish and Welsh Kinship*, particularly pp. 78-82.

16. Obviously, genealogical constructs are at play here, but it is noteworthy that Owain himself does not appear in Perfy's elegy.

17. K.L. Maund, *The Welsh Kings: Warrior, Warlords and Princes* (2006), p. 182.

18. Gerald of Wales, *Journey through Wales*, pp. 192-93.

19. Ibid., p. 76.

20. R.H. Bloch, *Medieval Misogyny and the Invention of Western Romantic Love* (1991), p. 14; Gerald of Wales, *Journey through Wales*, p. 90.

21. Turvey, *Llywelyn the Great*, pp. 25-28.

22. A subdivision of a *cantref*, or hundred. Similar to a wapentake.

23. *History of Fulk Fitz-Wairne*, pp. 28-29.

24. For a good summary of early years, see Turvey, *Llywelyn*, pp. 19-42. Also see generally Maund, *The Welsh Kings*, pp. 181-204.

25. Turvey, *Llywelyn the Great*, p. 32.

26. See R. Chapman Stacey, 'King, Queen and *Edling* in the Laws of Court', in T.M. Charles-Edwards, M.E. Owen and P. Russell (eds), *The Welsh King and His Court* (2000), pp. 29-62.

27. Not comital barons, however.

28. For an engaging discussion on the subject see I. W. Rowlands, 'King John and Wales', in S.D. Church (ed.), *King John: New Interpretations* (1999), particularly pages pp. 243, 276-77, 279.

29. *HW*, ii, p. 614.

30. See D. Fisher, *Royal Wales* (2010), pp. 14-15.

31. In return, the English king recognised that if any dispute concerning the lands were to arise, Welsh law would be deferred to for resolution.

Chapter Three – Marriage, Queenship and the Roles of Women in Wales

1. *Littere Wallie: Preserved in Liber A in the Public Record Office*, ed. J.G. Edwards (1940), pp. 92, 101.
2. *BS*, pp. 180-81; *BT, Pen20*, p. 126; *BT, Pen20Tr*, p. 70; *BT, Pen20Tr*, pp. 164-65.
3. Gir. Camb. *Op.*, vi, p. 134; Gerald of Wales, *Journey through Wales*, p. 193.
4. *Gwaith Llywarch ap Llywelyn 'Prydydd y Moch'*, ed. E.M. Jones (1991), p. 14. It is highly unfortunate that not one poem survives either written for Joan or in which is referred to because it is inevitable that several were written and performed in many a Welsh court during her lifetime.
5. See C. McAll, 'The Normal Paradigms of a Woman's Life in the Irish and Welsh Texts', in *The Welsh Law of Women*, pp. 7-22; T.M. Charles-Edwards, *Early Irish and Welsh Kinship* (1993), pp. 177, 186.
6. See E. Searle, 'Possible History', *Speculum*, 61/4 (October, 1986), pp. 779-86.
7. D. Stephenson, 'The Laws of the Court: Past Reality or Present Idea?', in *WKHC*, p. 402.
8. See *AWR,* nos. 200, 202, 205, pp. 333-38, 490. Many of the grants were subsequently confirmed by Owain. The witness lists to both Emma's and Dafydd's charters are most likely complete.
9. A letter by Pope Innocent III dated 17 February 1205 indicates as much. *Die Register Innocenz' III*, ed. O. Hageneder *et al.* (1964–), vii, no. 200, p. 385.
10. *HW*, ii, p. 636.

Chapter Four – Princess to Queen

1. *Magni Rotuli Scaccarii Normanniae sub Regibus Angliae*, ed. T. Stapleton, 2 vols (1840–4), ii, p. 569.
2. *Calendar of Documents Preserve in France, 918–1206*, ed. by J. Horace Round (1899), no. 418, p. 139. This grant was witnessed by William de Braose IV and made in his Welsh lordship of Gower.

3. Eileen Power, *Medieval Women*, edited by M.M. Postan (1995), p. 68.
4. *Rot. Regn. John*, 145.
5. Assuming this was actually where she was born and raised as our only indication of this is the record of her actually sailing from Normandy to embark on her new life as a princess of Wales. Just because she sailed from Normandy does not unequivocally mean that was her homeland.
6. In October 1204, Vieuxpont became the High Sheriff of Nottinghamshire, Derbyshire and the Royal Forests. Could this have been the John's way of rewarding the man who had charge of some of the king's most precious treasures?
7. *Rotuli Litteratum Clausarum in Turri Londinensi Asservati A.D. 1204–A.D. 1227*, ed. T.D. Hardy, 2 vols (Record Commission, 1832–44), i, pp. 12; *Annales Cestrienses*, ed. R.C. Christie, *Record Society of Lancashire and Cheshire*, 14 (1887), pp. 48-49; '*Annales Prioratus de Wigornia*', in *AM*, iv, p. 394.
8. *The Letters of Pope Innocent III (1198–1216) Concerning England and Wales: A Calendar with an Appendix of Texts*, (eds) C.R. Cheney and M.G. Cheney (1967), nos. 168, 469, 600; *HW*, ii, p. 616
9. His personal (and spiritual?) connection to Worcester ran so deep that it was his wish to be buried there, which he was in 1216.
10. For a good discussion on Welsh hospitality see L.B. Smith, 'On the Hospitality of the Welsh: A Comparative View', in *Power and Identity in the Middle Ages: Essays in Memory of Rees Davies*, (eds) H. Pryce and J. Watts (2007), pp. 181-94.
11. Gir. Camb., *Op.*, vi, pp. 182-83; Gerald of Wales, *Description of Wales*, pp. 236-37.
12. See *Gwaith Cynddelw Brydydd Mawr I*, (eds) N.A. Jones and A. Parry (1991), i, nos 16 and 21.
13. Walter Map, *De Nugis Curialium*, ed. M.R. James, rev. C.N.L. Brooke and R.A.B. Mynors (1983), pp. 184-85.
14. *Vita Griffini,* pp. 76-77, 154; *HGK*, p. 22.
15. T.M. Charles-Edwards, 'Food, Drink and Clothing in the Laws of Court', in *WKHC*, pp. 328-30, 332-33.
16. P. Russell, '*Canu i Swyddogion Llys y Brenin*', in *WKHC*, pp. 552-55.
17. Ibid., p. 554.
18. There are many examples found in the *Mabinogion* alone, as well as in the Lives of Saints. For the argument that queen was isolated

in her chamber, sitting at her table across from her own priest, see Robin Stacey, 'King, Queen and *Edling*', p. 59, note 118.

19. T.M. Charles-Edwards and N.A. Jones, '*Breintiau Gwŷr Powys*: The Liberties of the Men of Powys', in *WKHC*, pp. 217, 220.
20. Oxford, Jesus College, Ms. 111, f. 241ʳ.
21. *The Mabinogion*, trans. S. Davies (2007), p. 16; *Pwyll Pendeuic Dyuet*, ed. R.L. Thomson (1957), p. 16.
22. *Mabinogion*, p. 52; *Y Mabinogion*, eds. D. Ifans and R. Ifans (Llandysul, 1980), p. 53.
23. H. Fulton, 'The *Mabinogi* and the Education of Princes in Medieval Wales', in H. Fulton (ed.), *Medieval Celtic Literature and Society* (2005), pp. 230-47.
24. Mostly due to sheer lack of evidence.

Chapter Five – Winds of Change

1. '*Domina Gwladus filia Lewelini principis Wallia, & Johanne filiae Johannis regis Anglie*'. '*Annales Prioratus de Wigornia*', in *AM*, iv, p. 222. Although the surviving manuscript is late-fifteenth century, it is based on a 1390s copy of the original believed to have been written in 1262. See I. Mortimer, 'Wigmore Chronicles', 10 February 2015. http://www.ianmortimer.com/essays/WigmoreChronicle.pdf
2. Roger of Wendover, *Flowers of History: Comprising the History of England from the Decent of the Saxons to A.D. 1235: Formerly Ascribed to Matthew Paris*, ed. and trans. J.A. Giles, 2 vols (1968), ii, p. 249.
3. Maud de Saint-Valéry; Moll Wallbee.
4. *BTPen20Tr*, p. 191.
5. Ibid., p. 84.
6. D. Powel, *The Historie of Cambria, now Called Wales: a Part of the Most Famous Yland of Brytaine, Written in the Brytish Language aboue Two Hundreth Yeares Past* (1811), p. 191.
7. Being not seven miles from Aberffraw, Rhosyr is an important site for the history of Joan and Llywelyn. The remains of the palace were only discovered in the 1990s. St Fagans National Museum of History has recently constructed a replica of a royal *llys* inhabited by Joan and Llywelyn royal, based on the archaeology of Rhosyr.

8. *Annales Cambriae*, pp. 67-68.
9. *BS*, pp. 204-05; *BT, Pen20*, pp. 156-57; *BT, Pen20Tr*, p. 85; *BT, RBH*, pp. 190-93.
10. Wendover, *Flowers of History*, p. 225.
11. See, for example, Hurlock, K., 'Counselling the Princes: Advice and Counsel in Thirteenth-Century Welsh Society', *History*, 34 (2009), p. 29.
12. D. Stephenson and C. Owen Jones, 'The Date and Context of the Birth of Dafydd II Ap Llywelyn', *Flintshire Historical Journal*, 29 (2012), pp. 29-30, 32.
13. An earlier precedent may have been set by the Lord Rhys of Deheubarth who wanted his eldest legitimate son by legal wife Gwenllian to succeed him and not his eldest illegitimate son.
14. T.J. Llewelyn Pritchard, *Heroines of Welsh History: Or Memoirs of the Celebrated Women of Wales* (1854), p. 511.
15. *Regesta Honorii Papae III*, ii, pp. 417-18; *Calendar of Papal Registers*, i, p. 109; *AWR*, no. 279, pp. 446-47.
16. L. Wilkinson, 'Joan, Wife of Llywelyn the Great', in M. Prestwich, R. Britnell and R. Frame (eds), *Thirteenth Century England X: Proceedings of the Durham Conference 2003* (2005), p. 86.
17. Similar to the entries in the *Annales Cambriae*, the *Brutiau* and *Brenhinedd y Saesson*.
18. *HW*, ii, p. 670.

Chapter Six – A Letter of Warning

1. *HW*, ii, p. 637.
2. See Stephenson and Jones, 'Date and Context', pp. 31-23.
3. Discussed in detail in Chapter Eight.
4. Messer, 'Uxorial Agency', pp. 248-300.
5. Cited in Stephenson and Owen, 'Date and Context', p. 24.
6. Powell, *The Historie of Cambria*, pp. 192-93.
7. Wendover, *Flowers of History*, p. 257.
8. Matthew Paris, *Flowers of History: Especially such as Relate to the Affairs of Britain: From the Beginning of the World to the Year 1307*, trans. by C.D. Yonge, 2 vols (1853), ii, p. 113.
9. Wendover, *Flowers of History*, p. 257.

10. Powell, *Historie of Cambria*, p. 193. Having served John in Normandy, Robert FitzWalter went on to be one of the leaders of the Baronial Rebellion in 1215, along with Eustace de Vesci and Stephen Ridell. In fact, the former two alleged that John had tried to seduce Robert FitzWalter's eldest daughter and Eustace de Vescy's wife.

11. However, Powell does reference Holingshed's Chronicles, first published in 1577.

12. See Chapter Twelve for discussion.

13. *History of Fulk Fitz-Warine*, p. 76. Although the *Legend of Fulk FitzWarin* confuses Joan's aunt, Joan of Sicily, the importance of the narrative cannot be overlooked.

14. Though fleetingly small, such examples as these help to underline the realms in which Joan exercised political agency and certainly with the vignette found in *The Legend of Fulk FitzWarin* we have an extremely rare and delightful illustration of Joan's political diplomacy.

Chapter Seven – To Worcester

1. *BTPen20Tr*, p. 89.

2. The dispute that began in 1207 over the appointment of the new archbishop of Canterbury was what led to England being placed under interdict. John had declared any supporter of Stephen Langton a public enemy. The whole situation was one of many that led to the Magna Carta.

3. *Rotuli Litterarum Patentium in Turri Londinensi Asservati*, I. i., *A.D. 1201–A.D. 1216*, ed. T.D. Hardy (Record Commission, 1835), i, 125a and 126a; *Foedera, Conventiones, Litterae etc.*, ed. T. Rymer, 4 vols in 7 (revd edn, Record Commission, 1816), I, i, p. 126; *AWR*, nos 277 and 278, p. 446.

4. A similarity in the origins related to *nawdd* and the Irish equivalent snádud means they may represent a concept that was common during the Celtic period as they both derive from the Celtic root snáid, meaning to protect. For a discussion on *nawdd* see H. Pryce, *Native Law and the Church in Medieval Wales* (1993), pp. 165-69.

5. *Cyfreithiau Hywel Dda Yn ôl Llyfr Blegywryd*, (eds) S.J. Williams and J.E. Powell (1967), p. 6; *LTMW*, p. 8.

6. *Calendar of the Patent Rolls preserved in the Public Record Office, 1232–47* (London, 1891–), p. 130; *AWR*, no. 281, p. 448. This Robert was accused of the death of William, son of a man referred to as Ralph of Credenhill.

7. *AWR*, no. 277, p. 446.

8. For example see Llywelyn's letter to Henry III dated late June 1219 × early July 1219 or early May 1220 or June 1221, *AWR*, no. 245, pp. 403–04.

9. *BTPen20Tr*, p. 90.

10. Turvey, *Llywelyn*, p. 60.

11. Ibid., p. 61.

12. *HW*, ii, p. 648.

13. It was perhaps in disgust of this display of unchecked power that Llywelyn's former adversary turned adherent, once again switched sides. Although Gwenwynwyn of Powys decided that an alliance with King John would prove more beneficial to his goals, he found the move to be the wrong one, when Llywelyn moved against him, calling on his new vassals to support his campaign and drove him out of Wales once and for all. It was in England where Gwenwynwyn died in exile, and his lands reverted to Llywelyn as the guardian of the former prince of Powys' underage heir.

14. *BTPen20Tr*, p. 93.

15. *HW*, ii, p. 650.

16. Ibid., pp. 650-51.

17. Reginald's was not the only Marcher defection to England at this time; others included Thomas Corbet of Caus and Fulk FitzWarin, among others.

18. This was much to the chagrin of the Crown who supported Reginald, either naively or ideally envisaging that Llywelyn would pass Gower on to Gwladus' husband.

19. *AWR*, no. 249, pp. 409-10; *The Great Roll of the Pipe*, 4 Henry III (Pipe Roll Society, 1884–), p. 189; *Foedera*, I, i, p. 152.

20. The market was originally held on Tuesdays, but changed to Fridays.

21. Rymer, *Foedera*, I, i, p. 150.

22. *HW*, ii, p. 654.

23. See discussion of the one surviving letter Joan wrote, which was to Henry a few short years before her death, in Chapter Thirteen.

24. And even as mother of his chosen heir.

Chapter Eight – Royal Female Authority

1. It was agreed that another meeting was required to lay-out the terms for a more long-lasting armistice.
2. On 16 August.
3. Rhys died the following month and Llywelyn divided his lands between his brother and uncle.
4. The next year, in June 1222, saw false reports of Reginald's death.
5. Only Rothley in Leicestershire remained the anomaly.
6. Perhaps a consequence of its strategic location which meant it was in the cross-hairs of the frequent boarder warfare. See *AWR*, no. 249, pp. 409–10.
7. Ibid.
8. *The Great Roll of the Pipe,* 5 Henry III (Pipe Roll Society, 1884–), pp. xxxiv-xxxvi.
9. *Rotuli Litteratum Clausarum in Turri Londinensi Asservati A.D. 1204–A.D. 1227,* ed. T.D. Hardy, 2 vols (Record Commission, 1832–44), i, 487a; *AWR*, no. 249, pp. 409-10; *HW,* ii, p. 657.
10. *HW,* ii, p. 657.
11. See *AWR*, nos 66, 251, 285, 454, pp. 202, 412, 454-55, 651-53.
12. Ibid., nos 28, 35, pp. 171-75, 180-83.
13. Senana was the mother of Gruffudd's sons Owain Goch, Llywelyn, Dafydd and Rhodri. The couple also had at least one known daughter named Gwladus. Their sons Llywelyn and Dafydd were to be the last reigning princes of independent Wales.
14. *Curia Regis Rolls,* (1923–), xvi, no. 1595.
15. *Matthei Parisiensis, Monarchi Sancti Albani, Historia Anglorum,* (ed.) F. Madden, 3 vols, (Rolls Series, 1866–9), ii, p. 483.
16. Matthew Paris, *Flores Historiarum,* (ed.) H.R. Luard, 3 vols (Rolls Series, 1890), vol. ii, ad 1067– ad 1264, p. 272.
17. *Calendar of the Liberate Rolls preserved in the Public Record Office for the Reign of Henry III,* 6 vols (HMSO, 1917–64), ii, pp. 81, 134, 141.
18. It is unknown whether Gruffudd's seal was in her possession from the start of his imprisonment or if it was brought to her by the royal side to be used in negotiations.
19. *Matthæi Parisiensis, Monachi Sancti Albani, Chronica Majora,* (ed.) H.R. Luard, 7 vols (Rolls Series, 1874), iv, pp. 316-18.

20. Examples are found in G.C.G. Thomas, ed., *The Charters of the Abbey of Ystrad Marchell* (1997).
21. See J.J. Crump, 'The Mortimer Family and the Making of the March', in M. Prestwich, R.H. Britnell and R. Frame (eds), *Thirteenth Century England VI, Proceedings of the Durham Conference, 1995* (1997), p. 126; Smith, *Llywelyn ap Gruffudd, Prince of Wales* (1998; repr. 2001), p. 42.
22. *AWR*, no. 440, pp. 635-38.
23. Messer, 'Uxorial Agency'.

Chapter Nine – The Legitimate Diplomat

1. Both Kinnersley and Whittington had received royal permission to upgrade in 1221, which may have been one of the reasons for the Welsh attack.
2. *History of Fulk Fitz-Warine*, pp. 64-65.
3. July also saw the Lacy rebellion in Ireland where Gwenllian, Llywelyn's daughter, was captured by William Marshal's forces at Cavan castle.
4. *HW*, ii, p. 664.
5. *AWR*, no. 255, pp. 417-19.
6. *Rot. Claus*, i, p. 622; *HW*, ii, p. 665.
7. *Rot. Claus.*, i, p. 621.
8. *CPR, 1216–25*, p. 471; *Rot. Claus.*, i, p. 622.
9. *Rot. Claus.*, ii, p. 18.
10. Rymer, *Foedera*, I, i, p. 70; *Rot. Claus.*, i, pp. 611, 623; ii, pp. 8, 16, 17.
11. See K. Hurlock, 'The Welsh wife of Malcolm, Earl of Fife (d. 1266): An Alternative Suggestion'. *Scottish Historical Review*, 88/2 (2009), 352-55.
12. Rymer, *Foedera*, I, i, p. 178.
13. *Rot. Claus.*, ii, p. 47; *HW*, ii, p. 655.
14. For an informative assessment of their relationship see Wilkinson, 'Joan', pp. 88-89.
15. *Rot. Claus*, i, p. 622. Reference to Joan as 'formerly' the wife of Llywelyn in this contemporary source is highly unusual. Most likely, it is a scribal error.
16. *CPR, 1225–32*, pp. 52, 56, 59.

17. *Regesta Honorii Papae III*, ii, pp. 417–18; *Calendar of Papal Registers*, i, p. 109; *AWR*, no. 279, pp. 446-47.
18. Llywelyn's faith and devotion to the church, including his amiable acquiescence to following papal political directives, encouraged the pope further in his decision to legitimise Joan.
19. *CPR, 1225–32*, pp. 52, 56, 59.
20. *Rot. Claus*, ii, pp. 18, 135; *HW*, ii, p. 665. It is possible that this prominent diplomatic role relates to the request for Joan to be legitimised at precisely this time.
21. *Calendar of the Fine Rolls*, 12 Henry 1227–28, no. 120; Henry III Fine Rolls Project, https://finerollshenry3.org.uk/content/calendar/roll_027.html, accessed 30 April 2019.
22. *Rot. Claus.,* i, pp. 51, 68-69.
23. *CPR, 1225–32*, p. 112.

Chapter Ten – Hostage and Homage

1. *CFR*, 1227–28, nos 119 and 120.
2. The Welsh lordship of Ceri neighboured Montgomery and the campaign was aimed at preventing the loss of Ceri to Anglo-Norman hands.
3. *Calendar of the Close Rolls Preserved in the Public Record Office*, 1 Hen. III, 1227–31 (1900–), p. 114; *Rotuli Litteratum Clausarum in Turri Londinensi Asservati A.D. 1204–A.D. 1227*, ed. T.D. Hardy, 2 vols (Record Commission, London, 1832–44), I, pp. 334-35.
4. *CFR*, 1227–28, no. 79.
5. See Chapter Eleven.
6. *BTPen20Tr*, p. 101.
7. *CCR*, 1227–31, p. 123; *CPR*, 1225–32, p. 230.
8. *CPR, 1227–32*, p. 248.
9. Ibid., p. 257. The Welsh chronicles tell us that by this time, Gruffudd had been imprisoned by his father at Deganwy castle, where he was to remain for six whole years, being released in 1234.
10. *CPR, 1227–32*, p. 263. It seems extremely unlikely that this unnamed sister would have been Gwladus who clearly of age and a noteworthy widow by this time as is evidenced in the May grant for safe-conduct.
11. *HW*, ii, p. 669.

12. Not quite £30,000 in today's money.
13. Segrave became England's justiciar after the downfall of Hubert de Burgh in 1232.

Chapter Eleven – Interlude

1. Although, this possession did not actually include the town of Limerick, itself.
2. Powell, *Historie of Cambria*, p. 204.
3. See The National Archives currency converter for the year 1270: https://www.nationalarchives.gov.uk/currency-converter/#currency-result
4. Powell, *Historie of Cambria*, p. 251.
5. Pritchard, *Heroines of Welsh History*, p. 519.
6. Ibid., pp. 519-20.
7. Easter Sunday fell on 7 April.
8. *BT, Pen20Tr*, pp. 101-02.
9. *Calendar of Ancient Correspondence Concerning Wales*, ed. J.G. Edwards (1935), p. 37; *Royal and Other Historical Letters Illustrative of the Reign of Henry III*, ed. W. W. Shirley, 2 vols (Rolls Series, 1862), i, pp. 365-67.
10. *HW*, ii, p. 670.
11. *CPR*, 1225–1232, pp. 336, 339.
12. J.J. Crump, 'Repercussions of the Execution of William de Braose: A Letter from Llywelyn ab Iorwerth to Stephen de Segrave', *Historical Research*, 73 (2000), p. 206.
13. Ibid., pp. 197-212, 200-03.
14. For example, see *The Itinerary in Wales of John Leland in or about the Years 1536–1539*, ed. L. Toulmin Smith, 3 vols (1906), iii, p. 79.
15. Namely documentary evidence from Llywelyn ap Gruffudd, or Llywelyn the Last, that references Garth Celyn as his residence.
16. T. Pennant, *Tours of Wales*, (ed.) J. Rhys, 3 vols (1883), iii, p. 100; A.B. Williams, *The Tourist's Guide Through the Country of Caernarvon, containing a Short Sketch of its History, Antiquities, etc.* (1821), pp. 29-30.
17. See Crump, 'Repercussions'.
18. *AWR*, no. 263, pp. 431-33. Einion ap Gwalchmai was one of the top Venedotian ministers.

19. Crump, 'Repercussions', p. 201.
20. Wilkinson, 'Joan', p. 92.
21. *AWR*, no. 261, p. 428.
22. *Annales Cambriae*, ed. J. William ab Ithel (Rolls Series, 1960), p. 77; *AnnCestr*, p. 56-57; *Brut, RBH*, pp. 228-29; '*Annales de Margan*', in *AM*, i, p. 38; '*Annales Monasterii de Theokesberia*', *AM*, i, p. 101; '*Annales Monasterii de Waverleia*', in *AM*, ii, pp. 308-09; '*Annales Monasterii de Wintonia*', in *AM*, ii, p. 85; '*Annales Prioratus de Wigornia*', in *AM*, iv, p. 421; Roger of Wendover, *Flores Historiarum*, ii, p. 383. Also see Crump, 'Repercussions'.
23. *AWR*, no. 262, pp. 429-31.
24. Crump, 'Repercussions', p. 201.

Chapter Twelve – Reckoning

1. Williams, *The Tourist's Guide Through the Country of Caernarvon*, pp. 29-30.
2. Louisa Stewart Costello, *The Falls, Lakes and Mountains of North Wales* (1845), pp. 66-69.
3. See T.M. Charles-Edwards, 'Honour and Status in Some Irish and Welsh Prose Tales,' *Ériu*, 29 (1978), pp. 123-41.
4. Pritchard, *Heroines of Welsh History*, pp. 515-16.
5. For important and enlightening discussions on the concept of the calumniated wife and the punishment of women who transgressed gender norms in Welsh literature see J. Hemming, '*Sellam Gestare*: Saddle-Bearing Punishments and the Case of Rhiannon', *Viator*, 28 (1997), pp. 45-64; J. Watson, 'Enid the Disobedient: The *Mabinogion*'s Gereint and Enid', in C. Levin and J. Watson (eds), *Ambiguous Realities: Women in the Middle Ages and Renaissance* (1987), pp. 114-32; F. Windward, 'Some Aspects of the Women in *The Four Branches*', *Cambrain Medieval Celtic Studies*, 34 (Winter, 1997), pp. 77-106; and J. Wood, 'The Calumniated Wife in Medieval Welsh Literature', *Cambridge Medieval Celtic Studies*, 10 (1985), pp. 25–38.
6. *TYP*, triad 80, p. 210. Triad 84, pp. 271-72 references Gwenhwyfar's feud with her sister Gwenhwy(f)ach, which led to the battle of Camlan and Arthur's death.
7. *LTMW*, p. 51.

8. Ibid.

9. Ibid. 103. Also see Stacey, 'King, Queen and *Edling* in the Laws of Court'; Ead., 'Divorce, Medieval Welsh Style', *Speculum* (October, 2002), pp. 1107-27; and N. Patterson, 'Honour and Shame in Medieval Welsh Society: A Study of the Role of Burlesque in the Welsh Laws', *Studia Celtica*, 16/17 (1981/2), p. 95.

10. Patterson, 'Honour and Shame', pp. 74, 86.

11. *LTMW*, p. 52.

12. *Llyfr Blegywryd*, p. 45; *LTMW*, p. 48.

13. *Llyfr Iorwerth*, p. 28; *LTMW*, p. 53.

14. Lewys Dwnn, *Heraldic Vistations of Wales and Parts of the Marches Between the Years 1586 and 1613*, 2 vols (1846), ii, p. 101, note 7. Also see Stephenson, *Governance of Gwynedd*, pp. 104-05.

15. Wilkinson, 'Joan', pp. 90-93. Also see Owen, 'Shame and Reparation', pp. 40–68; Pryce, *Native Law and the Church*, p. 91.

16. Gir. Camb. *Op.*, vi, pp. 15, 20, 48-49; Gerald of Wales, *Journey through Wales*, pp. 76-77, 80, 109.

17. *AnnCestr*, pp. 56-57.

18. *LTMW*, p. 57.

19. *Ancient Laws and Institutes of Wales*, ed. A. Owen, 2 vols (Record Commission, 1841), i, p. 218.

20. Stacey, 'Divorce, Medieval Welsh Style'; *LTMW*, p. 154; *Llyfr Iorwerth*, p. 73.

21. See Pryce, *Native Law and the Church*, p. 93.

22. *Llyfr Iorwerth*, pp. 31-32; *LTMW*, p. 60. There were different rules of compensation for adultery based on the type of adultery committed. See Owen, 'Shame and Reparation', p. 52.

23. *Llyfr Iowerth*, p. 1; *LTMW*, p. 5. See Owen, 'Shame and Reparation', p. 46.

24. *AnnCestr*, pp. 56-57.

25. It is, however, possible that the unnamed daughter of Llywelyn who married Malcolm II, earl of Fife could actually have been a child born of Joan's affair with William.

26. Kate Norgate, 'Joan (d. 1237)', *Oxford Dictionary of National Biography*, vol. 29 (1885–1900).

27. 'Cynferth', pp. 442-43, 466-47.

28. *Vitae Sanctorum Britanniae,* pp. 136-39, 198-201, 216–19.

29. *BT, Pen20Tr*, pp. 282-89, 117.

30. 'Cyfnerth', pp. 444-45.
31. Ibid., pp. 450-1; *Llyfr Iorwerth*, pp. 9-10; *LTMW*, p. 16.
32. G.R.J. Jones, '*Llys* and *Maerdref*', in *WKHC*, p. 299.
33. *Llyfr Iorwerth*, p. 16; *LTMW*, pp. 29–30.
34. 'The Laws of the Court from Latin B', ed. and trans. P. Russell, in *WKHC*, pp. 500-01. 'Cyfnerth', pp. 466-67.
35. *Llyfr Iorwerth*, p. 10; *LTMW*, p. 20.
36. For an opposite viewpoint see Stacey, 'King, Queen and *Edling*, pp. 57–62.
37. *Llfyr Blegywryd*, p. 6; *LTMW*, p. 8.
38. *Vitae Sanctorum Britanniae,* pp. 136-39. Also see Davies, *Mabinogion,* pp. 68, 81, 139–40, 153.
39. *TYP*, triad 54, pp. 153-55. In 'Peredur' a goblet, the symbol of the queen as a peace-maker, is struck from her hand. *Mabinogion,* p. 68.

Chapter Thirteen – On Bended Knee and Shedding of Tears

1. *AnnCestr*, pp. 56-57.
2. '*Annales Prioratus de Wigornia*', in *AM*, iv, p. 421.
3. *CCR*, 1227–31, p. 368; '*Annales Prioratus de Dunstaplia*', in *AM*, iii, p. 117. It seems unlikely that Joan would have been able to attend either or both of her children's nuptials.
4. 'Between the Wye and the Severn'.
5. De Burgh was accused by Matthew Paris of poisoning Marshall.
6. Wendover, *Flowers of History*, p. 221.
7. *AnnCestr*, pp. 56-59.
8. *CFR*, 1230–31, nos 205 and 206.
9. *CCR*, 1227–31, pp. 523-54; *Calendar of the Charter Rolls preserved in the Public Record Office*, Volume 1, Henry III, 1226–1257 (1903), p. 135.
10. *AnnCestr*, pp. 56-57.
11. See Chapter Fourteen for the other possible date.
12. Translated in *Letters of Medieval Women*, ed. A. Crawford (2002), p. 54. [Karis]simo suo domino et fratri suo karissimo H. Dei gratia regi Angl(ie), domino Hib(er)n(ie), duci Norm(annie) et Aquit' et comiti And' I. domina Wall(ie) salutem et se ipsam. Sciatis, domine, quod tanta anxietate contristor quod nequaquam possem exprimere,

eo quod inimici nostri immo et vestri prevaluerunt seminare discordias inter vos et dominum meum. Super quo non minus doleo propter vos quam propter dominum meum, presertim cum sciam quam sincerum affectum habebat et adhuc habet dominus meus erga vos, et quam inutile sit nobis et periculosum, salva reverentia vestra, veros amicos amittere et inimicos pro amicis habere. Hinc est quod, tanquam flexis genibus et fusis lacrymis vestram rogo maiestatem quatinus in melius mutare consilia velitis et eos qui inseparabili dilectionis vinculo coniunguntur vobis reconsiliare non omittatis, quo facilius possitis et discatis et amicos diligere et inimicos gravare. Ad hec sciatis, domine, quod iniustissime suggerunt vobis nonnulli suspicionem habere de Inst(ru)cto et vestro et domini mei clerico, quo non credo vos posse habere in Angl(ia) vobis fideliorem clericum, sic me Deus adiuvet; nec ideo minus fidelis est vobis, si fideliter agit negocia domini sui, quia eodem modo se habet in agendis vestris coram domino suo; nec vos nec aliquis in ipso posset confidere, si domini sui tepide vel negligenter negocia tractaret. Si itaque in aliquo mihi credere velitis, in hoc mihi fidem adhibere velitis. Valete. *AWR*, no. 280, pp. 447-48.

13. *AWR,* no. 292, pp. 460-61.
14. *Annales Cambriae,* p. 82; '*Cronica de Wallia* and Other Documents from Exeter Cathedral Library MS. 3514', ed. T. Jones, *Bulletin of the Board of Celtic Studies*, 12 (1946), p. 38.
15. *BS*, pp. 230-33; *BT, Pen20*, p. 196; *BT, Pen20Tr*, p. 104; *BT, RBH*, pp. 234-35.
16. Cf. 'Lady of the Well', Davies, *Mabinogion*, pp. 124-28.
17. '*licet etiam propter hoc David Anglicano fulciretur auxilio, puta qui sororem regis Henricis secundi sibi matrimonio copulaverat*'. Gir. Camb., *Op.*, vi, p. 134; Gerald of Wales, *Journey through Wales*, p. 193.
18. *BS*, pp. 180-81; *BT, Pen20*, p. 126; *BT, Pen20Tr*, p. 70; *BT, RBH*, pp. 164-65. The poet Prydydd y Moch refers to her as Dafydd's wife (*gwraig*) and mother of Owain. *Gwaith Llywarch ap Llywelyn 'Prydydd y Moch'*, ed. E.M. Jones (Caerdydd, 1991), p. 14.
19. *AWR,* nos. 202, 203, pp. 334-36.
20. Ibid., nos. 432-46, pp. 629-33; Smith, *Llywelyn ap Gruffudd*, pp. 189, 398, 448-49.
21. *AWR*, p. 78.

22. There is difficulty in determining the date of the earliest document that accredits Llywelyn with the designation prince of Aberffraw, lord of Snowdon. The document in question is suggestive of a date of 1225, which would, in fact mean, that the change in titles for Joan and Llywelyn was not a consequence of events in April 1230. Nevertheless, the authenticity of the document itself is called into question. As such, discounting it means that the earliest dated document is 1 May 1230, the day before William's execution. *AWR*, nos 256, 260, pp. 419-21, 424-28.

23. Huw Pryce, 'Negotiating Anglo-Welsh Relations: Llywelyn the Great and Henry III', in B. Weiler (ed.), *England and Europe in the Reign of Henry III (1216–1272)* (2002), p. 20.

24. *AWR*, nos. 193, 194, 196, pp. 324-25, 327-28.

25. The Instructus found in records may have actually have been two different individuals with the same name over the course of time.

26. Professor Louise Wilkinson is an advocate for the probability that it was Instructus who 'helped Joan to keep in touch with her father'. Wilkinson, 'Joan', p. 89, n. 29.

Chapter Fourteen – Lady of Wales

1. *Rot. Pat.*, ii, p. 466; *CCR*, 1231–1234, p. 39.

2. John's life-like effigy that remains in place to this day is unique in being the oldest royal effigy in England.

3. *Rot. Pat.*, ii, p. 476.

4. Ibid.

5. *CPR*, 1232–47, p. 41.

6. Myddle lies between Ellesmere and Shrewsbury. The result of the treaty also saw Llywelyn officially maintaining his old over Cardigan and Buellt, the latter of which had long been an ambition of his and necessary to establishing genuine authority within Wales.

Epilogue

1. *AWR*, no. 281, p. 448. Credenhill, Hereforshire.

2. Ibid., no. 272, p. 442.

3. Although the formidable Joan who stood at his side as his paramour and counsellor and could never be replaced, the *Legend of Fulk FitzWarin* says that Llywelyn did remarry, to a daughter of Fulk. In every guise, however, this union, if it did take place, was short-lived given Llywelyn's physical state and death three years after Joan.

4. *BS*, pp. 230-33; *BT, Pen20,* p. 196; *BT, Pen20Tr,* p. 104; *BT, RBH,* pp. 234-5; *AC,* pp. 82-83. It is noteworthy that Joan's obits mirror those for Llywelyn after his own death in April 1240 in a fundamental way. It is to be expected that Llywelyn given considerable lamentation and praise on his death, who like the Lord Rhys, is compared to classical and mythological heroes. In particular, Llywelyn is praised for his character, as a defender of justice and for skills as a warrior, never mind his heavenly devotion to God. When measured with Joan's, the symbolic significance of their union and their roles as husband and wife, king and queen, is based on the titles and designations used to identify them.

Conclusion

1. R. Turvey, *Llywelyn the Great* (Llandysul, 2007), p. 1.
2. *TYP*, triad 97, pp. 244-45.
3. Also known as Menai Bridge, the shortest sailing distance between the mainland and the island.
4. For a discussion on the queen in the Iorwerth redaction see Stacey, 'King, Queen, and *Edling*', pp. 61-62; Stacey, *Law and the Imagination in Medieval Wales*, pp. 66-73, 143, 149, 219.
5. Joan's female lineage, in fact, comprises no less than two Holy Roman Empresses, Isabella and Matilda in the twelfth century.
6. Although no poems exist from this time dedicated to royal women or about royal women does not mean they were not composed, which, in fact, they most certainly were. They just have not survived.
7. Wilkinson, 'Joan', p. 86.
8. Richards, *Welsh Noblewomen in the Thirteenth Century*, pp. 132-33.
9. Ibid., 205.
10. *HW*, ii, p. 685.

Select Bibliography

Primary Sources

Sources for Joan

The Acts of Welsh Rulers 1120–1283. Edited by H. Pryce (Cardiff, 2005)

Annales Cambriae. Edited by J. Williams ab Ithel (Rolls Series, London, 1860)

Annales Cestrienses. Edited by R.C. Christie. *Record Society of Lancashire and Cheshire*, 14 (London, 1887)

Annales Monastici. Edited by H.R. Luard, 5 vols (Rolls Series, London, 1864–9):

'*Annales de Margan*', i, pp. 3-40

'*Annales Monasterii de Theokesberia*', i, pp. 43-180

'*Annales Monasterii de Wintonia*', ii, pp. 3-125

'*Annales Prioratus de Wigornia*', iv, pp. 355-564

Brenhinedd y Saesson, or The Kings of the Saxons: BM Cotton Ms. Cleopatra Bv and The Black Book of Basingwerk NLW Ms. 7006. Edited by T. Jones (Cardiff, 1971)

Brut y Tywysogyon Peniarth MS. 20. Edited by T. Jones (Cardiff, 1941)

Brut y Tywysogyon, or The Chronicle of the Princes Peniarth 20 Ms. Version. Translated by T. Jones (Cardiff, 1952)

Brut y Tywysogyon, or The Chronicle of the Princes Red Book of Hergest Version. Edited and translated by T. Jones (Cardiff, 1955)

Calendar of Ancient Correspondence Concerning Wales. Edited by J.G. Edwards (Cardiff, 1935)

Calendar of the Close Rolls Preserved in the Public Record Office, 1227–37 (London, 1900–)

224

Calendar of Entries in the Papal Registers Relating to Great Britain and Ireland: Papal Letters, A.D. 1198–1304. Edited by W.H. Bliss, 5 vols (London, 1893), i

Calendar of the Patent Rolls preserved in the Public Record Office (London, 1891–)

Close Rolls of the Reign of Henry III Preserved in the Public Record Office, 1227–42, Vols. 1-4 (London, 1902–38)

'*Cronica de Wallia* and Other Documents from Exeter Cathedral Library MS. 3514'. E.T. Jones. *Bulletin of the Board of Celtic Studies*, 12 (1946): 27–44

Foedera, Conventiones, Litterae etc. Edited by T. Rymer, 4 vols in 7 (revd edn, Record Commission, London), vol. I, part: i

The History of Fulk Fitz-Warine. Translated by Alice Kemp-Welch (London, 1904, 2001)

Letters of Medieval Women. Edited and translated by A. Crawford (Stroud, 2002)

Magni Rotuli Scaccarii Normanniae sub Regibus Angliae. Edited by T. Stapleton, 2 vols (London, 1840–4)

Matthæi Parisiensis, Monachi Sancti Albani, Chronica Majora. Edited by H.R. Luard, 7 vols (Rolls Series, London, 1874)

The National Archives. E. 163.4.47, m. 6

Powel, Dr Davd. *The Historie of Cambria, now Called Wales: A Part of the Most Famous Yland of Brytaine, Written in the Brytish Language aboue Two Hundreth Yeares Past* (London, reprint for John Harding, 1811)

Regesta Honorii Papae III. Edited by P. Pressutti, 2 vols (Rome, 1885–98)

Rogeri de Wendover, Liber Qui Dicitur Flores Historiarum Ab Anno Domini MCLIV. Annoque Henrici Anglorum Regis Secundi Primo. Edited by H.G. Hewlett, 3 vols (Rolls Series, London, 1887)

―――. *Chronica, sive Flores Historiarum*. Edited by H.O. Coxe, 4 vols (London, 1841–44)

Rotuli Litteratum Clausarum in Turri Londinensi Asservati A.D. 1204–A.D. 1227. Edited by T.D. Hardy, 2 vols (Record Commission, London, 1832–44)

Rotuli Litterarum Patentium in Turri Londinensi Asservati, I.i., *A.D. 1201–A.D. 1216*. Edited by T.D. Hardy (Record Commission, London, 1835)

Royal and Other Letters Illustrative of the Reign of Henry III. Edited by W.W. Shirley, 2 vols (London, 1866)

Wynn, Sir John. *The History of the Gwydir Family* (Cardiff, 1927)

Secondary Sources

Useful for in medieval Wales and Welsh history

Carr, A.D. *Medieval Wales* (Houndmills, 1995)

Cavell, Emma. 'Widows, Native Law and the Long Shadow of England in Thirteenth-century Wales'. *English Historical Review*, 133 (Dec. 2018): 1376-1419

———. 'Periphery to Core: Mortimer Women and Negotiation of the King's Justice in the Thirteenth-century March of Wales'. *Journal of the Mortimer History Society*, 2 (2018): 1-19

———. 'Emma d'Audley and the Clash of Laws in Thirteenth-century Northern Powys'. In Patricia Skinner (ed.), *The Welsh and the Medieval World: Travel, Migration and Exile*. (Cardiff, 2018), 49-74

———. 'Intelligence and Intrigue' in the March of Wales: Noblewomen and the Fall of Llywelyn ap Gruffudd, 1274–82'. *Historical Research* (2014): 1-19

———. 'Welsh Princes, English Wives: The Politics of Powys Wenwynwyn Revisited'. *Welsh History Review*, 27:2 (2014): 214-52

Charles-Edwards, T.M. *Early Irish and Welsh Kinship* (Oxford, 1993)

———, M.E. Owen and P. Russell (eds). *The Welsh King and His Court* (Cardiff, 2000)

Costello, Louisa Stewart. *The Falls, Lakes and Mountains of North Wales* (London, 1845)

Davies, R.R. *The Age of Conquest: Wales 1063–1415* (Oxford, 1991; first published as *Conquest, Coexistence, and Change: Wales 1063–1415*, 1987)

Doan, James. 'Sovereignty Aspects in the Roles of Women in Medieval Irish and Welsh Society'. In P. Jefferiss and W.J. Mahon (eds), *Proceedings of the Harvard Celtic Colloquium*, 5 (Harvard, 1985): 87–102

Given-Wilson, C. and A. Curteis. *The Royal Bastards of Medieval England* (London, 1984)

Hagger, M. *The De Verdun Family in England, Ireland and Wales, 1066–1316: A Study.* Unpublished PhD Thesis (University of St Andrews, 1998)

Hurlock, K. 'Counselling the Princes: Advice and Counsel in Thirteenth-Century Welsh Society'. *History*, 34 (2009): 20–35

————. 'The Welsh Wife of Malcolm, Earl of Fife (d. 1266): An Alternative Suggestion'. *Scottish Historical Review*, 88/2 (2009): 352-55

Insley, C. 'The Wilderness Years of Llywelyn the Great'. In M. Prestwich, R. Britnell and R. Frame (eds), *Proceedings of the Durham Conference 2001: Thirteenth Century England IX* (Woodbridge, 2003):163–74

Jenkins, D., and M.E. Owen (eds). *The Welsh Law of Women* (Cardiff, 1980)

Johns, S.M. 'Seals, Women and Identity'. In Paul Schofield, Elizabeth New and Susan M. Johns (eds). *Seals and Society: Medieval Wales, the Welsh Marches and their Border Region* (Cardiff, 2015), 91-104

————. *Gender, Nation and Conquest in the High Middle Ages: Nest of Deheubarth* (Manchester, 2013)

————. 'Nest of Deheubarth: Reading Female Power in the Historiography of Wales'. In J.L. Nelson, S. Reynolds, and S.M. Johns (eds), *Gender and Historiography: Studies in the History of the Earlier Middle Ages in Honour of Pauline Stafford* (London, 2012): 91–100

————. 'Beauty and the Feast: The Cultural Constructions of Female Beauty and Social Interaction in Twelfth-century Wales'. *Proceedings of the Harvard Celtic Colloquium* 30 (2011):102–15

————. *Noblewomen, Aristocracy and Power in the Twelfth-Century Anglo-Norman Realm* (Manchester, 2003)

Lloyd, J.E. 'Who was Gwenllian de Lacy'. *Archaeologia Cambrensis*, 74 (1919): 292-98

————. *A History of Wales: From the Earliest Times to the Edwardian Conquest*, 2 vols (London, 2nd edn,1912)

MacEwen, A.B.W. 'Elen, Countess of Chester: A Daughter of Joan, Princess of North Wales'. *The Genealogist,* 4 (1983): 137-38

Maund, K.L. *Princess Nest of Wales: Seductress of the English* (Stroud 2007)

————. *The Welsh Kings: Warrior, Warlords and Princes* (Stroud, 2006)

Messer, D.R. 'Welsh Queenship in the Twelfth and Thirteenth Centuries'. *Encyclopedia of the Global Middle Ages: Core Case Study.* London: Bloomsbury Academic (2019). Bloomsbury Medieval Studies. Web

————. 'A Model of Welsh Queenship: Joan of England and the Medieval Court of Gwynedd'. Special Edition on Medieval and Early Modern Queenship, ed. Louise Wilkinson. *Women's History Review* (Forthcoming, 2019)

———. 'Impressions of Welsh Queenship in the Twelfth and Thirteenth Centuries'. In Elena Woodacre (ed.), *Global Queenship* (Leeds, 2018): 147–58

———. 'Joan (d. 1237), princess and diplomat'. *Dictionary of Welsh Biography Online.* <https://biography.wales/article/s12-JOAN-TYW-1237?&query=joan&lang[]=en&sort=score&order=desc&ro, ws=12&page=1>, accessed 30 December 2018

———. 'Eleanor de Montfort (c. 1258–82), princess and diplomat'. *Dictionary of Welsh Biography Online*. https://biography.wales/article/s11-ELEA-WRL-1200, accessed 30 December 2018

———. 'The Uxorial Lifecyle and Female Agency in Wales in the Twelfth and Thirteenth Centuries'. Unpublished PhD Thesis (Bangor University, 2014)

———. 'Medieval Monarchs, Female Illegitimacy and Modern Genealogical Matters: Part II: Joan of England, c. 1190–1237'. *Foundations*, 1/4 (July 2004): 294-98

Newton, P. *Gwenllian: The Welsh Warrior Princess* (Llanrwst, 2002)

Norgate, K. 'Joan [Siwan], (d. 1237)'. Revised by A.D. Carr. *Oxford Dictionary of National Biography.* https://doi.org/10.1093/ref:odnb/14819, accessed 30 December 2018

Penman, S. 'The Mother of Joanna of Wales, wife of Llywelyn ab Iorwerth' (2009). <http://sharonkaypenman.com/blog/?p=88>, accessed 30 December 2018

Pennant, Thomas. *A Tour in Wales*, 2 vols in 4 (London, 1784)

Pryce, H. 'Negotiating Anglo-Welsh Relations: Llywelyn the Great and Henry III'. In B. Weiler (ed.), *England and Europe in the Reign of Henry III (1216–1272)* (Aldershot, 2002): 13-29

Reitwiesner, W.A. 'The Children of Joan, Princess of North Wales'. *The Genealogist,* 1/80 (1980): 80–95

Richards, G. *Welsh Noblewomen in the Thirteenth Century: An Historical Study of Medieval Welsh Law and Gender Roles* (Lewiston, 2009)

Roderick, A.J. 'Marriage and Politics in Wales, 1066–1282'. *Welsh History Review*, 4 (1968): 1–20

Sheppard, W.L. 'Joan, Princess of Wales, Daughter of King John: Ancestress to Bulkeley, James, Mellowes, Welby, Whittingham, Haugh, and St. John-Whiting Families'. *The American Genealogist,* 25/29 (1959): 29–33

Stacey, R. Chapman, 'Divorce, Medieval Welsh Style'. *Speculum* (October, 2002): 1107–27

———. *Law and the Imagination in Medieval Wales* (Philadelphia, 2018)

Stephenson, D. 'Empires in Wales: From Gruffudd ap Llywelyn to Llywelyn ap Gruffudd'. *Welsh History Review,* 28/1 (2016): 26–54

———, and C. Owen Jones. 'The Date and Context of the Birth of Dafydd II Ap Llywelyn'. *Flintshire Historical Journal,* 29 (2012): 21–32

———. *The Governance of Gwynedd.* Cardiff: University of Wales Press, 1984

Swallow, R. 'Gateways to Power: The Castles of Ranulf III of Chester and Llewellyn the Great of Gwynedd'. *Archaeological Journal,* 171 (2014): 289–311

Turvey, R. *Llywelyn the Great* (Llandysul, 2007)

———. *The Welsh Princes: The Native Rulers of Wales, 1063–1283* (London, 2002)

Wilkinson, L.J. 'Joan, Wife of Llywelyn the Great'. In M. Prestwich, R. Britnell and R. Frame (eds). *Thirteenth Century England X: Proceedings of the Durham Conference 2003* (Woodbridge, 2005): 81–93

Williams, P.B. *The Tourist's Guide Through the Country of Caernarvon, containing a Short Sketch of its History, Antiquities, etc.* (1821)

Index

Gwynedd): mother of; Philip le Boteler; Roesia; Susanna ferch Llywelyn ap Iorwerth (Gwynedd)

Nicholas, 15-16, 127-28; *see also* Bertram; Clemence; Roesia

Roesia, 16; *see also* Clemence; Nicholas

de Warenne, family,
Adela (?), 16; *see also* Hamelin; Richard FitzRoy (of Dover, natural son of King John)
Hamelin, 16; *see also* Adela (?)
William (Earl of Surrey), 142

Deganwy, 20, 60, 75, 82, 106, 216 n. 9

Denbighshire, 105

Descriptio Cambriae (*The Description of Wales*), xvi

diplomacy, 44, 63, 88, 113, 170, 175

divorce, 157, 158, 200; *see also ysgar* (separation)

Domesday Book, 14, 16

Dorsetshire, 132

dower, 72, 73, 103, 105, 108

dowry, 85, 103, 168

Dyffryn Clwyd, 103

E

edling (heir/successor), xiii, 6, 9, 24, 31, 33, 50, 65, 66, 67, 73, 85, 98, 105, 122, 128-29, 131, 150, 175

Ednyfed Fychan (Gwynedd), 174, 177, 180; *see also* Gruffudd ab Ednyfed (Gwynedd)

Edward I (King of England), viii, 17, 47, 81, 194, 195

Edward the Confessor, 19

Egerton, 134

Einion Fychan, 143, 177

Eldgyth (wife of Gruffudd ap Llywelyn, King of Wales), 19; *see also* Gruffudd ap Llywelyn (King of Wales)

Eleanor of Aquitaine, x, 150, 159, 197; *see also* Henry II (King of England); Louis VII (King of France)

Eleanor of Brittany (Fair Maid), 11; *see also* Arthur of Brittany; Constance (Duchess of Brittany); Geoffrey Plantagenet (Duke of Brittany)

Eleanor of England (Queen of Castile), x, 197

Eleanor of Provence (Queen of England), 196; *see also* Henry III (King of England); Poitevins

Elen ferch Llywelyn ap Iorwerth (Gwynedd), 105, 151, 176, 177, 13, 35, 55, 56, 95, 97, 99, 102-03; *see also* Dafydd ap Llywelyn ap Iorwerth (Gwynedd); Gwladus ferch Llywelyn ap Iorwerth (Gwynedd); Joan (Lady of Wales; Gwynedd); John the Scot; Llywelyn ap Iorwerth (Gwynedd); Marared ferch Llywelyn ap Iorwerth (Gwynedd); Susanna ferch Llywelyn ap Iorwerth (Gwynedd)